HOWARD J. STODDARD

HOWARD J. STODDARD, 1901–1971.

# Howard J. Stoddard

## FOUNDER, MICHIGAN NATIONAL BANK

Richard D. Poll

Michigan State University Press
East Lansing
1980

Library of Congress Catalog Card Number: 79-89980
ISBN 0-87013-220-2

★ ★ ★ ★ ★

Manufactured in the United States of America

# Contents

# Preface

This biography of one of the most colorful and significant figures in Michigan banking history has been written at the invitation of Howard J. Stoddard's family. It accents the positive, but the reader will have no difficulty discovering why Howard Stoddard was a controversial figure in the financial community of his adopted state. He was a stout believer in capitalistic enterprise, but he was no defender of the *status quo*. In aggressively building a family financial empire on the basis of consumer-oriented services, he influenced the course of banking in Michigan and America.

The book is the history of a man and an institution. Because Howard Stoddard's background, interests, personality and religious faith profoundly influenced his business career, they receive rather extensive attention. This is not a conventional business history, but it relates the main developments in Michigan National Bank's first thirty years, identifies many of the key personalities, and gives enough quantitative data so that, it is hoped, a clear picture emerges.

Indispensable to my research, as she was in gathering and organizing the extensive business files and personal scrapbooks on which the research is primarily based, has been Howard Stoddard's secretary and multi-purpose helper for more than three decades, Gladys H. MacGregor. Among his close associates, Russell Fairles, who was with Michigan National from the beginning, James B. Alley, who worked with Howard during the Detroit banking crisis and later as M.N.B. legal representative, and Waldo I. Stoddard, who was a collaborator and confidant as well as a brother, provided much information and read drafts of one or more chapters. Members of Howard's immediate family—Jennie Creer Stoddard and her children, Howard Preston, Stanford Creer ("Bud"), Virginia Claire Peery and Charles Creer—were cooperative, informative, and as circumstances permitted, very hospitable. The names of many others who submitted to interview and helped in other ways are given in the bibliographical note.

Because the primary sources are uncatalogued correspondence and interview transcripts, formal annotations have not been provided. Where quotations are from published materials, sources are indicated in the text. Where other documents are quoted, authors are identified and dates or time contexts are provided. Written documents are quoted precisely; excerpts from transcripts of interviews and public addresses have been edited to eliminate repetitions and obvious verbal lapses and transcribing errors. Efforts to locate the source for "The American Creed," quoted in Chapter 16, have been unsuccessful. All unpublished materials, including audiotapes and transcripts, are now in the possession of Michigan National Bank or Mrs. Stoddard.

The editorial advice and assistance of Jean Busfield and Lyle Blair, for Michigan State University Press, is gratefully acknowledged. The responsibility for such shortcomings as the book may have is, of course, mine.

RICHARD D. POLL
Western Illinois University

May 16, 1979

CHAPTER 1

# An Introduction

Take the heritage of generations of Scottish coal miners and English factory workers, transfuse it with a religious faith centered in an American land of promise, transform it among the pine forests of eastern Oregon, transplant it in Michigan, and what do you get?

Howard James Stoddard.

The innovative financier whose monument is Michigan National Bank was a man of faith—in God and in hard work, in people and in economic competition. He was devoted to his family, his church, his friends, his community and his country. And to his bank and those who worked with him to make it, at his death in 1971, one of the fifty largest in the United States.

Howard Stoddard liked to tell how he selected his vocation because of the "bankers hours" which were posted on the door of the little bank in the little Oregon town of LaGrande. Since the illusion of short working days was quickly shattered, it is well that he found banking a fascinating and rewarding career. He never tired of his work, and in time he extended the working days of many of his competitors.

Banking, to Howard Stoddard, had a pivotal relationship to all kinds of people and enterprises. He enjoyed lending money for all constructive purposes, and he pioneered in such consumer-centered fields as mobile home, FHA mortgage, credit card and installment financing. He saw the connections between corporate and national wellbeing. Inflation, federal fiscal policy, the Vietnam war and other problems drew him into the field of public affairs as publicist and lobbyist. His concern for the financial health of his adopted state made him adviser to governors and constitution-maker. It all came together in the slogan which he adopted for his company:

"Banking that is building Michigan."

Howard Stoddard was an uncommon banker because he was an uncommon man. Outstanding natural gifts, a favorable background and deep religious convictions were assets from the beginning. He decided early that he wanted to make money and to be his own boss. His approach to his vocation was influenced by the bitter lessons of the banking crisis of 1933 and by the ideas of such financial innovators as A.P. Giannini, Jesse Jones and his own cousin, Marriner Eccles. He was tough-minded to the point of stubbornness, but he listened before deciding and he gave subordinates wide latitude in doing their jobs. He was serious in his nature—some found him austere, even frightening at first—but he was not humorless and he had a remarkable ability to inspire loyalty. He admired the intellectually honest and disliked those who lacked scruples or did not defend their principles. He stood firm in his own convictions and he influenced many by his counsel and actions. He died at a moment of major triumph, when new state legislation had just opened the way for the statewide operations which he had envisioned when he began to bring together the elements of Michigan National Bank thirty years before.

Brought up amid stately trees, Howard Stoddard carried a love of finely-crafted wood through his life. The handsome paneling and furnishings of the home and offices of his affluent years were among his few personal indulgences. At selecting, shaping and polishing both forest and human timber he was adept, and in the process he fulfilled the destiny expressed in one of his favorite hymns:

Know this, that every man is free
To choose his life, and what he'll be;
For this eternal truth is given
That God will force no man to heaven.

He'll call, persuade, direct aright
And bless with wisdom, love and light.
In nameless ways be good and kind,
But never force the human mind.

Freedom and reason make us men.
Take these away—what are we then?
Mere animals, and just as well.
The beast may think of heaven or hell.*

Howard Stoddard chose banking because it challenged his analytical mind and provided an essential service. He pursued his career with such

* *Hymns* (Church of Jesus Christ of Latter day Saints: Salt Lake City, 1948), p. 90.

energy, ingenuity, tenacity and success that by the time of his death he was one of Michigan's most prominent citizens—heartily disliked by a few, envied by a few, and admired by many.

"Maverick" was the journalists' favorite word for him—"an independent individual who refuses to conform to his group."

CHAPTER 2

# Heritage of Faith and Work

Howard Stoddard left his home to seek his fortune, but he never left his heritage. The stubborn, sturdy Scots who came to America in the mid-nineteenth century, and the maternal forebears who came from England at about the same time and for the same reasons, brought an humble birthright and a vision of a land of promise. The same combination of faith, loyalty and hard work with which they pursued that vision tempered his own career. To understand Michigan's maverick banker requires looking at his Mormon pioneer background.

The Stoddarts—they spelled the name with a "t" in Scotland—had been miners in the collieries around Edinburgh for several generations when Howard Stoddard's great grandfather was born in 1795. John Stoddart grew up in the years when Sir Walter Scott's novels were romanticizing the heroic aspects of Scottish resistance to England. John almost certainly did not and perhaps could not read the stories, but at the age of 39 he served three months in prison for refusing to inform on a fellow Scotsman who had publicly denounced the bounty system by which the British army purchased recruits.

John and his wife, Janet Kerr Stoddart, produced ten children for a squalid world in which men and women toiled together in the mines for a few pence a day. (Half of Edinburgh's children died before they were five.) The men dug the coal and the women and older children carried it to the surface on their backs. Not until 1833 did the Factory Act prohibit children under nine from working and limit those under twelve to twelve hours per day. One of the Stoddart girls, the recently-wedded Ellen, was crushed to death on Christmas Eve 1834 in a mine rockfall. Eight years later another reform law forbade women to work underground.

John Kerr Stoddart, the youngest son of John and Janet, was born in

Penston, East Lothian, on June 8, 1836. For twelve years he shared the fortunes and misfortunes of his parents, learned a boy's work in the mines and scrambled for a little schooling. His family frequently moved as collieries closed or landlords exercised their arbitrary powers of eviction. One of the moves made them neighbors of a family named Nibley, who introduced them to a new religion and whose son, Charles W., later became young John's business associate and close friend in America.

The event which radically changed the Stoddarts' prospects was their encounter with missionaries of The Church of Jesus Christ of Latter-day Saints. Mormon proselyters first appeared in the Edinburgh area in 1840, and young John's fourteen-year-old brother, David, accepted baptism in June 1844, the same month in which the founder of Mormonism, Joseph Smith, was killed at Carthage, Illinois. Subsequently, John, both his parents and an older brother, Alexander, and his wife also joined the new movement.

To the Stoddarts, Nibleys and thousands of other Latter-day Saint converts in the British Isles now came a call to "gather" with the main body of the church in the American West. Brigham Young had led the majority of Joseph Smith's followers from Illinois across Iowa to the banks of the Missouri River, and a vanguard had established a new Zion in the Great Salt Lake Valley in 1847. From Council Bluffs, where Young was sustained as president of the Mormon Church, came a "General Epistle," dated December 27, 1847, to "all Saints in England, Scotland, Ireland, and Wales and adjacent islands and countries." The counsel was direct:

> . . . come immediately and prepare to go west—bringing with you all kinds of choice seeds, of grain, vegetables, fruit, shrubbery, trees and vines, everything that will please the eye, gladden the heart, or cheer the soul of man. . . . Also the best tools of every description . . . or models and descriptions of the same . . . and every implement and article within their knowledge that shall tend to promote the comfort, health, happiness and prosperity of any people.

The Mormon Stoddards—the "t" became "d" sometime prior to the arrival in America—had little to bring but their knowledge of mining and their conviction that God was calling them to a new life. Late in 1848 John, Janet and their sons David and John sailed with 307 other passengers from Liverpool on the ship "Sailor Prince." In those days an Atlantic crossing for the fugitives from European poverty meant paying only for water and space on ships designed primarily to carry freight. The "passengers" provided their own bedding, cooked their own food, performed their own birth, marriage and burial services, and had no problem deciding how much to tip the stewards.

"Sailor Prince" arrived in New Orleans late in October and, according to David's reminiscence, his family sailed up the Mississippi in time to reach St. Louis a few days before Christmas. Alexander, now twenty-six, and his small son John joined them in 1849, his wife Ellen and baby daughter having died at sea of cholera. Shortly after Alexander arrived in St. Louis he became ill, and a doctor administered a fatal overdose of laudanum, the standard pain reliever of that era. His young son was brought to Utah and raised by the Stoddard family.

Until 1851 the Stoddards were members of the Mormon community in Missouri, and some of the men worked in the nearby coal mines. One way or another they had to save money for the anticipated trip "across the plains." (In 1850 the Perpetual Emigrating Fund Company was organized to assist Mormon converts with loans and services so that they could make uninterrupted journeys to Utah, but the Stoddards benefitted only from the organizing, outfitting, ferrying and other services which the P.E.F.C. performed along their route west.)

Under the church-appointed leadership of John Easton, an emigrating party of ten families, the Stoddards among them, was organized at St. Louis in April 1851. At Council Bluffs they became part of a caravan of fifty wagons, but the pace was too slow for the Easton group and so, after a week or two, their ten wagons proceeded alone. This increased the risks, but neither the stampeding buffalo nor the begging Indians encountered along the way did them harm.

The John Stoddard clan reached Salt Lake City on Friday, October 5, 1851. The work experience which they had gained in Scotland determined what happened next. Brigham Young, bent on achieving a self-sufficient economic commonwealth in the Great Basin, was organizing a colonizing mission to exploit the iron and coal recently discovered in southern Utah territory. The Stoddards were called to participate in the Iron Mission—as generations of Stoddards would be called to accept church assignments in the future. David and John completed their first Utah home, a one-room cabin at Coal Creek, later Cedar City, and their father and mother moved in on Christmas Day, 1851. They were three hundred miles from Salt Lake City and almost twenty times that far from Edinburgh.

A time of testing followed. The miners and smelter builders at Coal Creek and the farmers at nearby Parowan lacked capital and worked under extremely difficult conditions. In the first season the iron missionaries cleared, fenced and irrigated several hundred acres, planted and harvested crops, cleared roads to the coal and iron deposits, opened mines and built a millrace, a water-powered furnace, a pattern shop, coke ovens, a blacksmith shop and an office. On September 30, 1852, they tapped the furnace and drew off the first iron manufactured west of the Mississippi River.

The colonists labored for several years trying to develop a viable iron industry, but capital remained insufficient and, in David's words, "the iron ore was too rich for the flux at their command." (Ninety years later the ore and eastern Utah coal would be the basis of the war-born Geneva Steel operation near Provo, Utah.) In 1852 the initial builders sold their interest to the church-sponsored Deseret Iron Company for about three thousand dollars in cash and stock credits. Among the signers of the contract was David Stoddard. John Kerr Stoddard's name did not appear, as he was only sixteen years old. Iron was intermittently produced for the next several years, but technical problems, a devastating flood and the sheer burden of survival finally prevailed. By 1857 the iron works virtually ceased operations.

The senior John Stoddard died at Cedar City in the spring of 1854. His boys carried on their assignment, looking after their mother and sharing the vicissitudes of life on the Mormon frontier. Church records show that on one occasion David contributed twelve pumpkins and one side of bacon, while John's tithe was fifteen cabbages and four squash. The sanctity of "the Lord's tenth" was a principle which later Stoddard generations would be taught in childhood.

Young John got along well with the Paiute Indians and was given an Indian name that meant Good Boy. Like other able-bodied males he became a member of the local militia, and he was apparently called to active duty when the Mormons mobilized to confront units of the U.S. Army in 1857. (The so-called "Utah War" was settled without bloodshed, a non-Mormon replacing Brigham Young as governor of Utah territory.)

John was eighteen when he married sixteen-year-old Esther Emily Kershaw. By the time the Stoddards left Cedar City in 1859, the first of Emily's seven children, James, had arrived and the second was on the way. John Henry was born in Beaver, fifty miles north of Cedar City, where his parents stopped temporarily on the way to a new home in northern Utah Territory. Wellsville was a Cache Valley village of less than a hundred people when the David Stoddards, the John Kerr Stoddards and the men's mother, Janet, settled there.

In Cache Valley, as elsewhere in pioneer Utah, plural marriage was being practiced in many households, and among the European Saints who moved into the valley in the 1860's were many women who had been converted to "the principle." Emma Eckersley, recently arrived with her family from Middleton, Lancashire, England, was one of them. The oldest of Joseph and Alice Eckersley's seven children, Emma had gone to work in a textile factory when she was eight. She was eighteen when John Stoddard took her to the L.D.S. Endowment House in Salt Lake City on July 2, 1864, to be sealed to him, as Emily had been, "for time and eternity."

Twelve children were born of this union. Howard Stoddard's father, George Eckersley Stoddard, was the first. He was born in Wellsville on July 12, 1865.

The culture of Mormon polygamy was the environment in which George Stoddard grew to manhood. Emily Stoddard was only thirty-one when she died, and her children who had survived infancy became part of Emma's family—George's half-brothers and sisters. Two years later John married Sarah and Elizabeth Yates, who added eleven children to John Stoddard's patriarchal family.

The ramifications of such a family enterprise were varied. The complex interpersonal relationships tested husband, wives and children, and it appears that John Kerr Stoddard's families handled them as successfully as most polygamous households. George Stoddard's sister Ellen, two years his junior, became the second wife of David Eccles, another convert Scotsman who was by then John Stoddard's business associate and well on the way to becoming Utah's first multi-millionaire. Ellen's oldest son, Howard Stoddard's cousin Marriner Stoddard Eccles, became a friend and advisor—one of the strong influences on Howard's concepts of banking and public policy. One of the factors which took both Emma Stoddard and Ellen Stoddard Eccles to Oregon with their children was the uncomfortable predicament of polygamous families in Utah in the years just before and after the L.D.S. Church formally stopped advocating and performing plural marriages in 1890.

George Stoddard grew up in a home dominated by discipline and hard work. Wellsville was his home until he married, but the logging camps operated by his father in various Utah and Wyoming locations were where he lived during the long timber-cutting seasons. Five of Emma Stoddard's children died in infancy, but the others all experienced the rigors—and adventures—of the pioneer lumber industry. As the nature of the business dictated, John moved his operations from place to place as the stands of timber were destroyed by the clear-cutting methods which were conventional in those days. Also, according to the nature of the business, he joined his gradually increasing capital with a variety of partners, the associations forming and dissolving as the years went on. George spent long hours as a boy at such menial lumber camp tasks as "edging shingles."

In the 1880's John Stoddard began the close relationship with David Eccles which was to powerfully influence the remainder of his life. Similar Scottish backgrounds and parallel lumbering interests had brought the two men together earlier, and their first business deal may have been David's purchase from John of the small sawmill with which he began to build the Eccles lumber empire in Oregon. At the time John and his sons—George's half-brothers—were cutting timber at various locations in Utah, Wyoming and near the Idaho-Montana line. In 1884 John purchased a lumber company in Ogden, Eccles' home town, and christened it John Stoddard and Son. Three years later he sold the firm to Eccles.

According to Sidney Hyman's *Marriner S. Eccles* (1976), John Stoddard and David Eccles shared economic philosophies as well as business interests. They personified that variant form of free enterprise capitalism which flourished in the American West in the late nineteenth century. They were non-typical only to the degree that their commitments to the Mormon Church affected their personal standards, patterns of financial contribution, and occasional participation in church-sponsored business ventures. "Indeed," says Hyman, "the whole of their world, aside from wives, children and Church, consisted of little more than work, and talk and worry about work, and plans for investments which could make money work as hard as they did personally." The lesson that you should make your money work as hard as you do was not lost on John's son George, or his grandson, Howard.

The tie that really linked the Stoddard and Eccles families together, however, was David's marriage to Ellen Stoddard. When they were secretly united in plural marriage in 1885, he was thirty-six and she was eighteen. By then John Stoddard had moved all of his families to Ogden, where Eccles was alderman and then mayor between 1885 and 1889.

George Stoddard was by then on his own. His father's strict discipline had always borne heavily on the boy, and it appears that the relationship was never close. Despite John Stoddard's pronounced religious zeal, George was not baptized a Latter-day Saint until he was twelve years old (the customary age is eight), and he did not develop a strong commitment to church activity until many years later. A naturally outgoing person, fond of sports and socializing, George frequently clashed with his stern, stubborn parent. Sometime in his teen years the tension reached the breaking point, described in Howard's memoir in these terms:

> It had been customary for him to give his father or mother his wages and when necessary he would ask for a small sum in return, to care for his own simple wants. Upon one occasion he was in Wells-

> ville and wished to attend a certain party being given by the younger folks of the village. The admission price was fifty cents but additional money would be needed for refreshments. Upon asking his father for this amount he met with a stern refusal. Nettled by this denial and smarting under what he considered an injustice, father left his home and moved across the street to some neighbors. Although his father later relented, saw his mistake and sent his boy the money, he refused to accept it and never returned to his home to live.

Afterwards father and son seemed to understand each other better and they were associated in many business activities until John's death in 1894.

Helping to cushion the relationship, probably, was George's marriage to Ellen Izatt. She was a Cache Valley girl, born on October 21, 1869, at Logan of parents who came to Utah from Scotland as teen-agers in the early 1860s. Ellen grew up on a farm home from which her father was often absent pursuing his trade as a stone mason. The Logan L.D.S. Temple and some of the lovely stone houses which stand today in Cache Valley incorporate Alexander Izatt's handiwork. At thirteen Ellen went to live in Wellsville, where her thrice-married maternal grandmother, Agnes Leatham Williamson Lawson, ran a small notions store while her crippled husband, Robert, went from village to village peddling notions from a donkey cart. Ellen lived with them for six years, taking care of grandparents, store, cart and donkey.

As romantic tradition has preserved the story, the Wellsville choir was rehearsing for a Christmas fund-raising concert when George Stoddard dropped in, just back from the lumber camp at Aspen. Among the singers were his sisters, Ellen and Sarah, and "a dark-haired, dark-eyed Scotch lassie" who captured his eye. He did not know her but remarked to one of his sisters that someday she was going to be his wife. An introduction was quickly arranged, and after a courtship conducted largely by mail, George became engaged to Ellen Izatt in February 1888.

The following June, George accepted a position with Utah Oregon Lumber Company, a timber-cutting operation in which his father had an interest. His assignment was to manage a small sawmill in Logan Canyon. Two cooks were required to feed the loggers and mill hands, so George asked Alexander Izatt if Ellen and her half-sister, Mary, could accept the jobs. As George later told the story, "he couldn't hire a cook so he married one." George and Ellen were married in Wellsville on June 19, 1888, when he was almost twenty-three and she was almost nineteen. Howard's short biography of his father describes what followed in these words (overlooking sister Mary's presence entirely):

> So the honeymoon started—father running a little sawmill during the day, repairing, filing saws and keeping books at night; mother cooking for a crew of twenty men. Their first home was a crude structure with a canvas wagon cover for a part of the roof, but the joy of working together, the splendid harmony that existed as they carried their burdens, looking ahead to the future, compensated for all of these hardships and their early days of married life were filled with the greatest happiness.

Certainly those years were full of change and movement. The summer assignment in Logan Canyon was successfully fulfilled but the following winter's venture in livestock raising at Wellsville was a disaster; the market declined and the forty head of cattle were sold for less than cost. Spring saw the young couple off to Aspen, where George ran a mill for his half-brother, Alexander, and Charles Moslander, who had taken him in when he left home. Then it was back to Logan for Ellen, to await the birth of her first child.

When George Earl Stoddard (he would always be called by his middle name) was born on November 17, 1889, his father was already in Oregon. John Stoddard had gone there two years before to operate the Eccles mill at North Powder, near the little town of Baker, and now Emma Stoddard, her daughter, Ellen Eccles, and her three unmarried children were joining him. As soon as George's Ellen was able, she followed her husband, and their story thereafter was intertwined with the growth of lumbering and Mormonism in the Pacific Northwest.

According to Leonard Arrington's *David Eccles* (1975), the organization of the Oregon Lumber Company in 1889 was the first major venture in the sometimes turbulent relationship between Eccles, John Stoddard and C.W. Nibley. Other Utah businessmen were also stockholders and served on the board of directors. Eccles was the majority stockholder, but the promotion-minded Nibley and the experienced Stoddard played important roles. They planned and built big, to match the demand for railroad ties and other lumber which was expanding as the Union Pacific Railroad pushed to complete a link between Cheyenne, Wyoming and Portland.

To process the timber a large sawmill was constructed in Baker. When completed in 1891 it was the most modern of its day, with two hundred horsepower engines instead of the twenty-five horsepower models upon which John Stoddard and his boys had trained. Soon the plant was employing three hundred men, and the waste lumber fueled the electric light plant which served the growing town.

To bring timber to the mill the Oregon Lumber Company visionary,

Nibley, persuaded his partners to build a narrow gauge railway to the rich timberlands of nearby Sumpter Valley. A favorable contract was arranged with the Union Pacific by which the railroad exchanged used track and equipment for Sumpter Valley Railway Company stock and also guaranteed to purchase 500,000 railroad ties for five years. Despite its decrepit rolling stock and roller coaster route, the S.V.R.C. paid fine dividends to its owners for a generation. That the people of eastern Oregon knew one of the reasons which brought its organizers to the region is witnessed by the nickname which the line carried in its early days: "The Polygamy Central."

When he first went to Oregon, George Stoddard operated as an independent timber cutter. He loved to tell the story of how he financed the small sawmill on Wolf Creek, about ten miles from North Powder. He purchased the machinery with borrowed money at eighteen percent interest. In the first year he cleared $12,000 on an investment of less than $2,000, plus the "sweat equity" represented by sawing timber for ten hours a day and then working far into the evenings on machinery and accounts.

In April 1890 Ellen set out for Oregon with a few possessions and the new baby. Her home at Wolf Creek was a log cabin. Other than a crude bed made of rough lumber, there was little furniture, and even papering the walls and cupboards with newspapers and hanging some white curtains at the two windows provided little comfort—nor did a summer of cooking for a mill crew of twelve men.

North Powder was their home for the next two and a half years. John Stoddard had moved to Hood River to operate another sawmill affiliated with Oregon Lumber Company, and he would shortly move to the main plant in Baker, where Emma had her home. George operated the North Powder mill in partnership with his half-brother Alexander, and in another rustic home Elmer Izatt Stoddard was born on May 21, 1891.

During a severe storm on Thanksgiving Day a year later the yard and mill at North Powder were destroyed by fire. A treasured family memory is that when George arrived at the scene he merely said, "It did a good job, didn't it, boys?" And in a half hour he came out of the bunkhouse with plans for a new mill.

The new start took him into partnership with his younger brother, Joseph, in Sumpter Valley. Under contract with Eccles and the S.V.R.C. they built a small mill on Clear Creek and produced lumber profitably until the nearby timberlands were exhausted. Then they borrowed a small engine from the railroad company and went into more distant tracts.

David Izatt Stoddard arrived on May 16, 1893, just before Ellen and

George took their little family to McEwan, as the logging camp on Clear Creek was called. There Ellen was again the pioneer mother until the need to introduce Earl and Elmer to such amenities as school and church took her and the three boys to Logan to spend the winter of 1895-1896 with Grandmother Stoddard. There Alexander Lester (who would also be known by his second name) was born December 8, 1895.

John Kerr Stoddard's career had by then come to an untimely end. With his family established in Baker and the names of John Stoddard, Charles Nibley and David Eccles becoming symbols of prosperity in the region, he was stricken with Bright's Disease. He returned to Logan for treatment and died there on August 18, 1894, at the age of 58. Emma thereafter resided in Logan until her death, January 22, 1936, being supported by her children when the changing fortunes of the Stoddard lumber enterprises in the late 1920s virtually wiped out the comfortable legacy which her husband left her.

Happy times followed Ellen's return to Baker in January 1896. She and the four boys moved into a new home—the first real home Ellen had ever had. The lumber business did well and George joined with Eccles and Nibley in forming the Oregon Sugar Company. John Izatt joined the family on June 24, 1898, and the first girl, Jeanette Izatt, was a most welcome addition on June 29, 1900. During the timber-cutting season George would spend the week at the mill in Sumpter Valley, but the week-ends and much of the long winters found the family together.

Again disaster struck when fire destroyed the $150,000 mill in 1900. Capital for reconstruction was furnished by David Eccles in return for one-third of the stock in the Stoddard Brothers Lumber Company. The new sawmill was built at Baker and the S.V.R.C. hauled logs to the plant from the cutting areas. The mill had about completed its first—and profitable—year when George and Ellen's seventh child, Howard James Stoddard, was born in Baker on November 1, 1901. His arrival coincided with boom times in eastern Oregon and with the opening of a new phase in the story of his family.

CHAPTER 3

# Son and Brother

Until Howard Stoddard went off to college, the predominant influences in his life were his family, his church and his father's businesses. Since the latter two shaped the family environment, they may appropriately be considered first.

Howard was only a few weeks old when a spiritual crisis in the life of his father gave a new priority to religious activity in the George Stoddard household. Howard later described the incident as he had many times heard it from his parents:

> Prior to this time he [father] had been more or less indifferent to religious activities. He was not interested in the church and preferred to spend his Sundays working at the mill or watching a baseball game. . . .
>
> It was in 1901 that he was stricken with a critical illness and suffered the most intense pain. All remedies seemed unavailing. Finally, he was asked by mother if he did not care to call the elders and have them administer to him. Feeling his position he disliked to ask for help from that source, but finally the elders were called and almost immediately following their prayer, rest and peace came to him. The same afternoon a prayer was offered by the members in church and during this time a spirit of supreme happiness seemed to take possession of his body.

Following his rapid recovery the church which was responsible for George Stoddard's being in Oregon became a major factor in his personal life. No longer was it left to Ellen alone to bear the responsibility of teaching her children the tenets of the Mormon faith and taking them to church when services were accessible. Howard grew up in a home permeated by Mormonism as well as a locality strongly impacted by that colonizing movement.

In an indirect way the Stoddard connection with Oregon went back to the first Mormon proselyting efforts in the lower Columbia River Valley in 1857-1858. They were minimally successful, but one of the missionaries, David Stuart, later led the emigrating party which brought the William Eccles family from Europe to Utah. Stuart's tales of the Northwest contributed to the decision which took David Eccles, his father and other kinsmen to Oregon City in 1867 to work in a new lumber mill. Church ties brought them back to Utah after two years, but the impressions of Oregon lingered with David and were doubtless communicated to John Stoddard and his family.

David Eccles, John Stoddard and Charles Nibley were by no means the only Mormons to follow the railroad-building boom into the Pacific Northwest in the 1880s. The founding of Oregon Lumber Company created job opportunities and the partners encouraged Utahns to accept them. Ten years later, in 1899, there were 57 church members plus 24 children under eight living in Baker, and others were scattered through Washington, Oregon, northern Idaho and western Montana.

Not surprisingly, John Stoddard was a leader in organizing Mormon activities in Baker. He and a relative, Grant Geddes, started a Sunday School around 1890, and in 1893 he was appointed president of the newly organized Baker Branch. (In the Mormon Church areas of membership concentration are organized into stakes and wards, while scattered members are formed into districts and branches under the supervision of missions.) When L.D.S. Apostle Franklin D. Richards installed President Stoddard, he predicted that the Baker Branch would be "but the nucleus of the great work to be done" in the Northwest. "There will be towns and cities inhabited by our people in these valleys. There will be a stake of Zion organized . . . and a tabernacle built. . . . "

John Stoddard died within a year, but George Stoddard's "conversion" brought him into the forefront of these developments. On January 22, 1902, George was rebaptized in the Logan Temple and he, Ellen and the seven children (Howard was two months old) were sealed in the Mormon covenant of eternal marriage. Two months later he was appointed bishop of the year-old LaGrande, Oregon, Ward. He was released from this position after five years to become a counselor to Union Stake President Franklin S. Bramwell, and in 1914 he succeeded Bramwell as head of the ecclesiastical unit which encompassed the wards in eastern Oregon. This post he held until his death.

The development which moved the center of Mormon activities from Baker to LaGrande was the establishment of a church-sponsored sugar factory in the Grande Ronde Valley in 1898. It was a spin-off from the successful production of beet sugar in Lehi, Utah, early in the decade—a venture sponsored by the L.D.S. hierarchy to provide a cash crop for Great Basin farmers.

David Eccles was persuaded, reluctantly, to invest in Utah Sugar Company, and when it succeeded he moved aggressively into this new field. In association with Charles Nibley, George Stoddard and others he organized Oregon Sugar Company, which built the first sugar factory in the state. The operation attracted some Mormons to settle in LaGrande and also contributed to missionary success among the local population. It also called George Stoddard's attention to the possibilities in the Grande Ronde Valley and led him to move to LaGrande shortly after Howard's birth.

Oregon Sugar Company, unfortunately, was not successful. The climate was right for sugar beets, but according to Arrington's biography of Eccles, the Oregon farmers "did not have the labor supply (not as many children) and preferred to grow wheat." The immigrants from Utah and Idaho who came with high hopes were never able to produce as much as half the tonnage required to make the plant profitable. The company was absorbed into Amalgamated Sugar Company, a part of the "Sugar Trust," in 1902, and after unprofitable operations for another decade the plant was moved to Rigby, Idaho. By then Stoddard and Nibley had become involved with Henry Havemeyer and other eastern capitalists in organizing Western Idaho Sugar Company, and that in turn had merged into Utah-Idaho Sugar Company, another element in the American Sugar Refining monopoly. The "trust" was broken up by the U.S. Supreme Court after 1911, but the two regional sugar companies continued to operate in the Intermountain West. Stoddard still held stock, but his active participation in the sugar industry ended with the closure of the LaGrande plant.

While it lasted, the LaGrande operation received George's major attention because of its economic importance to the new Mormon communities at Union, Cove, Mount Glen, Alicel, Imbler and Nibley, in the eastern end of the Grande Ronde. All became wards, along with Baker and LaGrande, when Union Stake was formed in 1901. George's interest as bishop and stake presidency member from 1902 onward made him work to keep the plant long after his interests as a sugar industry investor ceased to benefit. Howard's memoir describes the denouement from his father's perspective:

> Perhaps no other day in his life was so dismal as that beautiful spring day . . . when final decision was made to move the sugar factory. As he walked home from a directors meeting, the number of idle men on the streets, the selfishness and short-sightedness of others who could make the venture a success, weighed upon his mind. . . . His vision of growth and development for the people, the establishment of homes and the building of a strong stake of Zion in Eastern Oregon seemed shattered. It seemed that he was alone and helpless. . . .

As he feared, some of the small wards did not survive and some good people moved away, but the church base remained. The stake center which Apostle Richards foresaw was built in LaGrande while George was bishop. Stoddard and Nibley lumber, dollars and perspiration were generously contributed to what L.D.S. historian Andrew Jenson would later describe as "a fine tabernacle." When Church President Joseph F. Smith came to LaGrande in June 1907 to dedicate the edifice, he also effected the stake reorganization which brought George into the presidency.

Howard's formative years were thus filled with awareness of the importance of Mormonism to his parents and family. His mother was always active as teacher or officer in one of the church organizations; from 1908 to 1932 she was president of the Union Stake Primary (children's program). His older brothers began going on missions for the church about the time he was old enough to be baptized. He doubtless found some of the meetings as tedious as did others in his peer group, but he was habituated to church-going from infancy and the foundations of a lifelong commitment to Mormon principles and practices were securely laid.

His father's success in the lumber business made it possible for Howard to grow up in comfortable circumstances. By the time of John Stoddard's death, Oregon Lumber Company was well along the course which would help to make the other two founders very wealthy. Stoddard Brothers Lumber Company, run by George and Joseph Stoddard, was one of several smaller firms which shared in the growth of the industry. As already noted, time and events brought George into business relationships with his father's associates. After the 1900 fire at the Stoddard Brothers mill on Clear Creek led to the investment ties with David Eccles and a temporary split between Eccles and Charles Nibley, George found himself drawn closer to Nibley. The trend was accentuated after Eccles took George's sister Ellen and her family back to Logan a few years later. Nibley also settled in Utah when he was called to be presiding bishop of the Mormon Church in 1907, but his friendship and business ties with George continued.

George Stoddard's lumber interests expanded rapidly in the first years of the twentieth century. Grande Ronde Lumber Company was purchased by Nibley and the Stoddards in 1902, with Nibley becoming president and George one of the directors. Its mill was located at Perry, a few miles from LaGrande. Its profits were $93,000 in 1903 and three years later it was capitalized at $650,000. With the Nibley-Eccles reconciliation, Eccles also purchased stock and became a director. Operations continued profitably until after World War I.

The Nibley-Mimnaugh Lumber Company was launched by two of the stockholders in the Grande Ronde Lumber Company to buy land and cut timber along the Grande Ronde River. Its mill was at Wallowa, also near LaGrande. Needing funds around 1911, the company borrowed from Eccles and also expanded its capitalization; the Grande Ronde Lumber Company, Stoddard Brothers Lumber Company and Eccles became major stockholders and Nibley sold out his interest. The firm operated profitably until the 1920s.

The last of the Stoddard lumber ventures was jointly undertaken with Nibley at Santa Cruz, California. The San Vicente Lumber Company was a disappointment almost from the start. The available timber proved of poor quality and the enterprise was a constant source of worry to George, who had the primary operational responsibility. He was in California when he died, and the company was disposed of not long afterward.

Meanwhile the Stoddard Brothers Lumber Company changed its name to the Stoddard Lumber Company and transferred its incorporation from Utah to Oregon in 1914. According to Arrington the company was worth about $400,000 at this time. It prospered for a decade before beginning to be affected by the vicissitudes of the other Stoddard companies. The final chapter of this story involved Howard directly and painfully. It will be told later.

The years of Howard's growing up, however, saw the Stoddard lumber interests generally doing very well. The development of the business network took George rather heavily into debt, but earnings and prospects were good and the children enjoyed the comforts and status which came with their father's financial and ecclesiastical advancement.

Certainly George Stoddard enjoyed an excellent reputation in industry, community and state. Twice elected president of the Western White Pine Manufacturers Association, he effectively represented the industry in rate-making hearings before the Interstate Commerce Commission. His testimony, Howard remembered, prompted one of the commissioners to say, "I have never heard such a remarkable, clear presentation of an intricate subject." By inheritance or observation Howard came to possess a similar skill.

As an unpaid lobbyist George powerfully influenced the adoption of workmen's compensation legislation in Oregon. He also worked for statewide prohibition. As a philanthropist he helped to build the LaGrande Y.M.C.A. and the community hospital. At the time of his death he was not only an executive in the several lumber firms but a director and one of the founders of the Oregon Life Insurance Company and a director of the Baker Loan and Trust Company.

Given the prominence of business, church and community activities in the life of his father, it is not surprising that Howard Stoddard grew up in a home in which the conventional middle-class allocation of parental responsibilities prevailed. George provided the livelihood while Ellen handled the domestic side. Waldo Izatt Stoddard, who joined the family on September 11, 1904, later expressed the relationship in these terms: "He left it up to Mother to raise the family and discipline us to a degree, except as the boys grew older he counseled and worked with them." Emma Jean, born November 12, 1906, died before her fifth birthday. Robert LaVon, born October 21, 1912, rounded out the family circle. David Stoddard remembered that his mother was once on the train to Logan with several of her ten children when she was asked if they were all hers or if it was a picnic. "She announced that they were all hers and that it was no picnic."

Ellen remembered the songs of Scotland which she had learned from her father and she taught them to her children. She prepared baskets of food and clothing for them to distribute to the poor at Thanksgiving and Christmas. She was thrifty and hard-working to the point of carrying out the dishpan water and pouring it on the flowers. She worried so much about her family's wellbeing that the characteristic is mentioned in the children's reminiscences. Yet she agreed with George that they should be given responsibilities and some latitude. Howard and later Waldo drove Ellen and other Primary officers from LaGrande to Salt Lake City—a three day trip at that time—when they were in their early teens.

From his experience with his stern and zealous father, George Stoddard was led to pursue a different tack with his children. Ellen concurred, and she was in fact the one who provided most of the moral and religious instruction until the boys were old enough to accompany their father on trips to the lumber camps or out-of-town church meetings. The children knew what was expected of them but discipline was not severe. Waldo remembers that his mother once or twice "boxed my ears," but he recalls no physical punishment from his father. George taught primarily by example. More than once Waldo heard him say to others, "Well, when I begin to smoke, or swear, or drink, then it will be all right for my boys to do so. . . ." Yet he did not flaunt his standards, unless an incident which occurred when he was president of the Western Pine Manufacturers Association be so regarded. As described by Howard, this is what happened at one of the convention banquets:

> Wine glasses were placed in front of each plate and filled by the waiters. As they came to father all eyes were upon him. Quietly he turned his glass upside down and ordered water. Shortly after, toasts were offered and he was called upon to respond. Lifting his glass of

> clear sparkling water he said, "Gentlemen, it is my intention to conduct my business on principles just as clear and untainted as this glass of water I hold in my hand. Come, let's drink our toasts to this platform."

Ellen Stoddard had no more than sporadic elementary schooling and George went no farther than into high school, but their commitment to self-education was life-long. Their trip to Europe early in 1912 was more than a junket to see their missionary sons and a balm to ease the pain of little Emma Jean's recent death of polio. It fulfilled a shared ambition to see the homeland of their parents and other of their Mormon kin and friends. As for the children, they were expected to do their best in school, but George was not a martinet about grades or attendance. He would take one or two of the boys out of school for a day or two occasionally to accompany him to one of the logging camps or sawmills. His explanation: "I'll teach you more out here doing things than you'd learn in school in a day or two."

Devoted though he was, George's religious commitments did not produce as rigorous a standard for Sunday observance as some of his L. D. S. associates. Even when he was stake president he would sometimes tell the boys—after they had attended their morning meetings—to take the car and go swimming, fishing or picnicking. "You can't keep a bunch of red-blooded, husky boys around here doing nothing", he would say. According to Waldo, "he knew what had to be done for boys to grow up properly, and not restrict them so they'd rebel."

If the parents ever vigorously disagreed, it escaped the notice of the younger children. The extent to which George consulted Ellen on business decisions is not documented, but it is clear that he had the final word on major decisions affecting the family's future. Ellen's domestic autonomy, on the other hand, was respected. That George might have done some things differently may be illustrated, and that he had a sense of humor is certainly illustrated, by a cherished family anecdote. On an occasion when Ellen was ill and the task of getting the younger children ready for Sunday School fell to him, he hunted unsuccessfully for some garments and then exclaimed, "If these children were mine, I would know where their clothes might be."

Except for the conventional sex-differentiation in the case of Jeanette, the treatment of the Stoddard children was apparently even-handed. All the boys went with their father to the camps and mills and often they were left to look after themselves while he attended to business. When Howard was about thirteen he and Waldo accompanied their father to a lumbermen's convention in Chicago. While there was no need for the children to produce income for the family, the boys were all expected to work in the summers, with some time off for fishing or vacation trips. George agreed to match the pay which the boys earned so that they could accumulate enough to meet their personal financial needs during the school year.

Unlike his austere father, George believed that fun was an important element of life. He liked to rough and tumble with the boys and he also taught them to play pool on the regulation-size table which was a fixture in the LaGrande home. To strait-laced critics he said, "I would rather have my boys doing something at home in a good atmosphere than have them going elsewhere to get such entertainment." Not only did the Stoddard boys learn to play well but some of the sons of the strait-laced neighbors did also.

Although George Stoddard's assets increased beyond $750,000, his family's life style was not ostentatious. The large red brick home which he built when they moved to LaGrande in 1902 continued to be their home until 1928, long after he was gone. They enjoyed one of the first automobiles in the town, a Winston Six touring car. (George lost the sight of an eye when one of the carbide lamps on the car blew up while being lit, but the injury slowed him down only temporarily.)

In a family of ten children the development of each was bound to be influenced by the personalities and activities of all. Certainly Howard Stoddard did not grow up in a tranquil or lonely social environment, though he was spared the stresses of frequent relocation experienced by the older brothers. The number of siblings is a little deceptive, too, because Emma Jean died as a child and the other nine were sufficiently spaced so that the oldest were on their own before the last arrived. As Waldo, the brother closest to Howard, put it: "By the time they started to go away to college and on missions, there were never more than six or seven at home at any one time."

Of the six older Stoddards, Elmer was perhaps the leader, but they were all different, all independent and all close to one another. All except Jeanette left home for school, missions or marriage while their father was alive, and in varying degrees he was for all the boys an example. That they should all become lumbermen was natural.

Howard and Waldo knew their father only as boys, and his death was the most traumatic experience of their adolescent years. This shared experience and the shared relationship with their widowed mother and much younger brother, Bob, helped to draw them together, although they were different in many ways. Of all the Stoddard boys their paths most closely paralleled, and those paths took them away from lumber, Oregon and the Mormon West.

It was, as Waldo put it, "a remarkable family." When the eight brothers got together for the annual golfing reunion in Sun Valley, Idaho, in 1960, the club professional announced that he was happy to waive the green fees for them and any comparable group that might come along. There is reason to believe that Howard shared Waldo's opinion: "If I as a boy had had a chance to choose a family and an environment to grow up in, I could not have made a better choice. . . ."

Bob wrote in 1961 that all the Stoddard boys had their share of ambition and drive, plus a bit of stubbornness. "But I think Howard had a singleness of purpose which was more intense than any of his brothers." At the same time Elmer credited the brothers with accusing young Howard of "not enjoying life." "But who knows," he added, "perhaps he had as much pleasure in his pursuit of life as we found in sports." According to Waldo, Howard "loved to read and was inclined to be a good student from the first day he entered school." Lester remembered that George Stoddard gave a dollar each month to the youngster with the best report card, and Howard usually won. "Probably gave him his start in banking."

An inclination and desire to work with his hands was expressed in a variety of activities. Howard and Waldo had a Meccano building set which grew with the years, and Howard bought an alcohol-burning steam engine to run the various mechanical devices which the young boys built. Howard won a prize in the LaGrande "pushmobile" competition; he called his little wagon a "road louse" because it was painted white with little black dots on it. Later he converted an old Model T Ford into a "bug" of which he was very proud.

Carpentry skills were honed in a high school manual training class and he built a one-runner sled on the basis of a picture in *Popular Mechanics*. Since commercial skis were not readily available, he spearheaded a project to have some of the young men make their own. He also built the diving boards for the swimming hole at the dam on the Grande Ronde River at Perry, using personally selected lumber from the sawmill there. (The house which he built in East Lansing years later had a work bench, tool cabinets and the other paraphernalia of a hobby shop. Howard made less use of it than he intended, but it permitted him to teach his boys a little about carpentry and a lot about orderliness and the proper care of tools.)

Howard indulged in a number of athletic activities, but he did not excell. Waldo reports that his brother was a pretty good swimmer but did not enjoy football very much. As for basketball, he played on some of the teams which used the hardwood floor which the Stoddard boys and others installed in the ward recreation hall, and he did well enough in high school to receive a letter.

Waldo's judgment on Howard's basketball skills: "Mediocre; he would round out the team." Hunting and fishing trips were frequent, often two or three-day camping trips into the nearby canyons and forests in which several of the brothers, and once in a while their father, took part.

As teen-agers Howard and Waldo worked summers as their older brothers had done. The trip to the box factory four miles up the canyon from LaGrande was made on bicycles until they accumulated money for a motorcycle with sidecar. They were normally paid ten cents an hour for a ten-hour day. On a piecework project Waldo remembers that they once nailed ends on a thousand cantalope crates in a day and received two dollars each for their record-setting performance. Howard also occasionally drove a lumber company truck. (His enthusiasm for mechanics found further expression in keeping the family car clean and operating smoothly.)

Not all the boyhood friends were Mormon, but Howard and Waldo found their closest friends among boys with similar backgrounds and expectations. There were Protestants and Jews among them. At the LaGrande High School, which had about 350 students then, the L.D.S. young people tended to be the leaders, and in the town the few "roughneck kids" rarely presented problems. Howard was generally an "A" student, preferring such courses as accounting, mathematics and science. He was president of the senior class and a participant in the class play. While he did some dating and, in Waldo's words, "enjoyed dancing to a degree," he had no special girl friend when he went off to college and then on his mission.

His serious interest in church activities and religious ideas developed early. He was capable of cutting a priesthood meeting or Sunday School class on occasion and of bearing the verbal reproofs from his father which were the consequence. But he generally took his church assignments seriously and the missionary experiences of his older brothers inclined him to prepare himself for a call which would come in time. Peter G. Johnston, who succeeded George Stoddard as president of Union Stake, once said to Ellen Stoddard: "Now that boy is a thinker. . . . He knows what he is talking about and he is going to accomplish something."

As already noted, the most distressing boyhood experience for Howard Stoddard was the death of his father. George Stoddard had gone to Santa Cruz, as he did frequently during the last two or three years of his life, to look after the faltering San Vicente Lumber Company. Emergency prostate surgery was followed by uremic poisoning and he died ten days later. Of his family only Ellen was with him when the end came on February 27, 1917. He was in his fifty-second year.

Howard never forgot the assessments of his father which were expressed at the funeral services in LaGrande. Charles Nibley, the close family friend and business associate who was still presiding bishop of the Mormon Church, declared:

> In all of my association with George I never found a single thought or idea, nor knew of a single action of his life that did not ring true. He was always candid and fair. His judgment I regarded as most sound. He was dependable and loyal to the core, always a hard worker. . . .

CHAPTER 4

# Student, Missionary and Bridegroom

Howard Stoddard grew up fast after his father's death. Although he was still in high school in LaGrande, he became the "man of the house" when his brother John left for the University of Utah in the summer of 1917. The older brothers were nearby and Earl and Elmer took the leadership in the lumber businesses, but only Jeanette, Howard, Waldo and Bob remained with their mother. Ellen Stoddard handled her loss well. George left his family well provided for, and the stained glass windows which he had given to the stake tabernacle across the intersection from the red brick home were a constant reminder of happy times and hopeful expectations. (The home no longer stands and the windows have been installed in a new Union Stake center. Only the old-timers now remember when the Grande Ronde Valley was Stoddard country.)

One consequence of their father's death was that Howard, Waldo and Bob found it possible to break the family pattern of going back to Utah to college. Many of their high school peers, Mormon as well as non-Mormon, were choosing the schools of the Northwest, and so in September 1918, when he was not yet eighteen, Howard enrolled at Oregon State Agricultural College (now Oregon State University).

Rather shy as well as young, Howard did not immediately become a leader on the Corvallis campus. He enlisted in the reserve officer training program, but World War I shortly ended and he did not complete the requirements for a commission or see active military service. Nor was he apparently affected by the influenza epidemic which swept many campuses and communities in 1919. Although he had sufficient means so that he did not have to divide time between classes and a job, and he was one of the few in his class who owned a car, he was only moderately active socially. On Waldo's testimony, Howard never had a serious attachment to any young woman during this period of his life. He joined Phi Delta Theta fraternity, where he formed several enduring friendships. A fraternity brother later described him as the best dressed man on campus and told of his taking some of the students to an out-of-town movie in his sporty roadster and getting back so late that some of the girls had their week-end dating privileges suspended.

The two years in which Howard pursued a liberal arts program at O.S.A.C. saw him consistently making "A" and "B" grades. Although enrolled in the commercial course, he took classes ranging from oratory to American government and history. His only "D" was in typing, but he raised the grade to "C" in the second semester and developed a competence which served him well for the rest of his life. At the close of his freshman year he spent the summer back in LaGrande, working in the family lumber enterprises and sharing such tales of campus life with Waldo that the younger brother headed for Corvallis as soon as he finished high school two years later.

There were few Latter-day Saints on the campus or in the town, but Howard spent part of his O.S.A.C. years reading the Bible and other Mormon scriptures, preparing for the mission call which he had been taught since childhood to expect. It came at the end of his sophomore year—to the Swiss-German Mission.

Mormonism had been preached in Switzerland and Germany for three-quarters of a century, but always it was associated with the same doctrine of "gathering" which had brought Howard's grandparents from Scotland and England.The branches of the church in Europe were rarely large, therefore, and the membership was constantly changing as the more dedicated converts made their way to America if possible and the less zealous drifted into inactivity. Missionaries from Utah, Idaho and Arizona were heavily relied upon for instruction and leadership, and when these were all withdrawn on the outbreak of war in 1914, the local congregations inevitably fell into some disarray. The mission president, Angus J. Cannon, remained in Switzerland during the war, keeping in touch with the members by mail and through the mission publication, *Der Stern.* But in 1916 the German government restricted such communication and the local congregations thereafter were virtually on their own. Local missionary work continued and the German membership actually increased by about five hundred, reaching 8,000 in 1918. In addition to the stresses of a conflict in which at least seventy-five German Mormons died, the local branches had to cope with problems of housing and differences over doctrine, procedures and management of funds. Many of the church members carried on steadfastly, but apathy and friction were widespread.

Not until 1920 was the Swiss-German Mission resupplied with missionaries from the United States. Serge F. Ballif, President Cannon's successor, served until April 1923, and his journal tells a great deal about the problems, tasks and opportunities with which missionaries and members had to contend. The mission extended from Geneva to Koenigsberg, and most of it lay in a Germany beset by defeatism and resentment, political tumult, poverty and a monetary inflation which eventually reached catastrophic proportions.

When Elder Howard Stoddard sailed for Europe with the Ballifs on the "Berlin" in October 1920, he was not yet twenty years old. Despite failure to obtain visas in Washington and again in Paris, the president and his wife remained unruffled. "The Lord called us, and we're going," was all the explanation they offered to their uneasy young companion. Many times during later years Howard told church audiences what happened when their train reached the German border:

> We all got off to go through the customs. We waited until a lot of people had gone through. Finally, we entered the customs office.
>
> The officer who approached us was quite abrupt. "Where do you want to go?"
>
> "We want to go to Frankfurt."
>
> "Well, why waste my time here. Go on." He never even asked to see our passports.

Howard's first assignment was in Bern, Switzerland, a lovely city which had once had a flourishing L.D.S. branch but now, according to Ballif, was "very backward." As a new missionary, Howard concentrated on learning the German language and the techniques of tracting door-to-door, holding street meetings and conducting church affairs. He was paired with companions who had been engaged in the work barely longer than he. He was one of the speakers at a conference in December attended by both the retiring and incoming mission presidents. Ballif's preliminary and premature judgment was that "the Berner is naturally slow, but we woke them up as much as possible." (A generation later Bern became the site of the first Mormon temple in Europe.)

Early in 1921 Howard was transferred to Frankfurt am Main, where he first encountered the impact of the war upon the German people. The church authorities in Utah had established Zion's Emergency War Fund to aid impoverished members in Europe, and when Howard shortly was appointed president of the Frankfurt branch he became involved in the distribution of funds and commodities. President Ballif had an early opportunity to size up the young Oregonian when they traveled together to Coblenz, in the American sector of the Allied-occupied Rhineland, to receive an installment of money "for our poor people in Germany." Unfortunately this allotment did not arrive on schedule.

Jean Wunderlich, then a member of the Frankfurt congregation and in 1949 the president of the West German Mission, recalls how Howard endeared himself to the members. The occasion was the traditional branch outing on the public holiday which followed Pentecost Sunday. It was May, the woods along the Main River were beautiful, and the young people were particularly excited at the prospects. As Wunderlich reports it:

> On the day in question, as we waited, we noticed that a young lady named Emma Kuhn, who was usually with us, had not yet arrived. We became apprehensive because we knew that her health was precarious . . . she was suffering from advanced tuberculosis. She lived with her widowed mother in a garret apartment. Howard, who was then president of the branch, was also absent. Knowing that we would not leave without him, he soon appeared and explained that Emma was desperately ill and he was staying behind to help her aged mother take care of her. When we returned at night we learned that Emma had died and that her mother and he were the only ones at her death bed.

Highlights of Howard's year in Frankfurt were visits by L.D.S. Apostles Orson F. Whitney and David O. McKay. In August Whitney addressed an audience of more than five hundred, 313 of them "friends" who had responded to the invitations and advertising generated by the small branch. McKay's visit in November was toward the close of a round-the-world tour of Mormon missions. When he returned a year later to preside over the European missions of the church, his son David Lawrence McKay was one of Howard's co-workers in the Swiss-German Mission. Charles W. Nibley III, a grandson of George Stoddard's long-time friend and business partner, was another.

Apparently recognizing Howard's potential as an organizer and trouble-shooter, President Ballif assigned him on January 1, 1922, to preside over the Berlin conference, the largest regional unit in the mission. More than five hundred people packed the hall in which, according to Ballif's journal, President Stoddard "was sustained by full vote of people." For the next fifteen months Berlin was Howard's home, with interruptions for conference tours and business trips from Stettin to Leipzig. By May 9 Ballif could note after an unannounced visit: "President Stoddard has things well in hand in his conference."

An incident involving a fellow missionary from LaGrande occurred in March when Elder Frederick Zaugg and his companion were expelled from Koenigsberg by the police for allegedly preaching emigration to the German Saints. Official church policy had deemphasized the "gathering" since the end of the 19th century. Now Ballif stressed to both missionaries and members that church and mission policy forbade advocating emigration to America. (Within a year runaway inflation robbed this counsel of its effectiveness. Between 1922 and 1930 occurred the greatest trans-Atlantic migration of German Mormons in the church's history, a volume exceeded only after World War II. Jean Wunderlich was one of the emigres who called on Howard and Jennie Stoddard in New York City in 1926 while en route to Utah.)

Howard was one of twelve conference presidents who made short talks at the opening session of a mission-wide gathering at Stuttgart, July 2, 1922. In a marathon five-and-a-half hour testimony meeting the next day all 140 missionaries were heard. On the evening of Independence Day the Americans put on a program for several hundred Germans and Swiss and all "had a glorious time." The next day the missionaries attended the Passion Play at Oberammergau.

Ballif's growing reliance on Howard is apparent in his participation in real estate negotiations in Leipzig and Dresden and the distribution of $40,000 sent to Berlin in September for the support of the mission poor. In Ballif's account of the conference meetings held at this time is such language as this: "President Stoddard made splendid outline for day's meetings." "Conference is in splendid condition advancing." And a sentence almost prophetic: "Stoddard gave some very valuable instructions on efficiency."

During this period Howard found time to send Waldo, then an Orgeon State sophomore, a beautiful leather-bound volume of the three modern L.D.S. scriptures, the Book of Mormon, Doctrine and Covenants and Pearl of Great Price. On the fly leaf he wrote: "Waldo, this book will be your best friend." Two years later the volume went with Waldo on his mission to South America.

The climax of Howard's German experience came in February 1923. First was the quarterly meeting of the Berlin conference, at which he had the thrill of addressing an audience estimated at thirteen hundred. Then two weeks later, February 17-18, David O. McKay met in Berlin with all the German missionaries. They numbered 207, and the instructions they received from McKay were "very impressive." The second day was Sunday, and large crowds heard the European Mission president both morning and afternoon. In the evening the three Berlin branch choirs performed Evan Stephens' oratoria, "The Martyrs," which commemorated the death of the Prophet Joseph Smith and his brother Hyrum. It is not recorded whether the rendition was in German or English. It is reported that 1800 people were in attendance and another 300 were turned away.

The experience gained in arranging so impressive an undertaking would stand Howard Stoddard in good stead when the time came to reorganize banks and prepare constitutional conventions. The mastery of the German language and the taste for opera and symphony were other missionary acquisitions which enriched his later life. And living with rampant currency inflation made an unforgettable impression. Each dollar which Howard took with him to Germany in 1920 bought about five Deutschmarks. Each dollar which he received from home on the eve of his departure was worth more than 50,000 Deutschmarks, and in another nine months German paper money was worthless.

*Der Stern,* April 1, 1923, carried an announcement that Howard J. Stoddard was honorably released from his missionary service. It also noted that he planned to visit the Holy Land on his way home. The projected round-the-world journey was cut short by dysentery and homesickness, however. After climbing one of the Egyptian pyramids—alone and miserable—Howard headed for home by the most direct route.

When Howard Stoddard decided to continue his college education at the University of Utah rather than returning to Oregon State, he made one of the crucial decisions of his life. He spent only one term on the Salt Lake City campus, but it made possible his introduction to Jennie Creer and it resulted in their honeymoon departure for New York City and a life adventure which they would share for almost half a century.

Like her husband-to-be, Jennie Creer came from pioneer Mormon stock. Her great-grandparents on the Creer line were among the earliest to accept the teachings of the Latter-day Saints missionaries who first came to England in 1837. Some of the maternal forebears on the Brockbank and Thomas lines joined the church in America; through them came Jennie's eligibility for membership in the Daughters of the American Revolution. All the lines converged in the 1850s in the little central Utah settlement of Spanish Fork.

Edward Creer, born in Bolton, Lancashire, November 13, 1813, and Ann Morris Creer, born in Chorley, Lancashire, December 27, 1814, were both textile mill workers when they encountered Mormonism. They had been married on June 26, 1835, and the first of their twelve children, William, had been born in Preston, Lancashire, on February 18 of the next year. To this small factory town not far from Liverpool came Elders Heber C. Kimball, Orson Hyde, Willard Richards and Joseph Fielding in the summer of 1837, and Edward and Ann were among the hundreds baptized in the ensuing year. William, Jennie's grandfather, was baptized in Preston at the age of eight, about the time he left school to become a loom tender in one of the cotton mills.

Local opposition to their new faith, the lure of America, and the admonitions to gather to Zion led Edward and Ann Creer to sail from Liverpool to New Orleans in 1847 on the "Charlotte." Six children accompanied them, along with Edward's widowed mother and four sisters. Seven years elapsed before they reached their journey's end in Utah, and by then the mother, one sister and two of the children had succumbed to the cholera which was then endemic in the Mississippi Valley. Edward and his sons Williams and Orson toiled in the coal fields near St. Louis while eking out resources for the journey across the plains. (The John Stoddard family was in St. Louis during part of this period, and it is likely that Stoddard and Creer children knew each other seventy-five years before Howard and Jennie linked the two names.)

The Creers went West with the 1854 migration, part of a train of twenty-five wagons organized by the Perpetual Emigrating Fund Company. The first year in Salt Lake Valley Edward, William and Orson worked for John Young, a brother of President Brigham Young, taking provisions for pay under the barter system then prevalent in the cash-poor Mormon settlements. William, Orson and their oldest sister, Mary, went to Spanish Fork in 1856 to seek their fortunes, while Edward worked in the temple quarry in the mountains east of Salt Lake City until the Utah War brought temple construction to a temporary halt. Edward and William then took the field together as members of the Nauvoo Legion, waging a campaign of harrassment against the U.S. Army units which marched toward Utah Territory. When Brigham Young's strategy changed in the spring of 1858, Edward and Ann and their younger children were among the thousands who abandoned homes in the face of the advancing troops. The "Move South" took them as far as Spanish Fork, and when peace returned to the northern Utah valleys, they did not go back.

On January 22, 1858, William Creer married Sarah Jane Miller Bradley and his sister Mary married John Banks in a double ceremony. All of William and Sarah's nine children were born in Spanish Fork. The eighth, John

Preston, who became Jennie's father, was the last born in the log cabin which was the family home for more than fifteen years. Soon after John Preston's arrival on July 27, 1875, the William Creers moved into the frame house which still stands on the log cabin site.

Edward and William, father and son, worked together on many construction projects, including the transcontinental railroad contracts which Brigham Young made with the Central Pacific and Union Pacific in northern Utah. Both participated in the sporadic Indian fighting of the pioneer era and Edward helped to build the Provo Woolen Mill, taking shares in the enterprise as part payment for his work and being employed there for twelve years as a spinner. Ann Creer died on December 19, 1877; Edward followed on January 12, 1886.

Spanish Fork remembers William Creer for his enthusiasm for music, law and public affairs. He was one of the founders and for forty years the president of the Spanish Fork Choir, an organization which gained regional renown. When a brass band was formed, William sold his only cow to purchase a second-hand instrument. (Sarah Jane's views on these priorities, as she looked after a growing family in a one-room cabin, are not recorded.)

William served as a city alderman from 1866 to 1875, and during these years he read law in books purchased with some of his railroad earnings. In 1877 he was admitted to the Utah bar and thereafter until the end of the century he was either city attorney or mayor of Spanish Fork. He also served six terms in the territorial legislature, and he was one of the strong advocates of woman suffrage in the Utah state constitutional convention in 1895. He was given a testimonial in recognition of his efforts and his name appears on the Utah State Constitution. When he died on August 10, 1900, he left his family in comfortable circumstances. His widow died on May 22 1902.

Jennie Stoddard's father, John Preston Creer, trained to be a school teacher at Brigham Young Academy, in Provo, and L.D.S. Business College, in Salt Lake City. He also served in the Southern States Mission from 1897 to 1899. There he may have developed the fluency of speech which matched his congenial personality. Jennie remembers him as the kind of person whom acquaintances would ask, "Will you preach at my funeral?" It is not surprising that gregariousness is a prominent trait among his children.

On September 4, 1901, John Preston married Mary Elizabeth Brockbank, a daughter of Samuel and Mary Jane Thomas Brockbank. Samuel had the distinction of being the first male child born in Spanish Fork. Mary Elizabeth was born on September 6, 1879, so she was 22 and her bridegroom was 26 when they began life together. After completing ten years of schooling, she had gone to work as clerk and buyer for the Spanish Fork Co-op, a general merchandise store. Quiet, efficient and hard working, she was often in complete charge of the store, and the experience which she gained made her an invaluable business advisor to her husband later. She did not plan to be, and according to Jennie she did not become, "just a housewife." Evidence of her enthusasm for self-improvement was the etiquette book which she not only owned and read, but quoted when it seemed appropriate.

Mary Elizabeth was also devoted to her church and community. She sang in the town choir, of which her future father-in-law, William Creer, was president. Of her service in the L.D.S. Mutual Improvement Association, first as counselor and then president, Mary later wrote: "In those days we didn't have janitors to make the fires, fill the lamps or clean the buildings. After I went home from work, I chopped an armful of wood, took over matches and paper and made a fire in the stove to warm the room. . . ."

The newlyweds settled in the Utah County hamlet of Mapleton, where John Preston had accepted the principalship of the local school at the memorable salary of $65 per month, plus the use of a four-room house for a monthly rental of $2.50. By 1904 they were back in Spanish Fork, he as superintendent of schools and she as a young mother. Seven children were born during their years in Utah County: two boys—John Preston Jr. and Frank, and five girls—Jennie, La Reta, Lucille, Clara and Mary. The father's namesake died in infancy. The girls and Frank developed ties which kept them close long after they left home, and Howard Stoddard was one of the in-laws who was in time brought into the Creer family circle. Frank was in the insurance business in Michigan for a time after his graduation from Harvard Business School, and Clara and Mary and their families became permanent residents of the Wolverine State after living in Illinois and New Jersey.

Speculation in mining stocks proved a profitable sideline for John Preston Creer during the pre-World War I boom years. From 1907 to 1910 he gave full time to these ventures, and a new home for his family and a business building on Spanish Fork's Main Street are monuments to that success. Appointment as superintendent of schools for Utah County drew him back into education, and he became the primary author of the 1911 and 1915 legislation which consolidated the high school districts and then all the public school districts of Utah—a reform of major significance for the state and nation.

Business beckoned again at the end of the war. Creer accepted the vice presidency of B.A. McMillan Paper and School Company and moved with his family to Salt Lake City. The educational opportunities afforded by the University of Utah were an important attraction; all of the Creer children eventually graduated from that institution. The McMillan firm subsequently became Utah-Idaho School Supply Company, and John Preston was associated with it for the rest of his life. He and Mary were active in civic and church affairs in Salt Lake City until their deaths on April 25, 1954, and October 20, 1967, respectively.

Jennie Creer had just finished her junior year at the university when a conspiracy brought her and Howard Stoddard together. The chief plotter was Howard's Aunt Jennie Beers, a matchmaker who sensed a potential union in two young people who, on appearances, hardly seemed meant for each other. Jennie was approaching her 21st birthday and savoring to the full the social aspects of a coed's life. The college classes received attention enough to insure graduation, but Jennie had been brought up in an era and environment which saw fulfillment for an attractive young woman not in a mortar board but in a man with a future. Howard had a future, no doubt about it, but he was new in town, more interested in academics than extra-curricular matters, and still shy in social situations despite the poise acquired in the mission field.

The dinner at Jennie and Will Beers' place must have been a "first date" of an unusual sort. As Jennie remembers it, business and monetary affairs were the topics of conversation:

> Howard told me about the conditions he had found in Europe. . . . Currency was unstable, and he saw the horrible results of inflation, where money became of no value, and he talked about the suffering of the German people. . . . He also told of learning the German language, how he learned to speak it fluently, understand opera and read German poetry.

Howard's verson of the evening is not available, but whoever knows Jennie will take it for granted that not all the time was devoted to such sad and solemn themes. Still, it was a new experience for both of them, and apparently mutually agreeable. They dated frequently after Howard returned from a summer of reunions and employment in Oregon. They were fellow students at Utah only for the fall quarter of 1923, but before Howard left for Columbia University at Christmas time he gave Jennie this diagnosis of their relationship and prospects: "I take the serious side of life and you take the fun side. I think we make a good couple and that we can make a go of it. Come to New York with me, and we will go to Columbia to school together."

Forty-eight years later Jennie Stoddard told the directors of Michigan National Bank, at a special meeting honoring her recently deceased husband, that she had said "Yes" very quickly, "for fear he might change his mind."

While Howard was in the East plans were made by correspondence for a summer wedding. Howard worked energetically on the courses required for admission into Columbia's School of Business, while Jennie completed the requirements for a baccalaureate degree and teaching certificate in speech and dramatic arts. (Apart from a year of practice at a Salt Lake City junior high school on the way to her degree, Jennie used her teaching training only in church classes. She never had time for amateur theatricals, but her flair for the dramatic found other expression.)

The marriage ceremony was performed in the Salt Lake L.D.S. Temple on September 4, 1924, with Apostle Orson F. Whitney officiating. The wedding reception that evening was a gala affair at the Creers' new home on Gilmer Drive, on Salt Lake City's east side. All the college friends were there, and a dance floor had been constructed in the back yard for their enjoyment. Jennie remembers wishing she could have joined them. Instead she and Howard stood for hours with her mother and father, greeting the relatives, business associates and friends who came to greet the bride and groom. Many of them had never seen Howard Stoddard before.

The honeymoon was a drive to LaGrande, where the Stoddard families held another big reception. This time it was Jennie's turn to be on display. Howard took her around to the lumber companies which his father had helped to found. Unfortunately, that very day the Grande Ronde Lumber Company mill burned to the ground. (It was one of a number of reverses which befell the Stoddard enterprises in the 1920s, and it reinforced Howard's resolve to carve out his own career in another field.)

As the young couple traveled by train to New York they shared their aims and ambitions. Jennie always insisted that she realized right then that Howard was destined to become chairman of the board of some company. What company she did not know, but she also knew that he would be chairman of the board in their family. "He would be the star of the show," she later told the M.N.B. directors, "and I would play a supporting role."

Whether it always worked out that way, those who knew Howard and Jennie best must judge. One who knew them very well for many years put it this way: "Howard picked out a great banker's wife!"

CHAPTER 5

# Fledgling Banker

The 1920s were exciting times to be in New York City. They were the years of the flapper, whom even a newlywed ex-missionary probably noticed, and the speakeasy, which the two teetotalers from the West knew only from such sources as *New Yorker* cartoons. The ticker-tape parades, the Ziegfeld Follies, Carnegie Hall and the old Metropolitan Opera House were far downtown from Columbia University, but the subways were safe and the gallery tickets to highbrow and middlebrow entertainments were cheap by today's standards. The movies learned to talk while Jennie and Howard were in New York, and they were already a favorite relaxation for the busy couple.

Columbia was an academic enclave on Manhattan's upper West Side. It was decades away from the confrontations with expanding Harlem. In the Golden Twenties the poetry of the Harlem Renaissance and the Black nationalism of Marcus Garvey were entertaining rather than provoking to students who were aware of them. The assimilation of the myriad of Slavs, Italians, Greeks and Jews who had come through Ellis Island before war and restrictive legislation checked the flow was seen as a problem by some, but these newcomers were congregated far downtown. The world into which Jennie and Howard moved in 1924 was remote from the squalor and strife which were also part of metropolitan life.

Columbia University in those days was a prestige institution for affluent and/or aspiring students. According to the prevailing pattern in higher education, its professional schools offered undergraduate as well as graduate degrees. So Howard spent his first term satisfying prerequisites. Then, with a new wife for additional motivation, he mingled with graduate students in some of the classes which led to his Bachelor of Science degree from the School of Business. Awarded on June 3, 1925, the diploma bears the signature of the legendary Nicholas Murray Butler. The transcript shows that courses in banking, economics and psychology apparently gave Howard no difficulty. It would be interesting to hear his explanation for the "C+" in Finance 101; legions of undergraduates can sympathize with the "C+" in introductory statistics. A research assignment, "Unit and Branch Banking," may have been his introduction to what became a career interest.

Howard and Jennie were fortunate in that the Stoddard lumber businesses were doing well enough to maintain them in a less spartan lifestyle than some of their contemporaries. Dividends and his portion of the George Stoddard estate meant that no part time jobs were necessary and that Jennie could sample a course or two at the university. Within a year they picked up a new Buick in Flint, Michigan, on the way back from a trip West. Howard had already rented a very comfortable furnished apartment on Amsterdam Avenue, near the campus, for their first home, and although they changed locations annually during their New York years, each place was a congenial setting in which to entertain their growing circle of friends. Jennie remembers that sometimes they saw a concert or play "from the best seats in the house," but usually they tailored their activities to the economic capabilities of those they knew best.

While a bachelor at Columbia College Howard had gravitated naturally into the group of New York City Mormons, many of them married students from Utah. Now Jennie joined the group. Two of the closest associates later became presidents of her *alma mater*, the University of Utah—A. Ray Olpin and James C. Fletcher. The Olpins were contemporaries, like the Howard R. Driggses, the G.P. Roses and the Claude Heiners. Jim Fletcher was a young teen-ager in Jennie's Sunday School class, and his father, Harvey, was already engaged in the accoustical research which would soon win him a worldwide reputation at Bell Laboratories. Harvey Fletcher was also president of the small L.D.S. branch in Manhattan when the Stoddards arrived.

Still filled with missionary enthusiasm, Howard entered actively into the affairs of the Mormon congregation, and when the Fletchers moved to Long Island he became president of the Manhattan branch. Dissatisfied with the inexpensive but unattractive rented quarters in which meetings were being held, he arranged finally for the Sunday morning use of Carnegie Hall. It was a happy circumstance not only for the Mormon "regulars" but also for the stream of visitors from the West and immigrant Latter-day Saints from Europe who passed through New York in those years. Howard's experience with poor church facilities in Europe had already convinced him that an attractive environment enhances both worship and the prospects for conversion, and he continued to promote that concept throughout his life.

Once the degree was in hand, Howard was anxious, as Jennie put it, "to get out in the world and see what experiences he could have." He entertained thoughts of additional schooling later, with perhaps a look at the law, but his immediate concern was for an exposure to banking in something other than a routine job. Through George F. Oglethorpe, a friend of his banking cousins, Marriner and George Eccles, he received an offer from Irving Trust Company, but it was his own persuasiveness which won him a post in the credit department. This gave him opportunities to analyze the financial condition of loan-seeking firms of many kinds. His time was divided between visiting business offices all over New York City and writing reports and discussing them with associates in the trust company offices at Number 1 Wall Street. It was great training for a banker who would never be office-bound. (It was also a good vantage point for watching the parade for Charles Lindbergh on his triumphant return from Paris.)

The pay was good enough, together with dividend income from Oregon, to permit Howard and Jennie to move in 1926 to a garden apartment in Jackson Heights, just across the East River on Long Island. The lawns, tennis courts and access to sun and sky made it seem more appropriate than Manhattan for rearing a family, and the first little Stoddard was on the way. Howard Preston Stoddard was born in Fifth Avenue Hospital, near Central Park, on April 14, 1927, having given ample notice so that his mother's concerns about the thirty minute trip from Jackson Heights proved unwarranted. He was the first grandchild in the John Preston Creer family, and the prospective grandparents were happy to send Jennie's sister, Lucille, to stay with her during the last days of waiting and the first days of adjusting. "None of us were very experienced in parenthood," Jennie recalls, but the healthy young son made only the usual complaints.

Two things changed later in 1927. Howard decided to take some night classes in law at New York University and moved his family to an apartment in Greenwhich Village to reduce the commuting time between home, school and office. At the same time the family lumber businesses came on hard times, cutting back that source of income and introducing new matters for concern. Within a few months the plans for night school had to be abandoned, and within a year New York City as well.

Several factors contributed to the economic reverses for the lumber operations in Oregon. Overriding everything was the fact that the housing boom of the 1920s passed its peak two or three years before the stock market crash ushered in the Great Depression. By 1927 lumber prices were declining, inventories were accumulating and retrenchment was becoming inevitable.

Unfortunately, the Stoddard enterprises had little room to maneuver. When Charles W. Nibley moved out of the lumber business in the early part of the decade, Stoddard Lumber Company acquired its assets along with some tax liabilities which eventually proved unmanageable. Grand Ronde Lumber

Company borrowed to buy Nibley's shares in that firm, and later on to acquire the foreclosed assets of Baker White Pine Lumber Company. Credit was also obtained to rebuild the sawmill which burned down during Jennie Stoddard's honeymoon visit to Oregon, and later to purchase some new timber lands to replace those which had been cut over. (Techniques of forest conservation had been talked about since the Progressive Era, but only a few firms with large assets and land holdings had begun to practice this long-term form of timber replenishment.)

The profitability of the two lumber companies in which Ellen Stoddard and her children held most of the four thousand shares of stock depended, thus, upon sales and prices high enough to meet loan obligations and fixed costs. By 1927 this relationship was being threatened, and in faraway New York Howard Stoddard learned that a credit problem of special poignancy needed his attention.

Several times during 1927 and early 1928 Howard went out to Oregon, taking leave from the trust company in order to see what might be done. Finally he concluded that the rescue—or salvage—operation required full time. Resigning from Irving Trust, he took Jennie and little Howard with him to Oregon. It was a tough decision, because his prospects looked bright at the bank, the Fletchers, Driggses and other friends were planning careers in the East, and when he had left Oregon it had been with the firm intention not to go back to the lumber business. But now he had acquired the very kinds of experience which might help to save the situation back home, and so he made the choice.

During the fall and winter of 1928-1929 the family lived in an apartment in LaGrande. Howard's mother was in Baker, only fifty miles away, and Jennie had her first real opportunity to get acquainted. Elmer, David, Lester and John Stoddard were in the Northwest and participated in varying degrees in the painful decisions which had to be made.

Ultimately the deteriorating lumber market defeated Howard's best efforts. Working with his brothers and with Eccles, who was both a stockholder and a creditor, Howard worked out a plan to merge Grande Ronde and Stoddard Lumber companies, with himself as "trustee" to handle the complex stock transfers, tax negotiations and loan renegotiations which were involved. Had there been larger holdings of standing timber and had it been possible to extend some of the loans for a while longer, the arrangement might have worked. But the history of the Great Depression is filled with such "ifs". Further borrowings and credit rearrangements kept the company afloat until March 1931, when the Stoddards' stock which had been pledged as collateral was sold for about 20% of its 1926 market value. When the terms of the trusteeship arrangement were finally executed against him in 1932, Howard was left with an obligation of over $16,000. Tax claims later added several thousand dollars to this burden, but it was all eventually paid. Some of the Stoddard brothers continued to be associated with lumber enterprises, but the family business which John and George Stoddard had built out of Oregon pine was at an end.

The experience in Oregon brought Howard Stoddard his first close contact with Marriner Stoddard Eccles, the oldest son of George Stoddard's sister Ellen and by now the chief manager of that part of the David Eccles estate which went to Ellen's family. It was a testing experience because the Eccles Investment Company was one of the major creditors and so Marriner was involved in one of the crucial "ifs". It was a testing time in another sense, for Marriner was sufficiently impressed with the ability and energy which Howard showed in a failing cause that an enduring relationship was formed on the basis of mutual respect and a sharing of many ideas.

Forty years later Howard would write:

> I cannot close this letter without expressing to you, Marriner, my deep appreciation for all that you have meant in my life. . . . each visit with you, particularly in recent years, has served to enrich my understanding of the problems as they were analyzed and expressed by you. You have indeed had a tremendous influence for many years, and I am most grateful to be numbered as a relative and a close, personal friend.

In a note to Jennie following Howard's death, Marriner wrote of the cousin who was eleven years his junior:

> As you know, Howard was like a brother to me. . . . I regarded him as an extremely able young man with great future possibilities, and was very happy to be associated with him briefly in the lumber business, and later in the banking business at Salt Lake. . . . Howard was always one of my very strongest supporters. We usually saw eye to eye with reference to the banking, economic, political and social problems.

The first spin-off from the kindling friendship was a new job for Howard Stoddard. Eccles and others were putting together what eventually became one of the intermountain West's largest financial networks, First Security Corporation, and a merger with National Copper Bank in March 1929 gave them entry into Salt Lake City. With the three small affiliates of National Copper, the merger added $8,000,000 in resources to the $37,000,000 represented by the twenty-one banks in Utah, Idaho and Wyoming already under

First Security control. In the shuffle of top personnel which took place at National Copper, Louis S. Cates was named president. He was not a banker but vice president of Utah Copper Company, whose open pit mine at Bingham, Utah, had already been described as "the richest hole on earth." His name added prestige to National Copper and its affiliates, but he took the position with the understanding that Eccles would provide someone else to direct the actual operations.

This was the post to which Marriner Eccles nominated Howard Stoddard —vice president (and *de facto* manager) of National Copper Bank. The First Security board approved the nomination on March 31, 1929. Not yet 28 years old, Howard Stoddard had his first bank.

Coming back to Utah was a homecoming, especially for Jennie. The first house she and Howard rented was on Gilmer Drive, quite close to the scene of the wedding reception. There had been visits to Salt Lake City almost every summer, but now the big Creer home and the loving parents and sisters were always accessible. When Virginia Claire Stoddard joined the family on September 8, 1929, there was no lack of caretakers for young Howard and helpers for mother and new baby. Howard's sister Jeanette was also in Salt Lake and before long Waldo and Lester came to town. As did Stanford Creer Stoddard, destined to be called "Bud"; he was born December 28, 1930. By then his parents had bought a home a little farther up on Salt Lake's "East Bench" and were settling in for what they anticipated would be a long stay.

Yale Ward, the L.D.S. ecclesiastical area into which Howard and Jennie moved, was described in a contemporary church encyclopedia as having within its limits "some of the most desirable residential sites in Salt Lake City, upon which are constructed many palatial homes, occupied by some of the most influential business and professional men of the city." The Stoddards belonged to the upwardly mobile residents of the ward, rather than those who had already arrived. Their home was hardly palatial, but the immediate neighborhood was full of young families of similar circumstances and aspirations.

Jennie quickly found that three small children made "homemaker" a full time vocation, even with help from a hired girl. Howard's income supported his family in comfortable style, but instead of dividends from stockholdings there were installments on the trusteeship debt; so there was little to spare. Hard times meant declining prices and Howard and Jennie were among the fortunate ones with constant or rising incomes who benefitted from that aspect of the deepening depression.

An indication of Howard Stoddard's ability to attract favorable attention was his appointment as an alternate member of the high council of the Liberty

Stake, of which Yale Ward was a part. The role of the twelve-man high council in the Mormon Church is to advise the stake president, the ward bishops and other organizational heads, to perform certain judicial functions, and to carry instruction and admonition to the ward congregations. A long-standing tradition among Mormons is that "high council night" is rarely exhilarating, since many able organization men are not great preachers. Howard, however, was as effective in the pulpit as in the council chamber, and most Sundays found him speaking to a church audience somewhere.

His being chosen for this position when he was not yet thirty, and in a stake with more than 500 high priests and 15,000 members, is remarkable. That Wilson McCarthy, a member of the Liberty Stake presidency, was an attorney for First Security Corporation may have had something to do with the choice. That McCarthy was also a Democrat would have great significance for Howard Stoddard a little later.

The Great Depression hit Utah hard. The state's two major economic activities, farming and mining, did not fully recover from the post-war depression of 1920-1921, and when the crash came in 1929 these areas were among the most severely affected. Between 1929 and 1933 the total production of minerals plummeted 80 percent, farm income declined by more than 60 percent, and the portion of Utah's work force without jobs rose to 35 percent. Of the 105 banks in the state in 1929, 32 failed during the next four years.

People like Howard and Jennie who were not directly hurt were nontheless touched by the widening circle of adversity around them. Members of both of their families were affected. Ellen Stoddard's estate had already disappeared and her sons gradually left Oregon to seek opportunities elsewhere. In 1934 she finally sold her small home and moved to Salt Lake, where she spent the last five years of her life. Her children were able to support her in modest circumstances and John built a home for her next to his own.

"No bank of the First Security Corporation ever closed during the Great Depression," Sidney Hyman notes, "and no depositor in them lost one cent of his deposits." Yet fifteen of the twenty-six banks in the system were running at a loss by 1933, and it required a blend of ruthlessness and bold imagination to keep the financial network solvent. When another Ogden bank failed in the summer of 1931, runs on First Savings Bank and First National Bank there were averted only by a mustering of cash and an ostentatious display of confidence. The following February the failure of Deseret Savings Bank in Salt Lake City threatened Deseret National Bank, which Brigham Young had founded sixty years before. When the L.D.S. Church and the larger financial institutions declined to intervene, Eccles arranged the merger of

Deseret National and National Copper into First National Bank of Salt Lake City, under the First Security Corporation umbrella.

It was a cliff-hanger operation and Howard Stoddard was right in the middle, for the combined banks were to operate out of the National Copper offices and all of the arrangements had to be completed between a Saturday afternoon and the next Monday morning. Approval for the merger was obtained by phone from the Comptroller of the Currency; by then he was dealing with bank crises on a daily basis. The agreement of Deseret National stockholders representing at least two-thirds of the shares had to be obtained, and they were scattered all over the nation. The phone bills were huge and the legal requirement of thirty days notice was simply ignored. The assets and records of Deseret National were moved and a consolidation of accounts was affected in one all-night operation. A publicity blitz was launched through the Sunday Salt Lake *Tribune*, and when the new bank opened its doors the next morning there was no run on deposits at all. Howard emerged as senior vice president of First National, with some valuable insights on how banks can be put together.

These and other experiences extended Howard Stoddard's general education in economics and business. When he had gone to Columbia particularly to study under the famous E.R.A. Seligman, economists were preoccupied with the firm and the market. (A wiseacre with an unsympathetic view of the "dismal science" pioneered by Adam Smith, David Ricardo and Alfred Marshall scoffed that one could produce an economist by teaching a parrot to say "supply and demand.") The unfettered movement of prices was assumed to direct production and distribution with an "unseen hand." The Federal Reserve System, founded in 1913 to curb the power of "Wall Street", was judged to have adequate powers to insure the health of the financial community. In fact, producers administered prices in large sectors of the economy, the New York banks dominated the Federal Reserve Board, and neither bankers, businessmen nor the academicians who taught banking and business courses were any better prepared than Herbert Hoover to cope with what happened in 1929.

Schooled by his observations in Germany to fear the consequences of unchecked inflation, Howard now discovered that deflation could be quite as traumatic. What had happened to the Oregon lumber market was now happening throughout the industrialized world, producing breadlines, bitterness and prospects of revolution. Like most of his contemporaries, Howard saw war as the usual cause of inflation and inflation as the eventual cause of deflation. The timing and severity of this business contraction therefore perplexed him.

Unlike the more conservative advocates of patience, he began to lose confidence that market forces would set everything right if given time, but he rejected the monetary panaceas which were coming into vogue on the political left. He must have heard some of the increasingly interventionist talks which Marriner Eccles began giving in 1931, he probably read some of the literature which Marriner was reading, and he may have had opportunity to discuss more than bank business with the man who would soon become a key figure in the New Deal. By the time he addressed the Utah State Bankers Convention in June 1932, Eccles was declaring: "There is only one agency in my opinion that can turn the cycle upward and that is the government."

Judging from an address which Howard Stoddard gave to a conference of the American Institute of Banking at about the same time, he was less sanguine about governmental remedies than his cousin. In a Los Angeles speech on "Bonds and the Purchasing Power of the Dollar," he likened a recently passed Congressional resolution asking the Federal Reserve Board to restore the 1926 commodity price level to an Indian rain dance—"actuated by worthy motives but inspired by false medicine men." He continued:

> It is indeed regrettable in the present babel of confusion, the political expediencies, that so little sane reasoning is being done by those charged with the political and business leadership of this people. One of the most, if not the most, pressing problems—the stabilization of the purchasing power of the dollar—has been considered and discussed largely with a woeful disregard of facts and conditions.

There followed a clear analysis of the function of money as a carrier of value and of the implications for debtors and creditors when declining prices made money increase in value. "If the purchasing power of the dollar had the same meaning for the debtor and creditor alike," then the decline in the price level since 1929 would not be so devastating. Since it was not the same, the total domestic bonded and mortgage indebtedness, which he placed at $161 billion, was a formidable barrier to recovery. "In one sense—and the most important one—to the extent of about 40%, we have transferred wealth in the form of increased buying power from one class in our community to the other, and the debtor is being sorely tried."

As to remedies, the talk was clearer about those which won't work than about better alternatives. Printing press money, silver-backed currency and "the mystical power that was supposed to reside in the central banks" to control prices by manipulating the discount rate were rejected. "At this juncture," said the young Salt Lake bank executive, "I venture the assertion that when a workable solution has been found it will be based upon the control of other basic factors and not upon money itself."

To this point he seemed in agreement with Eccles and the "new economics" which would come into vogue later in the 1930s. But in the end his memories of depreciating Deutschmarks and his fundamental optimism about the American economic system led him to a conclusion closer to what both Hoover and Franklin D. Roosevelt would advocate in the upcoming presidential campaign:

> Deflation has taken its toll. Let us not forget that inflation, once undertaken, may also get out of control. To use an old expression, we may find that we have leaped from the frying pan into the fire. The disease from which we are suffering did not develop over night and its eventual cure will not be found in a hysterical supplication to the rain gods.
>
> Purchasing power of the dollar will doubtless be stabilized on or about the present level. Adjustments will be made on this basis, slowly at first, then with increased rapidity. The weaker bonds and mortgages will go, the others remain. We will enter a period of wholesome prosperity strengthened, not weakened, by the present difficulties.

A few months later Howard Stoddard was in Washington and Detroit, finding the adjustment of purchasing power more complicated and the weeding out of weak debtors more painful than he may have anticipated. He entered the governmental battle against the depression a year before Marriner. He did so not because of any conversion to an interventionist philosophy, but because of the course which his own fortunes seemed to be taking.

During Louis Cates' presidency at National Copper Bank the Stoddards and Cates enjoyed an excellent social relationship and Howard had wide latitude in managing the bank. But in 1930 Cates accepted the presidency of another big copper enterprise, Phelps Dodge Corporation, and moved to New York. Roy Bullen, the First Security director who succeeded to the presidency, also gave Howard a free hand, but he held the post for less than a year. During this period Waldo Stoddard came to Utah for the summer after a year of night classes at Columbia University and employment at New York's National City Bank. Howard arranged a job for him as a bookkeeper at National Copper and shortly afterward Eccles offered him a position in the credit department of First National Bank of Ogden. Waldo soon married Winifred Holmgren and a few years later the couple responded to Howard's invitation to come to Michigan. The relationship thereafter would be very close and mutually beneficial, as the brothers applied the lessons both had learned about banking in perilous times.

With Bullen's death the trend of Howard's work in Salt Lake City gradually frustrated his career aspirations. First Security Corporation took over Bankers Trust Company and Central Trust Company, merged them in 1931, and moved Charles Smith, the former president of Central Trust, into the top spot at National Copper. (Howard was still too young to head a major unit in a business so tradition-bound and image-conscious as banking, even Eccles style, and Smith was both a banker and an important stockholder.) Smith was an active president, and in 1932 he took the same role in the new First National Bank. As Eccles later described the situation in a letter to Stanford Stoddard: "I do not believe the relationship between Charles Smith and Howard was a very happy one—they were entirely different personalities and Charlie was very much older and much more conservative." Unwilling to carry on in an uncomfortable situation until other deaths or banking upheavals created new opportunities, Howard began to look around. Eccles wrote to Jennie after Howard's death: "I regretted exceedingly that he decided to leave First Security . . . ; however, under the circumstances, I did not blame him."

The opportunity came late in 1932, when the federal Reconstruction Finance Corporation was given extended life and expanded its professional staff in an effort to cope with worsening economic conditions. Wilson McCarthy was one of the R.F.C. directors, having been appointed by President Hoover because the board needed a Westerner and a Democrat. Whether Howard sought out McCarthy or *vice versa* is uncertain. The invitation to join the R.F.C. staff as an examiner came during the busy pre-Christmas season, and before the end of the year Howard had resigned his bank position and was off to Washington.

It was not, apparently, a hard decision for Howard. Washington was displacing New York as the center of decision-making for the American banking community, and in the fluid situation created by the economic malaise and the election of Roosevelt anything might happen. Howard was at least nominally a Republican, but the Democrats had the ball and he had no doubt of his ability to make some points for himself under their game plan.

As for Jennie, what she was called upon to leave was much more tangible than what Washington might bring. But she had already learned that "there was one way to live with Howard, and that was to go where he went." She waited until May for Howard Jr. to finish kindergarten and Howard to decide where his R.F.C. assignments made it advisable for them to light. Then she left Utah with her six, three and two-year-olds, and with her fingers crossed.

Except as frequent visitors, she and Howard never came back.

CHAPTER 6

# Depression and Bank Holiday

Washington in the winter of 1933 was a far different place from the tranquil Southern-style town on the Potomac which Howard and Jennie Stoddard had visited in the middle 1920s. Calvin Coolidge was in the White House then, and the nation responded to his credo: "The business of the United States is business." Coolidge's decision not to run for reelection in 1928 was later interpreted by some as prophetic foresight, but the man whom the Republican Party picked to succeed him was quite as capable of inspiring confidence that prosperity would endure indefinitely.

Herbert Hoover took office in the nation's capital at about the same time Howard Stoddard went to work at National Copper Bank. Four years later Howard came to Washington as Hoover was preparing to leave. The depression which destroyed the political career of a President created an opportunity for an ambitious young banker who was still looking for a place to make his mark.

In January 1933 Washington was a capital in crisis. More than twelve million people—almost 25 percent of the country's work force—were unemployed. The gross national product—a concept which economists were just beginning to study seriously—had fallen almost 50 percent in four years, from $103 billion to $56 billion. (It did not pass $100 billion again until 1941.) Prices of the things most people bought were down by about 20 percent, but since average weekly wages for those who still had jobs were down almost a third, only a relatively few Americans enjoyed what Howard and Jennie had experienced in Utah—a real increase in purchasing power. Banks were failing at a rate of five or ten a day—1,352 in 1930, 2,294 in 1931, and 1,456 in 1932. The decline in failure rate in 1932 was due in part to the efforts of the Hoover administration and particularly to the Reconstruction Finance Corporation.

The situation deteriorated late in the year and that was when Wilson McCarthy invited Howard to join the fight.

By present day standards of bank solvency and depositor security, the record of the American banking system had not been good for years before the great crash. Business optimism and Federal Reserve Board policies encouraged credit expansion in the 1920s, and since major industries like automobiles, appliances and utilities financed much of their expansion out of earnings or stock sales rather than short-term borrowing, commercial banks shifted more and more of their funds into securities and real estate. They also put their own earnings into these markets and sometimes organized investment companies to handle the placement of their own and their depositors' money. When the securities market soared in the latter part of the decade, banks provided many of the brokers' loans which finance the speculative buying of stocks and bonds.

Such investments were at least nominally backed by collateral, but unlike the short-term business loans which had earlier been the chief stock-in-trade of commercial banks, these assets could not be turned into cash by rediscounting them at the Federal Reserve banks. Nor could they be sold for cash without loss if the stock, bond or mortgage markets declined, as they did in the years of the great deflation. Lack of liquidity had been a problem for some banks in the 1920s, when "frozen assets," imprudent loans, inept management and outright fraud led to the failure of more than 5,000 banks. Most of these, however, were small state banks, unaffiliated with the Federal Reserve System and not subject to the constraints and examinations—lax as they were—which went with national bank charters. With the collapse of the stock market late in 1929, major banks with tens of millions of dollars in deposits began to face liquidity problems. The 9,000 banks which suspended operations in the next four years included some of the most prestigious.

According to Susan Estabrook Kennedy's *The Banking Crisis of 1933* (1973), when the pretentiously-named Bank of United States failed in New York City in December 1930, it revealed "two flaws in the American banking structure: first, a need for fundamental reform of bank organization, operation, and supervision; and second, the unique relationship between credit and finance, on the one hand, and public confidence and fear on the other." Panic swept in intermittent tides through cities and whole regions during the next two years. As the spectre of depositors lining up to make withdrawals haunted the dreams of bankers, they contracted their loans, unloaded assets for what the market would bring, foreclosed on defaulters—both businessmen and homeowners, and in general contributed to the failure of confidence. Facing the desperate urgency to save their own banks, boards of directors were unlikely to be swayed to other courses by the exhortations which were Washington's first response to the crisis.

Hoover saw the depression primarily as a problem of confidence and urged voluntary and cooperative actions to meet it. He and his financial advisers considered some of the comprehensive changes in national banking laws which were being advocated by a few academicians, legislators, and radical bankers like Eccles—Federal Reserve membership for all banks, statewide or trade area branch banking by national banks, and separation of commercial and investment banking. But in the face of heavy opposition, he did not push for reforms until very late in his term, and then unsuccessfully.

Eugene Meyer, the chairman of the Federal Reserve Board, urged that Hoover ask Congress to revive the War Finance Corporation, which had been organized in 1918 to mobilize the nation's financial resources for war production and had not wound up its affairs until 1929. Instead the President urged bankers to form a voluntary National Credit Corporation, which would muster credit to support banks which were in trouble. Such an organization was formed in October 1931. Banks joined by subscribing to its capital fund and could then obtain loans on the basis of sound assets which were not eligible for rediscount at the Federal Reserve banks. (Mortgages which were not in default and the stocks and bonds of solvent companies represented real economic value, but they were not the kinds of negotiable paper which could be sold to the Fed—at a discount—when more cash was needed.)

Loans from National Credit Corporation helped banks in California and Louisiana almost at once, but the caution with which the directors disposed of the $500 million available and the burgeoning demand for help quickly made it clear that other remedies were needed. Seven hundred banks failed in December 1931 and January 1932 while Congress acted upon Hoover's next recommendation.

The Reconstruction Finance Corporation was approved by Congress and the President on January 22, 1932. Its capital stock of $500 million was to be subscribed by the United States Treasury, and it was authorized to raise another $3 billion through the issue of notes and bonds. Its resources were to be used primarily to aid banks, other financial institutions, and railroads with liquidity problems by making loans on the security of a wide range of sound assets. The board of directors appointed by Hoover was chaired by former Vice President Charles G. Dawes and included two *ex officio* members, Secretary of the Treasury Ogden Mills and Federal Reserve Board Chairman Meyer. The other four members were Wilson McCarthy, Harvey Couch,

Gardiner Cowles and Jesse Jones. A successful banker and a flamboyant Texas Democrat, Jones became R.F.C. chairman in the Roosevelt administration, and he and McCarthy were the directors with whom Howard Stoddard would have most to do.

R.F.C. was also authorized to use up to $200 million—the amount was later increased—for the reorganization or liquidation of banks which were already closed, in order to help them pay off their depositors. A bank's closing did not mean that its assets had become valueless, only that in a depressed economy they could not be turned into sufficient cash to meet the needs of panicky depositors. What R.F.C. was authorized to do in such a case was to make a loan, secured by some of the bank assets, large enough to relieve acute depositor distress, and to help develop a plan for the orderly disposal of the remaining good assets over a period of time. A relatively sound bank might be reorganized on the basis of an R.F.C. loan, new capital funds from its stockholders or depositors, and negotiated arrangements for the deferred payment of some deposits. A weaker bank might be liquidated, its depositors being paid in part from the proceeds of the sale of its best assets and from stockholder assessments, and additional payments to depositors being made over time as remaining assets could be disposed of. It was this phase of Reconstruction Finance Corporation operations which shortly gave Howard Stoddard his entree into Michigan banking.

At about the same time Stoddard was wrapped up in the Deseret National Bank merger, Congress also authorized the Federal Reserve Board to rediscount more kinds of commercial bank obligations and to issue Federal Reserve notes on the basis of United States government bonds. These provisions of the Glass-Steagall Act sought to stimulate business activity by making it easier for banks to loan money. This action, like the President's efforts to talk prosperity back from "just around the corner," accomplished little because the state of the economy discouraged investment of any kind. Virginia Senator Carter Glass—the "father of the Federal Reserve System"—was by now pushing for more comprehensive banking reforms, but Hoover and the Federal Reserve Board both opposed this effort. In consequence the Fed and R.F.C. spent most of their energies trying to prevent bank and business failures. Initially the response was hopeful; there were only 46 bank failures in March 1932.

Most R.F.C. bank loans in this period were large, the logic being that the failure of a major city bank would have repercussions throughout a state or region. One loan got the agency into political hot water and produced repercussions which hampered freedom of action thereafter. Three weeks after Dawes resigned from the R.F.C. board in June, a loan of $90 million was made to Central Republic National Bank of Chicago, of which he had been and was now again an officer. In strictly economic terms it was a sound loan, ultimately repaid in full. But the charge of "favoritism" came easily in a land distraught, disillusioned, and in the midst of a presidential campaign.

When Congress revised the R.F.C. statute shortly afterward, it included a provision sponsored by Speaker of the House of Representatives—and Democratic presidential contender—John Nance Garner requiring full publicity for all loans. Hoover at first refused to accept the bill for this and other reasons, but ultimately he accepted a publicity provision with congressional assurances that information about loans would only go to concerned government agencies, who would keep it confidential. By the time Stoddard joined its staff, R.F.C. was so sensitive to possible adverse publicity that it adopted a more cautious and conservative approach than the dimensions of the nation's financial problems probably required.

The revised law also authorized $300 million in R.F.C. loans to states which were running out of relief funds for the unemployed, and up to $1.5 billion in loans for self-liquidating public works to generate jobs. The relief loans were quickly made, but the public works program was barely moving when the Roosevelt administration moved both unemployment relief and "pump priming" to other agencies. That left R.F.C. with its primary mission of administering credit transfusions to certain sectors of the American economy. (During the campaign critics called it "a breadline for business" and censured Hoover for his reluctance to provide similar relief for the poor.)

In its first eight months R.F.C. approved almost $1.5 billion in loans to about 6,000 financial institutions, including almost 5,000 banks and trust companies. Closed banks received $44 million in reorganization and liquidation loans. Most of this aid was to small banks which had been forced to close their doors when city banks called loans in order to protect their own liquidity. (This was the kind of hard-nosed banking which enabled most of the major metropolitan banks and several aggregates like First Security Corporation to weather the storm.)

Revisionist historians, no longer awed by the New Deal's charismatic leader, cite R.F.C. as evidence that Herbert Hoover was moving in unprecedented directions despite limitations imposed by an election-minded, opposition-controlled Congress and his own distrust of "statism." As the political campaign progressed, the differences between the Hoover and Roosevelt prescriptions for depression fighting were more in style and rhetoric than in substance. But the veterans of the "bonus march," the residents of the "Hoovervilles," and millions of other Americans believed it was time for a change and said so in the November 1932 election.

By then the banking situation was deteriorating again. First Security Bank of Boise had survived a run brought on by the closing of several other Idaho banks. Nevada banks were in trouble and the governor of the state closed them all late in October. When they reopened after the election, several were in reorganization under plans developed with R.F.C. participation. No other bank moratoriums followed immediately, but a precedent had been set.

In December Hoover extended the R.F.C. charter to January 1934. Other extensions followed under Roosevelt and Truman, and the corporation did not go out of existence until 1953. During the depression and World War II it loaned, spent and gave away more than $35 billion, with negligible losses on its loans and investments. Of the $3.4 billion it made available to all American banks during the financial crisis, 13 percent went to Michigan institutions, and most of that was in the form of reorganization and liquidation loans with which Howard Stoddard was closely involved.

When Stoddard went to Washington, he had a general idea of what he was getting into. As an examiner he would be looking at the portfolios of banks seeking R.F.C. help. He would be making the recommendations upon which loans would be made or denied—upon which closures or reorganizations might depend. He did not know that he would be sent immediately into the most complex, serious and frustrating banking mess that the Reconstruction Finance Corporation would ever face. Nor did he anticipate that he would be in the middle of a nation-wide financial upheaval which would change the character of American banking forever.

Had he known what the next few months would bring, Stoddard might have responded less casually when he was assigned to the Kentucky-Ohio-Michigan R.F.C. region, under Jesse Jones' general oversight, and sent immediately to Detroit. More than thirty years later *Michigan Manufacturer and Financial Record,* in a lead article on "Stoddard's Billion-Dollar Banking Empire," carried this anecdote:

> "It's quite a challenge up there," Jones told him; and when Stoddard accepted, Jones asked him how much salary he wanted.
>
> "Pay me what you think I'm worth," was the quick answer.
>
> Jones grinned. "You can't live on that!"
>
> "There were times when I thought he was right," Stoddard comments now.

Actually the R.F.C. salary supported him and his family in comfort. Further, as the same October 1964 article pointed out, "the Detroit experience paid big dividends."

The state of Michigan was in a singular predicament in 1933 because both the strengths and the weaknesses of the Great Prosperity had been exaggerated there. Automobile production—the most important single factor in the postwar economic growth of the United States—came to be concentrated there. More than 5,600,000 cars, trucks and buses rolled off the assembly lines of Detroit, Dearborn, Pontiac and Flint in 1929. Workers and their families flooded into the factory towns and residential suburbs, attracted by the high wages symbolized by Henry Ford's "five dollars per day." While the nation's population increased by 17 percent in the 1920s, Michigan grew by 32 percent and her urban areas by 47 percent. Detroit soared from 1,000,000 to 1,600,000; Dearborn had 2,000 people in 1920 and 50,000 a decade later, when unemployment haunted many of its heavily mortgaged subdivisions.

This growth, like that of America from the days of the Founding Fathers, was built in part on optimism, speculation and credit. Bright ideas, natural resources and hard work were fundamental, of course, but if the capitalization of future prospects were not also part of the process, there would be little need for bankers (and no Howard Stoddard story).

Michigan's banking system was ill-equipped to cope with the 1920s. The problems and the flawed manner in which they were handled are best described in "The Detroit Banking Collapse of 1933," a 1972 New York Univeristy doctoral dissertation by John J. Holland, Jr. This study, which places less emphasis on human error and villainy than earlier works on the same subject, notes that a conservative state banking code, little changed since the late nineteenth century, forbade what is now called "full service banking." Commercial, saving and trust functions were more sharply segregated than in most states. While state authorities were cautious about chartering new banks, the regulation of financial institutions was not stringent and that of trust companies was particularly lax. Firms in the money business in Michigan were small, serving limited markets. Few of the banks had either national bank charters or affiliation with the Federal Reserve system. Because the agricultural depression of the 1920s hit Michigan relatively lightly, the state experienced few bank failures. But the automobile boom presented new challenges.

Simply stated, the commercial banks, savings institutions and trust companies of Michigan had difficulty finding uses for the funds which an expanding economy entrusted to them. Industrial firms followed the national pattern of financing expansion through reinvestment of profits or through stock and bond sales. They relied on the money markets of New York and Chicago for capital transactions, but they placed substantial operating funds in the local banks of Detroit, Flint, Grand Rapids, Battle Creek and other factory centers. Workers saving for homes, furniture, cars or "a rainy day" poured money into savings banks, savings and loan associations and postal savings accounts. Individuals, firms and estates with larger cash resources found the higher earnings promised by trust company certificates an attractive alternative to investing—or speculating—directly in stocks, bonds or real estate.

Competitive pressure led the commercial banks to the point of excess in two directions. The first is illustrated by the pattern of loan expansion in the 1920s: Traditional commercial loans increased about 25 percent, real estate loans (mortgages, construction advances and commercial building bonds) doubled, and security loans trebled. To the extent that safety was preferred over earnings, U.S. government securities and municipal bonds, particularly those of Detroit, were purchased. The second response was for each bank to open branches in the new factory and residential areas of its home city, as was permitted to state banks. The number of branches in Detroit more than doubled before the real estate boom peaked in 1927, just at the time national banks were given the same branching privilege.

The axiom of both international diplomacy and profit maximization—"If you can't lick 'em, join 'em"—eventually produced a drive toward consolidation in Detroit's financial community. Between 1927 and 1930 a number of holding companies were formed to bring diversified saving, lending and investment services under unified direction. At first the activities were confined to the city, then they expanded to embrace suburban and out-state cities. Two major groups emerged.

Guardian Detroit Union Group, Inc., was the holding company from among the post-1933 fragments of which Howard Stoddard would one day put together Michigan National Bank. Its founders included such illustrious men as Edsel Ford, Henry's son, and Roy D. Chapin, who soon became Hoover's Secretary of Commerce. Its centerpiece was Guardian Detroit Bank, founded in 1927. By an intricate series of mergers and stock trades the "Guardian Group" acquired control of 31 banks and trust companies, with many branches, and brought most of them under national charters. They included National Bank of Commerce, Union Guardian Trust Company and Michigan Industrial Bank, in the metropolis, and these out-state institutions: City National Bank & Trust Company, Battle Creek; Union Industrial Bank and Union Industrial Trust Company, Flint; Grand Rapids National

Bank and Grand Rapids Trust Company; Capital National Bank, Lansing; First National Bank & Trust Company and Federal Commercial & Savings Bank, Port Huron; and Second National Bank & Trust Company, Saginaw. All of them later came to know Stoddard very well.

Detroit Bankers Company, the last and largest of the aggregates, was not put together until 1930, when Michigan's industrial boom had passed its peak and the repercussions of the stock market made retrenchment seem the best approach to preserving earnings. Main units in the "Detroit Bankers Group" were First National Bank, Peoples Wayne County Bank, Bank of Michigan and Peninsular State Bank, with almost 200 branch offices in Detroit. Trust and investment affiliates in the city and banks in the suburbs also came under the tightly-controlled holding company; out-state interests were minimal. This is the group with which Stoddard gained his first experience with Michigan banking after leaving the Reconstruction Finance Corporation.

At the end of 1931 the two Detroit banks in the Guardian Group merged to form the Guardian National Bank of Commerce, with assets having a book value of almost $200 million. Peoples Wayne County Bank also merged with First National Bank, giving Detroit Bankers Company a multi-branch commercial operation with resources book-valued at almost $600 million. Both new banks were under national charters, which meant closer scrutiny by examiners than some of their activities had received from state authorities.

These were the years when the Samuel Insulls, Richard Whitneys and Ivar Kreugers were showing how far from the "straight and narrow road" the pursuit of wealth could lead imaginative entrepreneurs. Breaches of faith and even of law were committed as the men who dominated the two Detroit holding companies tried to maintain profitability and then solvency in a contracting economy. Dividends were maintained at levels unjustified by the earnings (or losses) of the operating companies, funds were shifted from bank to bank to camouflage problems, and deceptive reports were issued to stockholders. More than forty officials were eventually indicted for violations of federal banking laws, but only three were finally punished lightly for technical violations.

The most profound consequences of the publicity which was given to these derelictions after the banking empires had collapsed was that it contributed to the public disillusionment with bankers. A story told by Michigan Senator Arthur Vandenberg and others during the crisis of 1933 went like this: "If you put three bankers in a barrel and sent them over Niagara Falls, there would be an s.o.b. on top all the time."

What brought Michigan banking to disaster was not skulduggery but a traditionally conservative and politically inhibited response to the problem already mentioned in connection with the Reconstruction Finance Corporation—lack of liquidity. To a much greater extent than banks in other metropolitan areas, the institutions of Detroit tied up their resources in loans and investments which could—and did—become "frozen." Union Industrial Trust Company was particularly vulnerable. Under imprudent management it ventured into such high-risk areas as real estate development loans, and by the time it came into the Guardian Group it was already in trouble. Its lavish $12 million, 36-story tower on Griswold Street was not completed until 1933, in time to be described by the Detroit *Evening News* as "the most concrete testimony to all banking mistakes in Detroit."

Ultimately, according to Holland, the efforts to bail out Union Industrial Trust imperiled the whole Guardian Group. In a time when public confidence was crucial the Guardian troubles then affected Detroit Bankers Group—and the repercussions spread far beyond Michigan.

The impact of the Great Depression was nowhere more severe than in Detroit, described by Commerce Secretary Chapin in January 1933 as "the gloomiest city in America." Economic activity fell to one-third of its 1929 peak. Employment in the metropolitan area declined from 270,000 to 60,000, and many of the employed were on short work weeks. More than 150,000 people left the city, and in two years about 87,000 homes and apartment houses were sold for delinquent taxes. Almost 40,000 families were on relief as 1933 opened, and the depletion of city and state resources had brought the weekly relief allowance down to $4.95 per family. In the face of falling income, the city slashed wages, cut back on employment, and still faced the possibility of having no funds to meet payrolls.

The smaller factory towns were in hardly better condition, and the depression this time hit the farming communities as well. A state-wide census in February 1931 reported almost 200,000 unemployed. By January 1933 the situation was appreciably worse.

If Michigan's banking system was inadequate for the 1920s, it was even less prepared for the 1930s. Between January 1, 1931 and January 25, 1933, 195 banks closed their doors. Most of them were small town state banks whose portfolios full of mortgages were already partially "frozen" before the crash came. The failure of Detroit's American State Bank was averted only by joint action of other banks, arranged by the Detroit Clearing House Association, in taking over some of its assets in exchange for funds to pay off its uneasy depositors. An index of the decline in public confidence was the increase in the amount of savings placed in U.S. postal savings accounts, behind which stood the credit of the federal government. In Detroit such deposits were a little over $1 million in 1929, and more than $41 million in 1933.

Government efforts to cope with the situation were more prophetic than productive. The Michigan legislature approved a law in 1932 to facilitate the reorganization of weak banks in order to prevent further failures. The "Michigan Plan" did not stem the tide, but it provided the mechanism for some of the reorganizations in which Howard Stoddard became involved. Congress passed a Federal Home Loan Bank Act, also in 1932, intended to unfreeze the mortgage market, but its resources and provisions were not broad enough to do the job. Its New Deal successors, the Home Owners Loan Corporation and the Federal Housing Administration, provided the guarantees within which Stoddard disposed of many mortgages for the benefit of Detroit bank depositors and later made such mortgages a profitable part of Michigan National's holdings. Reconstruction Finance Corporation made a $9 million loan to Union Guardian Trust Company in July 1932, but at the year's end it seemed clear that this weakest link in the Guardian chain was about to break.

It was an R.F.C. responsibility to avert such happenings, and in January 1933 Howard Stoddard was among the examiners and lawyers sent to Detroit to see what could be done. Jennie remembers his sentiments on facing this formidable task: "I had nothing to lose. If I could help, I had everything to gain."

John K. McKee, who later became a Federal Reserve Board member and a critic of Stoddard's bank-building activities, headed the group. James B. Alley, who became a close friend and later an attorney for Michigan National Bank, was the chief legal representative. Charles T. Fisher, Jr., head of the Detroit R.F.C. office, was one of Stoddard's close collaborators, and the Fishers and Stoddards became good friends. Later Fisher became prominent in Detroit banking circles and from that perspective he, too, opposed Stoddard's unconventional approach to building and managing a banking empire.

At the time they were a group of close co-workers, engaged in the exciting and awesome task of putting together the data and recommendations upon which the fate of the two largest banking groups in the motor capital of America would depend. Some of them shared apartments, their families being in Washington and elsewhere. Stoddard lived in a hotel with other R.F.C. men, not far from the bank skyscrapers where they often worked far into the night. Letters and phone calls were his only contacts with Jennie and the kids "back home."

The technical responsibility of the twelve R.F.C. examiners was to evaluate the assets of the Guardian Group in order to establish the basis for another loan. Their work went on against a background of intricate political and business maneuvering and increasing public clamor. The details are involved and morbid; the outcome was traumatic and profound.

The laws creating the Reconstruction Finance Corporation authorized it to make loans to banks and other financial institutions on the basis of sound collateral. The question which defied answering was how to evaluate the assets offered as collateral. If a mortgage for $10,000, for example, were accepted at face value, then the Guardian Group had more than enough collateral to support the loans needed to meet foreseeable depositor demands. If it were accepted at current market, or liquidating, value, then much of the group's paper was almost valueless in early 1933, even though monthly installments or interest charges were being paid and the long range prospects for full recovery were good. Some kinds of subjective and pragmatic judgments had to be made, and the constraints under which Stoddard and his fellow examiners operated were the cautious terms of the R.F.C. statute, which required a finding that every loan would be fully and adequately secured.

One of the complicating factors was the publicity which attended loans and the rumors about loan applications which inevitably followed the Garner amendment. The merest hint that a bank anywhere was seeking R.F.C. assistance was likely to generate depositor pressure, and the press and politicians scrutinized each loan for signs of favoritism.

Another complicator was the reluctance of bankers, stockholders and large depositors to take risks in a situation so fraught with peril. Adam Smith had built a case for the free enterprise system on the premise that each individual's seeking his own economic advantage would produce a healthy national economy. The Great Depression seemed to prove that, in the short run at least, it wasn't necessarily so.

A third problem was the tension between the outgoing and incoming national administrations. Hoover wanted Roosevelt to endorse proposed emergency actions and remedial legislation and the President-in-waiting refused to do so, partly because of the political risks involved and partly because his own approach to the financial crisis was far from formulated. Only in the latter part of February 1933 did the two Secretaries of the Treasury, retiring Ogden Mills and incoming William Woodin, establish effective liaison, and by then the first fateful R.F.C. decisions had already been made.

Adding fireworks as well as complexity to the situation was the bitter hostility between Michigan Senator James Couzens and Henry Ford. The two had been business associates, but a variety of disagreements led Ford to buy out Couzens' interests in the automobile company. Couzens then went into politics while retaining an active interest in Detroit financial affairs. In the crisis winter the Senator once threatened to publicly denounce any further loan to the Ford-dominated Guardian Group. When Couzens later attacked the R.F.C., saying that he saw no reason to rescue unsound banks, Ford commented, "For once in his life, Jim Couzens is right." Finally, when the Senator agreed under heavy administration pressure to participate in an R.F.C. reorganization plan, Ford refused and the project aborted. (Years later Howard expressed the opinion to his brother, Waldo, that the Detroit closings could have been avoided if Couzens "hadn't been so antagonistic.")

At the same time the Senate Committee on Banking and Currency was holding hearings on the national financial debacle. Crusading committee counsel Ferdinand Pecora put leading New York financial leaders through interrogations which disclosed how "insiders" had taken advantage of their positions during the speculative orgy of the late 1920s and the following deflation. The testimony further undermined public confidence. Virginia Senator Glass expressed a reaction with a Southern twist: "One banker in my state attempted to marry a white woman and they lynched him." Another manifestation was the rantings of the Detroit radio priest, Father Charles Coughlin. Expounder of conspiracy theories which later led him to endorse Hitler, Coughlin now blamed the "bankocrats" for the problems threatening to swamp the nation.

In this context the R.F.C. examiners followed conservative guidelines in evaluating the collateral available for the requested $42 million Guardian loan. Certainly they were stricter than the intuitive judgment Jesse Jones had used eight months earlier in recommending the Dawes loan. But in the politically charged atmosphere, McKee and the R.F.C. board stuck by their judgment that the proposed collateral was insufficient. This meant that about $6 million in local capital had to be found between February 11, when the banks closed for the Lincoln's Birthday week-end, and February 14, when the Guardian banks could not open without R.F.C. help.

Late that Saturday officers of Detroit Bankers Company learned of the seriousness of the Guardian predicament and realized that they, too, must mobilize cash in order to survive the runs which would certainly develop Tuesday. They asked R.F.C. for $100 million, pledging assets which Stoddard and his fellow examiners judged to be adequate, but the R.F.C. board declined to go along without some participation by local capital.

After two days of frantic negotiatings, involving Treasury Under-secretary Arthur Ballantine, Chapin, McKee, General Motors President Alfred P. Sloan, Walter Chrysler, Henry Ford and others, no acceptable plans were found for closing the gap between what R.F.C. would loan and what local bankers judged that the emergency situation required. To avert runs on virtually every bank in Michigan, the concerned parties finally appealed to Governor William Comstock to adopt the device which Nevada had pioneered a few months before.

At 1:32 a.m. on Tuesday, February 14, Governor Comstock declared a moratorium on all banking operations in Michigan except for such hardship transactions as might subsequently be approved. The closure was initially for eight days, but it continued until it merged into the national "bank holiday" which launched the New Deal.

When Franklin D. Roosevelt told a distracted country on March 4, 1933 that "the only thing we have to fear is fear itself," the state of the nation's banks was by no means the least of the problems which he had on his mind. Thirty-four states had no banking facilities or only restricted services. The governors of New York and Illinois suspended operations hours before the inauguration when it became apparent that the great central city banks could no longer stand the panic-generated withdrawals by correspondent banks as well as other depositors. In Michigan 550 national and state banks, representing $1.5 billion belonging to 900,000 depositors, had been under moratorium restraints for three weeks. Depositors had been permitted to withdraw 5 percent from their accounts to meet emergencies, but no acceptable formula for R.F.C. aid to the Detroit banks had been developed.

Representatives of Roosevelt and Hoover worked all night March 3-4 putting together a response to the bank debacle. Ultimately it was agreed that the President should use an obscure provision of the 1918 Trading-with-the-Enemy Act as the legal basis for closing all the banks in the country, and then call a special session of Congress to validate this action, extend the holiday if necessary, and pass legislation to reopen the banks.

On March 6 Roosevelt suspended "all banking transactions" for four days. Emergency regulations issued by the Treasury Department governed this period and the extensions which followed after Congress had acted. Banks might allow access to safety deposit boxes, cash U.S. government checks, accept payments and receive segregated new deposits. There was much talk about using "bank scrip" as substitute money but instead the supply of Federal Reserve notes was expanded to meet the need. Public morale held up remarkably well. Susan Kennedy notes that "the governor of California deferred two hangings because 'a bank holiday is no time to hang a man.'"

Roosevelt came to the White House conservative in his economic leanings and neither well informed nor deeply interested in "the dismal science." From among the many plans offered, he rejected the nationalizing of the banks and the insuring of bank deposits, sending to Congress a bill based primarily on Ogden Mills' proposal to Secretary Woodin—a plan which Hoover had previously rejected.

The Emergency Banking Act of 1933 went to Congress on Thursday, March 9. It was signed by the President at 8:36 that evening—one minute less than eight hours after his message was read to both houses.

Title I validated the bank moratorium and gave the President authority to extend it.

Title II, which Howard Stoddard soon knew almost by heart, was the "Bank Conservation Act." It followed the Mills plan of a three-phased reopening of the banks. Those found to be sound upon quick scrutiny would be permitted to open immediately. A second group would follow within a few days or weeks as examination revealed them to be safe. A third group would not be permitted to reopen without reorganization. A conservator would be appointed for each such closed bank, to direct limited operations and develop a reorganization plan. What depositors and stockholders might expect to recover from these banks would depend upon the available assets, the details of the reorganization plan, and ultimately upon whether economic recovery would cause the assets to recover their lost value. Authority to license reopening was divided. The Treasury Department was given jurisdiction over national banks and state banks which were Federal Reserve members; state banking authorities licensed the rest, and they generally followed Treasury guidelines.

Title III permitted national banks to sell preferred stock and capital notes in order to strengthen their capital structure. Undercapitalization had been a common bank problem since the 1920s. This provision permitted R.F.C. to assist banks by purchasing such obligations as well as making loans, a permission utilized in many of the reorganizations with which Stoddard was associated.

Title IV broadened the range of assets upon which Federal Reserve Banks could make cash advances to member banks. U.S. government bonds were prominent on the list, and this convertibility feature strongly influenced the pattern of Michigan National Bank investments for many years.

On Sunday evening, March 12, Roosevelt made his first "fireside chat" to an anxious and hopeful radio audience. It was a clear, reassuring and persuasive account of what was happening to the banks; according to Will

Rogers, "even a banker could understand it." During the next three days more than 5,000 banks reopened with Treasury licenses. They held about 90 percent of all the bank assets in the Federal Reserve system. Within a month almost 7,500 state banks reopened. By the end of the year less than 2,000 of the 17,300 commercial banks which had held federal or state charters in March were still unlicensed. Some had simply expired, some had merged with other banks, and some had been taken over by new institutions. Two of the largest in the last category were in Detroit.

First National Bank and Guardian National Bank of Commerce had not actually been under great depositor pressure when discussions with R.F.C. about the second Guardian loan began. John Holland argues that if the efforts which went into achieving "liquidity" for the banks in the Guardian Group had been devoted to cutting loose the insolvent Union Guardian Trust Company, the holiday and subsequent reorganization of the banks in the Guardian and Detroit Bankers groups need never have occurred. In November 1934 a Detroit *Free Press* interview with Jesse Jones about a pending loan to allow partial payment to depositors in the defunct First National Bank produced this exchange:

> "In view of the fact that everything indicates a payoff of 100 cents on the dollar in the Guardian National, would you say now that a mistake was made when that bank was closed?" was the question.
>
> "That's all buried now; why revive it? The Guardian is being cleaned up," Jones countered.
>
> "But, Mr. Jones, the closing of the Guardian National precipitated the national bank disaster, and it seems inconsistent that a bank able to pay out 100 per cent should have been denied the right to reopen when the new licenses were issued," was the next suggestion.
>
> "Well, there may have been mistakes made when banks were being reopened, but by and large I think the program was a good one," replied the RFC chairman. "There is no use going into that now."

Operating within the narrow limits dictated by the preoccupation with liquidity, Howard Stoddard was very much involved in the R.F.C. actions which helped to bring on the "bank holiday" and in the subsequent decisions not to reopen Guardian National Bank of Commerce and First National Bank. Later, according to several of his close associates, he came to regard the closures as unnecessary and wrong, and in 1969 he so stated publicly. But the wisdom of hindsight was not available when the R.F.C. statute was written, revised and applied amid the politics and panic of 1932 and early 1933. At the time the closures may have seemed consistent with the concept of "weeding out" which Stoddard had recently expressed to the bankers in Los Angeles.

In any event, the new situation presented new challenges—and new opportunities.

CHAPTER 7

# Michigan's "Mister R.F.C."

"In no other large city was the drama of the banking crisis so prolonged or so tense as in Detroit." This retrospective judgment by Jesse Jones is amply borne out by the events of 1933 in which Howard Stoddard was intimately involved. For weeks he and his fellow R.F.C. examiners searched for liquidity among the assets of the Guardian and Detroit Bankers groups. The portfolios of the two key banks were swollen with mortgages, and in the process Stoddard began to develop a special expertise on real estate loans. As the examiners worked, bank officers moved assets around and took other measures to put as good a face as possible on a deteriorating situation. Then they played "button, button, who's got the button" with leaders of the business community in a quest for additional capital to secure R.F.C. reorganization loans. A sampling of Detroit headlines during the winter days when Michigan's banks were closed suggests the flavor of the time:

EARLY BANK RELIEF IS IN SIGHT (*February 15*)
COMSTOCK'S FAMOUS CHUCKLE HELPS HIM WEATHER STORM (*February 16*)
MICHIGAN PLAN IS EVOLVED TO REOPEN BANKS (*February 17*)
COMSTOCK GIVEN DICTATOR'S POWER OVER STATE'S BANKS AS LEGISLATURE VOTES ADOPTION OF EMERGENCY MEASURES (*February 21*)
DECIDE BANK FATE TONIGHT: ASK RFC 150 MILLION LOAN (*February 22*)
NEW BANK PLAN IS JEOPARDIZED BY PRESS LEAK (*February 24*)
BANK OPENING DUE NEXT WEEK (*February 25*)
STATE DEPOSITS PERILED: BANKERS FIGHT GOVERNOR (*February 25*)
PRESIDENT SIGNS COUZENS BANKING BILL (*February 26*)
(Making national banks eligible to participate in legislation covering state banks)
BANKS OPEN WEDNESDAY UNDER CONTROL OF FORDS (*February 27*)
COUZENS COMING TO AID OF BANKS (*February 28*)
LEGISLATORS BLOCK BANK PLAN (*March 3*)

State to Probe Detroit Banks (*March 7*)
Comstock Sees New Bank Era (*March 8*)
Decision on Opening Detroit Banks Due Today (*March 11*)
First National, Guardian Close in 245 Million U.S. Bank Plan (*March 13*)
Conservators on Job Handling Bank Situation (*March 15*)
RFC Spurns Plea to Save Bank Deposit: Depositor sues Bank on Holiday Check: 7 of Guardian Banks Open (*March 16*) (Guardian out-state banks among first-phase licensees)
Woodin Hears 2 Bank Plans (*March 18*)
RFC Announces New Detroit Bank (*March 21*)
Hundreds Jam New Bank to Open Accounts (*March 24*)

During the Michigan bank holiday it became apparent that by the applicable liquidity criteria neither Guardian National Bank of Commerce nor First National Bank could reopen without reorganization and new capital. When the Emergency Banking Act established the program for licensing, the banks went almost automatically into group three. It then became the responsibility of all concerned to give Detroit adequate banking services as soon as possible. (Only four small banks in the city were licensed in the first three-day period in March.)

On March 15 the Reconstruction Finance Corporation's Detroit task force recommended to the R.F.C. board that a new bank be formed, based on the purchase of the best Guardian National and First National assets. R.F.C. and Detroit capitalists would purchase the new bank's stock and an R.F.C. loan would permit the bank to pay for the transferred assets and the conservators of the unlicensed banks to pay off a percentage of their depositor claims. Subsequent plans to dispose of the remaining assets and satisfy the remaining claims against the closed banks would be worked out by the conservators. Howard Stoddard, for the examiners, and Henry Persons, for the R.F.C. legal staff, were the primary authors of this proposal.

The R.F.C. board and Treasury Secretary Woodin quickly approved the plan. It was announced on March 21 and three days later the new National Bank of Detroit opened for business in the old First National Bank headquarters. (The fate of the Guardian Building and the Ford banking interests will be considered later.) Common stock in National Bank of Detroit—$12,500,000 worth—was purchased reluctantly by General Motors. R.F.C. paid an equal amount for preferred stock. (In the late 1940s both G.M. and R.F.C. shares were purchased by others, and both organizations made a little money on their investments.) R.F.C. loaned an additional $120 million to finance the transfer of assets and a 30 percent payoff to anxious and angry depositors of the closed banks. (This loan was also repaid in full.) A confidence-inspiring Kansas City banker was persuaded to come and head the new bank, but the chief operating positions were taken by men from the Guardian and Detroit Bankers groups. National Bank of Detroit was an immediate and enduring success, despite the crowd noises which attended its birth.

When Guardian National and First National were denied licenses and conservators were appointed, critics attacked the action in the courts, without success. Others launched a search for villains, with the Detroit chief of police and Father Coughlin as oddly-matched antagonists in one headline-making controversy. The state legislature authorized a probe, and a one-man grand jury conducted by Wayne County Circuit Judge Harry B. Keidan ruled in September that the banks were solvent at the time they were closed. Senator Couzens, who disapproved of the Keidan inquiry, carried the subject to the Pecora Committee, whose investigations continued into 1934. The indictments and penalities growing out of the Senate hearings have been previously mentioned. Neither legal proceedings nor public controversies affected anything but the political and psychological environment in Detroit.

A picture in a Detroit paper on April 13, 1933, is the first of Howard Stoddard to appear in any Michigan newspaper. He is with Jim Alley and Henry Persons in a conference with National Bank of Detroit President Walter S. McLucas, First National Conservator C.O. Thomas and Guardian National Conservator B.C. Schram. The occasion was the transfer of $131,201,000 worth of assets from the old banks to the new in order to make possible the payments to depositors.

Once the Detroit plan was in implementation, John McKee and Alley went back to Washington, while Stoddard and Charles Fisher were placed in charge of R.F.C. participation in the reorganization of out-state banks. According to Jennie, who joined her husband in May, Jesse Jones called Howard every Sunday morning for a report. She also recalls that executives from some of the closed banks came to the Alden Park Manor apartment, desperate for word about the status of the examinations or loan applications upon which the fate of their institutions depended. A number of banks had already reopened, some with the aid of R.F.C. loans aggregating $20 million. By mid-April more than 250 of the out-state banks were still closed, and many of them could not be licensed without R.F.C. loans or preferred stock purchases. They required a special kind of scrutiny—not only of their portfolios, but also of their personnel and their long range potential.

This was the assignment in which Howard Stoddard began to win the nickname of Michigan's "Mister R.F.C." It was also the assignment which inspired first thoughts of "Banking That Is Building Michigan." He told Jennie at the time: "If I only had a million dollars I could buy all the banks that are for sale." To which she pragmatically replied: "Howard, you're dreaming. I need money for the pediatrician and the dentist, and besides I would like a few new clothes to go places with you, and you say you need a million dollars!"

A memorandum to Jones and McKee, dated May 29, 1933, outlined the situation as Stoddard perceived it. Eighteen examiners were in the field, concentrating on the ten cities in which half of the total out-state deposit liability was located. Six of them became Michigan National Bank cities in the next nine years—Battle Creek, Grand Rapids, Lansing, Port Huron, Saginaw and Flint. Stoddard agreed with the Michigan commissioner of banking that all of them would need help, but he disagreed about the method:

> The State Banking Department has been working with the so-called Michigan plan which permits the retention in the reorganized bank of good assets and places in the hands of trustees those which are not acceptable. This plan will not succeed because of the lack of liquidity and also the fact that most of the State banks are already borrowing heavily or have large secured deposits. In my opinion, final reorganization in most places must come through the formation of a new bank, with that institution buying acceptable assets from those now closed.

The direct, unadorned style was typical of Stoddard's business communications throughout his career. The succinct summary of conditions in each of the ten cities was also typical. The statement about Lansing bears quoting because it introduces several key elements in the Michigan National story:

> *Lansing* Population 78,300
>
> Capital National Bank is a new bank being formed and matters should be perfected this week. Will give only a 15% liquidation to former banks with the Reo Motor Company appearing as the largest holder of new common stock. Preferred stock application now awaiting action in Washington.

As the people in Detroit were already discovering, this "new bank" plan was rigorous. Stoddard described the plan and his role to a group of Pennsylvania bankers years later:

> The pattern was simple. The RFC would put up the preferred stock, and it was my job to go to a community, to sell General Motors, Chrysler, Ford or some rich individual such as Kellogg of Battle Creek, to put up the common stock. We would establish a new bank, take the good assets out of the closed bank through immediate liquidation. Then the new bank, as rapidly as possible, would serve the process of taking the closed bank's assets into the new bank, and over a period of time we were able to restore sound banking.

This program promised viable banking facilities, but it required that large depositors subordinate part of their claims in order for small depositors to be paid off first, and it asked local firms and individuals—including depositors in the closed banks—to buy stock to match R.F.C. preferred stock purchases. It also forced depositors to wait while the liquidating of "frozen assets" gradually generated funds, and it sometimes required stockholders in the defunct banks to pay assessments, under their double liability obligation, to satisfy outstanding claims. Because the plan offered and sometimes pressured depositors to accept stock in satisfaction of their claims, it produced a number of unenthused, even disgruntled, stockholders. Stoddard quickly learned this, and he even became acquainted with some of the reluctant shareholders in the more than 25 out-state banks which he personally helped to organize.

While conducting these examinations, Stoddard came to know Senator Arthur Vandenberg, who was a director of Grand Rapids Savings Bank and understandably interested in the whole banking situation. Like Couzens, he was a Republican, but he was not a curmudgeon. Of Stoddard's work in building Peoples National Bank from the salvageable remnants of Grand Rapids Savings and two other institutions, Vandenberg wrote: "No matter what else you may do in connection with your difficult responsibilities in Michigan, I shall always believe that your labors in this particular instance will always be a monument to your good judgment and your courage and your ability." The same August 10, 1933, letter spoke of "the confirmed assurance that you would come to Grand Rapids and become the active President of the Peoples National Bank," and added: "You are sure of a hearty welcome and I know you will find this to be a most happy place to live, and labor, and play."

It is tantalizing to speculate about what might have happened if this plan had been carried through. Howard changed his mind, according to Jennie, because the proposed appointment was announced while the key R.F.C. loan to the Grand Rapids bank was still pending, creating suspicions of impropriety. There was little grieving, however, because Jennie and the children had come to Alden Park Manor, and the situation in Detroit was still quite fluid.

Stoddard's next assignment gave him a short time to get reacquainted with his family. The receivers—formerly conservators—of Guardian National and First National banks had requested a reassessment of their remaining assets as the basis for further R.F.C. loans, and many Detroiters had been pressing for a reopening of the banks on the ground that such a reassessment would show what the Keidan grand jury was also trying to establish—that the banks had been solvent when they were denied licenses in March. Stoddard and Fisher directed the reaudit and took their report to Washington early in July. After review by the R.F.C. board and Treasury officials, Jesse Jones coupled an announcement of new loans with a vigorous defense of the actions which had been taken in March. He noted in his July 13 statement that R.F.C. would loan up to $25 million to the Guardian National receiver and up to $50 million to the First National receiver. In connection with releases made during the bank holiday and the following R.F.C. loans, this would permit both banks to pay off 60 percent of their depositor liabilities. Stockholder assessments and the liquidation of remaining assets would have to generate the remaining 40 percent. R.F.C. would consider any reorganization plans which mobilized new local capital, but it would not support the reopening of the banks in their present condition.

In a bid to mollify local sentiment, Jones praised the auto magnates for efforts to provide Detroit with banking service—General Motors' Alfred P. Sloan, Jr. and Donaldson Brown for capitalizing National Bank of Detroit, Walter Chrysler for indicating his willingness to participate, and the Fords for taking part in a pending effort to create a second new bank, based on some of the Guardian Group banks which had not been drawn into the March liquidation. They had all made it clear, he noted, "that they have no desire to engage in the banking business. They have made these investments for the sole and only purpose of giving to Detroit proper banking facilities and to release as much as possible of the deposits in closed banks."

Stoddard and Fisher were directly involved with the Ford negotiations which in August gave birth to Manufacturers National Bank, merging the assets of several suburban Guardian banks which were still awaiting licensing. Under the agreement worked out with Edsel Ford, $5.25 million in new capital would be subscribed by Ford interests, the new bank would purchase the assets of the merged banks and take over their deposit liabilities, and at the same time R.F.C. would loan enough to permit the new bank to pay an additional dividend to the depositors of Guardian National Bank of Commerce. The new bank was established without R.F.C. stock purchases, and Stoddard then helped to work out the plan for using an R.F.C. loan of about

$14 million to pay off all the small Guardian National deposits and reduce the balances owed to the remaining 6,000 depositors.

Detroit thus had two major banks again, and Thomas and Schram were left with the remains of the predecessor institutions. Guardian Detroit Union Group, Inc., and Detroit Bankers Company were also in receivership, and their failure left an impression about holding companies which dominated public policy in Michigan for more than thirty years.

An interesting by-product of Stoddard's apparently effective relationship with Edsel Ford was the Roosevelt administration's effort to use the R.F.C. connection to persuade Henry Ford to participate in the newly-formed National Recovery Administration. As later recalled by Stoddard, Roosevelt sent Jesse Jones to Detroit and Stoddard arranged an appointment for both of them. They checked into Dearborn Inn under assumed names—the Ford hold-out against the N.R.A. "Blue Eagle" was headline news at the time—and were soon in the great man's presence. What followed is described in the 1964 Stoddard story in *Michigan Manufacturer and Financial Record*:

> Each time Jones started to steer the conversation toward his mission, Ford would deftly change the topic and continue talking. After an hour and a half, Ford jumped up and commented gaily:
>
> "It was wonderful for you to come all the way here to see me, Mr. Jones. I've enjoyed every minute of it. Good bye now."

And with that he disappeared through the door.

The fate of the bank receiverships continued to receive Stoddard's attention, because both R.F.C. and the depositors were eager to wind them up quickly, once the possibility of reopening was eliminated. During the summer he suggested one possible solution. Since about two-thirds of the remaining First National assets and almost one-half of the Guardian National assets consisted of real estate mortgages, he proposed that "a properly organized mortgage company would be the proper instrumentality . . . to handle the liquidation, rather than the protracted continuation of the National Bank Receiverships." The company he envisioned would take over the mortgages, arrange payment plans where amortization schedules did not already exist, handle collections (and foreclosures if necessary), sell mortgages to other investors whenever the market was favorable, and make payments to its owners (including holders of unsatisfied bank depositor claims). Complete disposal of the mortgage assets would take time this way, but it would be more profitable than a quick sale in a depressed market.

The plan was not adopted at the time, but the close association with Schram, Thomas and Detroit mortgages profoundly influenced Howard Stoddard's later career.

At the end of the summer Howard and Jennie moved to Washington. It was what they had had in mind when the R.F.C. offer was first accepted and what Jennie had anticipated when she brought the children east in May. With the agency now moving from crisis management to financial reconstruction, the nation's capital was the logical place for a middle-level bureaucrat with at least nominal responsibilities in three states—Michigan, Ohio and Kentucky—and an interest in opportunities anywhere. Besides, there were friends from the West and from New York in the L.D.S. Washington Branch, and an impressive new chapel with a broad activity program for the three growing children and their parents.

It did not work out as planned. Jennie and the children spent six months in a semi-furnished apartment which had been rented "temporarily." Stoddard was gone much of the time. He continued to be the examining division's top authority on Michigan, and he still spent much time with the problems of the banks which he had left behind. Capital National Bank of Lansing sought a reorganization loan to permit a 50 percent payoff, and Senator Vandenberg appealed to Stoddard for the $4 million loan which had been requested. The tone of the September 30 letter was a little cooler than the August correspondence about Grand Rapids:

> I understand that this Bank has about 90% of the money of the people of Lansing impounded and it certainly would be sound public policy to make every possible effort to start a new Bank as quickly as possible. . . .
>
> Meanwhile, I am particularly anxious that these Lansing people should understand the situation and I am hopeful that you can find an early opportunity for another and more enlightening interview with them.

A new Lansing National Bank was eventually formed along the lines of Stoddard's proposal. Not everyone was satisfied with a plan which was businesslike but hardly generous, and Stoddard's later entry into the banking field in the state capital encountered more resistance than in some of the other towns where Michigan National Bank was launched.

Stoddard also worked out a plan for reorganizing the capital structure of Detroit Savings Bank, which had been licensed after the bank holiday but still needed to dispose of some shaky assets. Joseph M. Dodge, who had been a First National officer, was now president of Detroit Savings and a close and collaborative associate in planning the loan. Later, as an officer in Michigan Bankers Association, he led the opposition to the formation of Michigan National Bank.

What apparently disillusioned Stoddard with Washington was the effort to develop plans for managing the July loans to the Guardian National receiver in order to pay off the small depositors and to use the remaining resources—mainly mortgages and stockholder double indemnity obligations—to retire the remaining claims of the large depositors. Ford, Parke Davis, Chrysler and other prominent corporate depositors approved the plan, but when Stoddard sought approval from the Comptroller of the Currency, he ran into a political thicket. Senator Couzens, still feuding with Ford and sensitive to criticism that he had not fought hard enough to reopen the two big Detroit banks, was part of the problem. At first, according to a memorandum which Stoddard made of the sequence of events, Couzens was "very enthusiastic." A week later he was "in unpleasant mood—stated he had just talked with Detroit—whole plan was to avoid stock assessments." Stoddard explained why it was impossible to complete the liquidation of either Guardian National or First National without assessing the stockholders, and Couzens finally agreed to cooperate. However, the promised interview with the comptroller did not materialize, and the final Guardian liquidation plan was not endorsed by all the concerned parties until the next November. It was not finally approved by the courts until April 1935.

The ways of politics were always strange and often uncomfortable to Howard Stoddard. Commuting between Washington and Michigan was disruptive to family life and the development of church and social ties. He was also discovering, as Jennie later put it, that "these government jobs were a little precarious, and unless you were strongly bent on moving up in governmental circles, it just took too much time." She recalls a big dinner with the Vandenbergs at which protocol determined seating and she and Howard speculated on the career implications of their position at the very foot of the table. When the conventional Christmas greetings and thanks came from Jesse Jones "on behalf of President Roosevelt and the Directors of this Corporation," Stoddard was already thinking of new possibilities.

"Life was always a challenge to him," Jennie remembers. This time the challenge seemed to call him back to Michigan. On January 2, 1934, Charles F. Meyler, one of the attorneys involved in the Detroit bank reorganizations, wrote to him:

> At this time I wish to express appreciation for the very sympathetic attitude you displayed toward our difficulties and the very able assistance which you rendered us in connection with same. I believe that no small share of the credit for the improvement in Michigan's banking situation is due to your efforts, and I am satisfied that the very hearty cooperation we received from you materially assisted us. We will be in touch with you later. . . .

When Jones learned that Stoddard was considering leaving R.F.C., he offered a position in his bank in Houston. "There's a great opportunity; you ought to try it," he said to the keen-minded young banker who seemed to have particularly caught his fancy. "I often wonder," Jennie reminisces, "what would have happened to us if we had made that decision. I know Howard would have gotten along very well because he just had that way of doing things." But Houston seemed remote from family and familiar things in a day when air travel was in its infancy, and the offer was declined.

On January 24, 1934, a Detroit newspaper carried the first solo picture of Howard Stoddard to appear in the Michigan press. Like the several dozen "mug shots" which would follow over the next thirty-seven years, it showed a serious countenance and bankerly dress. The hairline was just beginning to recede. The story fitted the sober expression: "STODDARD QUITS POST WITH RFC. TO HANDLE MORTGAGES FOR FIRST NATIONAL."

Apparently his Michigan friends had been "in touch." According to the account, First National Bank Receiver C.O. Thomas had sought Stoddard's services to "administer the liquidation of mortgage assets of the First National, involving some 50,000 separate accounts." Stoddard was described as an experienced banker, instrumental in securing more than a quarter of a billion dollars in R.F.C. aid for Michigan institutions and knowledgeable about recent federal deposit insurance and mortgage insurance legislation. He was giving up his post as R.F.C. district superintendent to accept the new assignment.

Two job changes and three family moves in barely a year, and now a position which by its very nature was self-liquidating—Stoddard obviously did not know exactly what his "big chance" would be. He was convinced, however, that he would find it in Michigan.

CHAPTER 8

# Liquidator of Banks

Going back to Detroit meant opportunity for the Stoddard family to settle down. For a few months they camped in Alden Park Manor while Jennie shopped the "houses for rent." The Grosse Pointe suburbs, along Lake Erie, were to Detroit in those days what Yale Ward was to Salt Lake City, and there in the fall she found a nice little furnished home on Lincoln Road. It offered a nearby school, proximity to some of the new friends she and Howard were making, and a base from which to look for more permanent housing as soon as it was time to start putting down roots. The little Mormon branch met twenty miles away, but they quickly reestablished the contacts of the previous summer. Despite the expanding business demands on his time, Stoddard served as branch president in 1936-1937, being released when the congregation was divided and a small branch was established on the east side of the city, closer to Grosse Pointe. The unfolding of the Stoddards' social, civic, church and family lives in Michigan is the subject of later chapters.

The banking world which Stoddard reentered when he became assistant receiver for First National Bank was being radically reshaped by legislation in Washington and Lansing. The Glass-Steagall Act of 1933 incorporated many reforms which had been discussed prior to the bank crisis, such as expanding the supervisory authority of the Federal Reserve Board and the Comptroller of the Currency and separating commercial from investment banking. It prohibited payment of interest on demand deposits and gave the Fed authority to set maximum rates on time and savings deposits—provisions which Stoddard later found unduly restrictive. (Two years later the scope and power of the Federal Reserve Board were more drastically enlarged. A primary architect of these changes was Marriner Eccles, a member of the board since 1933 and its chairman since November 1934. Stoddard's R.F.C. boss, John K. McKee, became a member of the reformed board in 1935.)

The Glass-Steagall Act also permitted national banks to have branches on a city-wide or state-wide basis within the limits set by state laws. Senator Vandenberg's amending language reflected the concern of small banks in

Michigan and elsewhere; it forbade the extension of branches into communities which already had adequate banking services, except where existing banks were absorbed in the process. The Michigan Banking Act of 1933 permitted state-wide branching, and when 1937 legislation withdrew that permission, it left a similar exception. Howard Stoddard and an aggressive industrialist-financier whom he would shortly meet—Charles B. Bohn—found these exceptions adequate for the branch banking venture which became Michigan National Bank.

An important feature of the 1933 federal legislation was the insuring of bank deposits. Long discussed in academic, political and financial circles, this concept was initially opposed by both President Roosevelt and Senator Glass as too radical. Small banks had by now come to favor it as a protection against branch banking competition, while large banks generally opposed it as a use of the resources of strong institutions to bail out weak ones. Vandenberg broke the log jam in the Senate by proposing a $2,500 insurance ceiling on individual accounts. When the bill was finally passed with much popular acclaim, the President was happy not only to sign it but to claim credit for the idea. The Federal Deposit Insurance Corporation took over the insurance operation in 1934, and within two years all national and Federal Reserve member banks were covered. In time almost all state banks were brought into the program, and the ceiling on insured accounts was several times raised.

F.D.I.C. profoundly influenced the banking environment in which Michigan National Bank was later built. It helped consumer-oriented banking because it restored confidence in small depositors like the legendary fellow who appeared at a teller window during a bank run and declared: "If you've got my money, I guess I really don't want it. But if you haven't got it, by God, I want it now!" Less than 500 banks failed in the next ten years and less than 150 in the following twenty-five, with negligible losses to small depositors.

Congress also created the Home Owners Loan Corporation to refinance mortgages. In less than four years the agency acquired $3 billion worth of mortgages and helped at least a million home owners. It bought more mortgages in Michigan than in any other state, and it bought a large part of these through Howard Stoddard. When C.O. Thomas sought Stoddard's services, it was to expedite the exchange of more than $90 million in mortgages for H.O.L.C. bonds. Since such bonds had the credit of the federal government behind them, they could be used as collateral for R.F.C. loans to fund further payments to First National depositors.

Between March and November 1934 Stoddard negotiated the exchange of about $50 million worth of mortgages and in the process became an expert on Detroit real estate and the intricacies and possibilities of the mortgage market. He discovered, among other things, that most of the problem mortgages in the First National portfolio were frozen assets because of their terms. They required a single lump sum payment at the date of maturity, with foreclosure as the lender's only recourse when hard times made such payment impossible. If, instead of foreclosing, the bank offered to rewrite the mortgage on an amortizing basis, both parties benefited. Years later, when he was building a banking dynasty on the basis of consumer financing, Stoddard stated the lesson in these words: "Any man can pay any debt if the monthly payment is small enough. There is nothing like amortization. It is the key to our future."

Stoddard also acquired two invaluable colleagues during this period. Gladys MacGregor became his secretary, general-purpose helper, and keeper of his history. Waldo Stoddard came from Utah to Michigan to become business associate, confidant and idea man to his older brother.

Waldo moved to Battle Creek in June 1934 because First National Bank there, newly formed with capital transfusions from W.K. Kellogg, was looking for a young and experienced outsider to head one of its departments. Howard knew all about the reorganization, and he also knew the man for the job. So Waldo moved into Howard's sphere of action and was his closest friend for the next 37 years.

Gladys MacGregor was working for Willard L. Elkins at the First National receivership when first she met "Mr. Stoddard." A native of Amherstburg, Ontario, she went from high school into the local bank, which later merged with Bank of Montreal. In 1925 she crossed the Detroit River to a better-paying position with First National Bank, and there she was when the bank closed. She had been working on mortgage liquidation for almost a year when a man whom she remembers as "literally tall, dark and handsome":

> asked to see Mr. Elkins, then walked through a room full of people already waiting, entered the office and closed the door. He stayed so long that people became restless. A few days later he repeated the performance, and that really aroused my ire. Then he took over a desk, opened a brief case and began to go through files, all the time observing everything that happened. No word of introduction or explanation. He was pleasant and agreeable, but wholly mysterious.

On March 1 Elkins suffered a disabling illness, and so the man who came to assist became the man in charge of mortgage liquidation. He called the staff together, introduced himself, and outlined a business approach quite like that which would later characterize his direction of Michigan National. As Gladys recalls:

> He reminded the men that many of them had been in the mortgage business much longer than he had, and therefore he would expect them to carry on their work. He would hold them responsible, each for his own job. Each would have to make decisions, but he would be available for consultation.

From the perspective of decades of effective and devoted association, Gladys MacGregor described this first encounter with Howard Stoddard in a leadership role: "They had come in like small, frightened boys, and they left like tall men."

One of the first assignments was housecleaning. Stoddard's penchant for a clean desk and tidy files became proverbial. With over 42,000 mortgages and related papers to keep track of, the wisdom of the new office rule soon became apparent: "The first time you put anything down, put it in its place. That way you never have to look for anything. If you have it, it is in its place. If it is not in its place, you do not have it." Over the years Gladys learned not to discard every paper her boss earmarked for the waste basket, but the business files for the years of the Stoddard-MacGregor collaboration (1934-1964) are remarkably lean and clean.

Once the work pattern was established, the processing of mortgages went smoothly. Exchanges were being made for H.O.L.C. bonds at a rate of about a hundred a day, and Stoddard estimated in one of his frequent letters to Jesse Jones that about 50 percent of the real estate contracts in the hands of the receivership would prove eligible for disposition in this manner. The painful business of foreclosing on delinquent accounts continued, since neither the transferring nor the insuring of mortgages relieved borrowers of the necessity to make scheduled payments. But the improving market made it easier for hard-pressed homeowners to refinance, and the modest upturn in the Detroit economy which attended the early New Deal recovery efforts put more money into the pockets of many mortgages. The establishment of the Federal Housing Administration in 1934 further strengthened the mortgage market. It insured mortgages up to 80 (later 90) percent of the appraised value of the property and paid off the creditors with government bonds when defaults occurred.

John McKee testified to the Pecora Committee that the R.F.C. examiners found the First National Bank's 1933 mortgages to be "about as clean . . . as we have ever seen, well cared for, well amortized. . . . They were good mortgages. There were very few in default." As he worked again with some of these accounts now, Howard Stoddard became strongly convinced that prudently handled, insured home mortgages were among the soundest investments that a bank could make. Haunted by memories of "frozen assets," many of his banking contemporaries took much longer to come to this opinion.

The routine nature of much of the work left Stoddard free to look at other aspects of the Detroit banking situation. He was approached by representatives of the Washington home financing agencies to help promote the formation of a savings and loans association. Such a federally insured agency could take over some First National and Guardian National mortgages, fund new home construction, and encourage saving. He endorsed such a project to associates in the local financial community, but he took no direct part in the reviving savings and loan movement. (Years later, when he battled against the income tax advantage enjoyed by savings and loan associations, Stoddard voiced the thought that he should, perhaps, have gone that way.)

As federal policies and economic conditions increased the value of both First National and Guardian National receivership assets, the federal courts decided that owners of stock in the two group holding companies were legally obligated to pay double liability assessments. Assessment action against the approximately 17,000 stockholders could produce as much as $35 million to satisfy remaining depositor claims.

These hopeful developments encouraged Stoddard to plan ways to wind up the receiverships and achieve the impossible dream of a 100 percent payout for both banks. As early as March 21, 1934, he sent Jesse Jones the broad outline of "a comprehensive programme which would clean up the entire Detroit situation." It involved these elements:

1. Large depositors would agree to subordinate their deposit claims—which meant that they would not insist on participation in the next round of payments generated by the receiverships.

2. On the basis of the improved mortgage market, R.F.C. would loan enough to permit an 80 percent pay-out by both receiverships, including payment in full to all small depositors.

3. Large depositors would form corporations to take over the two sets of assets, manage the stockholder assessments, and make payment of their claims in installments over a period of time.

4. The receiverships would be dissolved, thus terminating the financial uncertainties and political battles associated with them.

By mid-summer exploratory discussions by R.F.C. and receivership personnel and key depositors had reached the point where Jones, on a visit to

Detroit, could discuss plans with the press. With regard to a new dividend for Guardian National Bank of Commerce, problems were "just about solved." A local liquidating corporation would be formed, financed mainly by R.F.C. The general pay-off level would be brought up from 68 to 81 percent by an R.F.C. advance of about $18 million. The still-pending (and finally unsuccessful) lawsuit by a group of First National depositors demanding a preferential 100 percent pay-off was delaying action with reference to this receivership, Jones stated. The much greater number of small depositors also posed problems. But he added: "The Guardian plan, if it is accepted and works out, will be used as a pattern in moves to eventually lift the First National receivership and turn the banks back to local interests. It is about three times larger and will take more time to work out."

A First National program was actually worked out before the end of the year, but it did not exactly parallel the Guardian approach. A Reconstruction Finance Corporation loan of $84 million cleared the way to pay off more than 500,000 depositors with accounts under $300 and to form a depositors committee to work with the receiver. (B.C. Schram replaced Thomas in that spot after the Guardian receivership ended, and he served until the First National liquidation ended in the early 1940s.) The R.F.C. loan was propitious. As a local journalist put it: "Detroit's 1934 edition of Santa Claus has pink cheeks and white hair but no whiskers. His name is Jesse H. Jones."

Jennie Stoddard had become well acquainted with Jones' telephone voice and outgoing demeanor during the R.F.C. days. While the R.F.C. chairman was working on the liquidating corporation loans, this friendship produced a spin-off which warrants telling in Jennie's own words:

> One morning I answered the telephone and it was Mr. Jones' secretary. He said that Mrs. Jones and Mrs. Woodrow Wilson had accompanied Mr. Jones to Detroit, and they would like to be at my disposal for the day. I gasped and said, "What an assignment!" . . . I called Howard and he told me to consult with Mrs. Charles T. Fisher, as Mr. Fisher was local head of the R.F.C. I called her, and her mother Mrs. Briggs had the day arranged for us. We had luncheon at the beautiful Briggs home in Bloomfield Hills, and I returned the ladies to Dearborn Inn. . . .
>
> Next morning another call came from Mr. Jones' secretary, asking if I would take care of Mrs. Jones and Mrs. Wilson. I felt they would not have asked if they had not wanted me to do something. They knew the circumstances under which I lived. They knew I was new in

> Detroit with a family of three, and if they wanted my company I was very flattered. So I drove my car to Dearborn Inn and picked up the ladies. Howard joined us later in the afternoon, and we drove all through the Grosse Pointe area to see some of the familiar landmarks I had studied as a new resident of Michigan. I asked if they would like to come to my apartment and meet my children, and they said they would. Anticipating this, the children were all scrubbed and dressed in their Sunday best. They were also warned to use their Sunday manners when the ladies arrived. We had a homey social half hour, and I remember Mrs. Wilson asking if I had a needle and thread, as the hem of her dress had caught and was falling down. I hemmed Mrs. Wilson's skirt . . . at my Alden Park Manor apartment.

Both liquidating programs were implemented, both finally paid off their participating depositors in full, with a little interest, and Howard Stoddard almost certainly could have gone with either. But the Guardian National project jelled first, and there he chose to cast his lot.

On November 1, 1934, Stoddard resigned from the First National receivership to accept the proffered position as secretary—in effect chief of operations—of the newly formed Guardian Depositors Committee. He told Gladys MacGregor that he would have a place for her within six months, and he told Jennie to start looking for a house to buy. She found the house just a little distance away on Lincoln Road. French style, with three upstairs bedrooms and a maid's room over the garage, it was a delight to redecorate. In memory, it is Jennie's favorite home.

With a salary of $10,000 (about $40,000 in 1979 purchasing power), prospects for good increases, and an apparently strategic situation in Michigan's reforming financial world, Howard Stoddard felt bullish about the future. That he had done a good job in his previous position is attested by a letter from his First National subordinates, wishing him success and expressing confidence that "with your genius for organization, it will be successful." Interesting in view of the facts that the mortgage unit was small and many of the staff were older than the 32-year-old supervisor is the salutation, "Dear Mr. Stoddard." Several comments showed the same blend of admiration, appreciation and social distance which mark many of the descriptions of "Mr. Stoddard" by his later associates at Michigan National:

> You have shown a human and personal interest in us which we tried to merit with our loyalty. When you assumed direction of this office you brought a sense of stability and security to the whole per-

> sonnel and so improved the shaken morale of all the employees. The feeling that you were our friend has endeared you to us.

The plan for terminating the Guardian National receivership was approved by the Comptroller of the Currency in August 1934. It consisted of these elements:

1. Collection of $5,040,000 from about 3100 stockholders—the amount which the comptroller estimated could be obtained out of a double liability obligation of $10 million without extended and costly litigation—and releasing the shareholders from further assessment liability.

2. Sale of remaining bank assets at a reappraised value, under a court order to prevent later legal challenge, to Guardian Depositors Corporation.

3. Assignment to G.D.C. by bank creditors of the unpaid balances of their claims, the issuance of participation certificate entitling them to *pro-rata* shares of proceeds from liquidating these assets.

4. Payment of a final dividend to creditors electing not to participate in G.D.C. (A minority of the remaining depositors chose this option and settled for a 19 percent dividend, which meant a total recovery of 87 percent of their deposits when the bank closed in February 1933.)

The assignment of Guardian Depositors Committee was to organize the corporation which would replace the receivership, and in the interim to cooperate with Schram, the receiver, in the ongoing liquidation of Guardian National assets. The committee included Packard Motor Company Treasurer Hugh J. Ferry, chairman; Howard J. Stoddard, secretary; and representatives of Ford Motor Company, Chrysler Corporation, General Motors Corporation and Murray Corporation of America. Detroit attorneys Clifford B. Longley and Henry E. Bodman, both with Ford and Guardian Group connections, were associated with the work of the committee. Ferry and Stoddard had drafted the plan which Stoddard now had the day-to-day responsibility to execute.

Stoddard's new headquarters were on the first floor of the very elegant but almost empty Guardian Building. His office was at the end of a long hall, heavily carpeted. He removed a six foot strip of carpeting nearest his door so that he could hear the footsteps of anyone approaching. It had the additional effect, according to Gladys MacGregor, of producing "a clacking sound which echoed in a manner frightening to callers, most of whom were already tense and nervous."

The work of the depositors committee was simplified by the earlier reduction in the number of depositor accounts. Late in 1933, in connection with an R.F.C. loan which raised the pay-off level from 60 to 68 percent, Stoddard and others persuaded a number of large Guardian National depositors to waive their rights to the dividend in order that about 135,000 claims of $1,000 or less could be paid in full. This was done at a cost of over $3 million, with the automakers providing the largest waivers.

By the time the requisite court order was issued on April 30, 1935, some 4400 depositors, representing 83 percent of the outstanding claims, had elected to go with Guardian Depositors Corporation. (They included the receivers for some of the out-state Guardian banks whose newly-formed successors later came into Michigan National Bank.) The solicitation of these agreements was not without difficulty, as extended correspondence between Stoddard and Senator Couzens shows. The reappraisal of Guardian National assets by the depositors committee showed a current value of 87 percent of face value, sufficient to produce the 19 percent cash dividend offered to non-participants in G.D.C. Couzens and others were confused by the fact that the committee projected a 94 percent pay-off to those who would accept G.D.C. certificates and wait for the collection of assessments and the orderly disposal of assets. In explaining the situation to Couzens, who actually wanted to conduct his private reassessment, Stoddard expressed his personal confidence in the venture:

> My own experience in Michigan has been confined to the months since the closing of the banks in February 1933, but I have been favorably impressed with the fundamental economic foundations of this City and I am personally optimistic concerning its future. For that reason and also because of my belief that there will be a broad general recovery in values, I share with the members of the Committee in believing that over a period of years it is to be hoped that these depositors who assign their claims may receive all of their unpaid balance in full.

In May and June 1935 the necessary steps to form Guardian Depositors Corporation were taken. Holders of participation certificates elected a board of directors, consisting of representatives of several major Detroit industrial and financial concerns, including Ford, General Motors and Packard. On May 17 the board selected William R. Cation, former managing director of the Detroit branch of the Federal Reserve Bank of Chicago, as president; W. Thomas ZurSchmiede, Schram's chief aide in the Guardian Naitonal receivership, as vice president and treasurer, and Howard J. Stoddard as vice president and secretary. The resolution approving the sale of the remaining Guardian National assets to G.D.C. was signed on June 6 by Schram, Cation and

Stoddard, and shortly thereafter G.D.C. assumed the outstanding loans with Reconstruction Finance Corporation.

A condition set by the Comptroller for forming the corporation was that the funds from the stockholders assessments be in hand. By the time court approval of the plan was obtained, Stoddard had done so well with these collections that it became feasible to borrow enough from Edsel Ford and Charles S. Mott, both of whom had a substantial interest in the successful outcome of G.D.C., to go ahead. On June 3 he borrowed $220,000 from each, on one-year notes bearing 2 percent interest, to put with the $4,600,000 previously collected from stockholders. Both notes were retired on schedule.

When the corporation was formed, its assets consisted largely of still uncollected assessments and a miscellaneous group of assets, mostly mortgages, from Guardian National Bank of Commerce. When the receiver took over the bank's assets in 1933, they had a book value of over $150 million, but successive sales to National Bank of Detroit, Manufacturers National Bank, and Home Owners Loan Corporation had disposed of most of them, including the best. The task of G.D.C. was to collect at least enough from the stockholders to cover the Ford and Mott loans and to dispose of the remaining assets in such a way as to maximize the return to those depositors who had cast their lot with the corporation.

So efficiently did the work proceed that by October 1935 it was possible for G.D.C. to cut its ties with the federal government by borrowing from local banks to pay the balance of a little less than $7 million still owed R.F.C. At that time the corporation, an unprecedented venture in American banking history, was expressly commended by the Comptroller, the R.F.C. board and President Roosevelt. Associates attributed much of the success to Howard Stoddard. By setting forth the facts and alternatives clearly and persuasively, he was able to enlist the cooperation of stockholders and large depositors and the necessary endorsements of Washington and Lansing agencies. The office work he handled meticulously.

By July 1937 Guardian Depositors Corporation had collected $5,179,000 from stockholders and this phase of operations was substantially finished. To handle some of the leg work on assessments, the corporation employed Ralph V. Free, who had been an assistant cashier at Guardian National and who later worked for Stoddard in acquiring bank stock and managing mortgages during the formative period of Michigan National. When the corporation was finally dissolved in 1942, it had paid its certificate holders in full, with some interest, and it had refunded part of the stockholder assessments.

Stoddard had long since left, after giving the Guardian liquidation his best efforts for almost three years. There is evidence that he was disappointed—perhaps even felt betrayed—at not being elected either president, treasurer or director of the corporation. He was not even able to redeem his promise to Gladys MacGregor, who spent the time at intrinsically distasteful work in the foreclosure department of the First National receivership while he supervised the largely routine collection and accounting operations at G.D.C. He had a plush office and an improving income. He and Jennie had contact, business and social, with some of the most important people in Detroit. But he did not have a base on which to build, nor did it seem likely that the fraternity of the financially powerful in Detroit would make a place for him soon.

A plausible hypothesis is that to the metropolitan banking establishment Howard Stoddard was still young, he was an outsider, he was as ambitious as he was able, and his very reputation as "Mister R.F.C." was a reminder of painful, even embarrassing, episodes. Key political figures like Couzens and ex-Governor Alex J. Groesbeck, receiver for the Guardian Group holding company, remembered his role in the First National and Guardian National closures, and the stockholders who paid double indemnity assessments rarely did it with enthusiasm. It is even possible that the kinship with Marriner Eccles was a drawback, for the major banking figures of Michigan were made very cautious and conservative by the 1933 crisis and the reforms being successfully advocated in Washington by the new F.R.B. chairman were not popular among them.

As the crisis environment of the panic months gave way to business and politics as usual in 1935 and 1936, it became clear to Stoddard that what he was looking for in Michigan would not come on a silver platter, and it probably would not come from the metropolitan area. So he sought it out-state, and when it came he resigned from Guardian Depositors Corporation without notice. His departure at the end of 1937, and the lack of a "Dear Howard"—or "Dear Mr. Stoddard"—letter, say something about his disillusionment. It would take him 18 years to get back into Detroit, and by then he would have his own power base.

## CHAPTER 9

# The Bohn Connection

When Louis Cates learned of Howard Stoddard's move from Utah he wrote: "I am delighted to hear that you have secured a position with the R.F.C. and am positive that it is a great step forward. With your ability for hard work, you will undoubtedly soon be in a position where your contacts will be of immeasurable value to you."

After almost three years with Reconstruction Finance Corporation and the two Detroit bank receiverships, Stoddard had become very well informed on who was who and what was what in Michigan banking, but he had still not found the winning combination for himself. Jennie remembers those tantalizing days well. By the time developments with Guardian National took their disappointing turn, Stoddard had "this idea of what he'd like to do." He knew where there were promising out-state banks to be had—if he had a million dollars. Lacking the resources, "he had to find a sponsor"—someone who was willing to risk quite a little money on his idea. "You just don't do that in a hurry," Jennie recalls. "You stick to your job, you meet people, you feel your way very carefully."

It was by no means all frustration. In addition to the delights and demands of family and church, there was the widening circle of friends and acquaintances in Grosse Pointe and Detroit society. Through the Charles Fishers they met some of the most prominent people while they were still with R.F.C. Howard joined the Detroit Club because that was where the bankers and businessmen went to lunch, and later on he and Jennie joined the Grosse Pointe Yacht Club. Still a relatively unsophisticated young mother from the West, Jennie "wasn't too anxious to belong to those clubs" at first. "But if there's where we were making our contacts, then that's what we should do, and that's what we did." Whatever her first impulses, she soon found that she enjoyed the social whirl as much as she had as a sorority girl in Utah. And she brought to it a considerable flair.

A highlight of 1935 was the week-end which L.D.S. Church President Heber J. Grant spent with the Stoddards. A prominent Utah financier as well as head of the Mormons, Grant had been invited to talk to the Detroit Club, an assignment which he apparently discharged with wit and competence. Howard invited eight or ten of his friends in the business community to breakfast with Grant at the Grosse Pointe home. "It was an experience for them," Jennie remembers, "like an audience with the Pope."

A social encounter with unforeseen consequences also took place in mid-1935 at a pot luck party given by Lincoln Road neighbors. Edna and George M. Endicott were there; the "M" stood for Monroe, and "Roe" and Edna became two of the Stoddards closest friends. An invitation to dine at the Endicotts resulted. Thirty-seven years later Jennie told the M.N.B. board of directors: "As I look back at that dinner party, I feel that a miracle happened." That's where Howard and Jennie met Charles B. and Elizabeth Bohn.

Bohn was Edna Endicott's father. He was also president of Bohn Aluminum and Brass Corporation, a self-made multimillionaire, and a man with an eye open for new opportunities.

Born in Toledo in 1880, Bohn was orphaned at 11 and a bookkeeper in a Cleveland brass foundry at 17. As he learned the business he was particularly intrigued by aluminum, then used principally for jewelry and so expensive that the company's limited supply was kept in a safe. He and three companions raised $2500 in 1900 to launch Allyne Brass Foundry Company, which became the first firm in America to offer commercial aluminum castings. In 1918 he organized Charles B. Bohn Foundry in Detroit, and his castings were used in the Army's "liberty" airplane engines. Mergers in the 1920s produced Bohn Aluminum and Brass Corporation, a national leader in its field and a pioneer in research on aviation uses of aluminum and magnesium castings. (It weathered the depression and boomed during World War II, operating 14 manufacturing plants in Michigan in the post-war period.)

Bohn was also an ardent sportsman, the secretary and principal stockholder of the Detroit Racing Association. (He later became co-owner of Bomar Stables, which produced one of the great American race horses, Grand Slam.) Perhaps it was the gambler in Charles Bohn which helped him to take a chance on Howard Stoddard.

Stoddard had previously contacted Bohn, one of the stockholders in Detroit's First National Bank, about a double liability assessment. The 54-year-old industrialist was no more enthused than others in the same predicament, but he was so impressed by Stoddard's presentation that he agreed, adding: "By the way, young fellow, if you ever see a good opportunity in banking for me to get some of the money back I lost in the First National, let me know."

Banking was the chief subject of conversation that evening at the Endicotts—as it tended to be in many social gatherings of which Howard Stoddard was a part. He never cared much for small talk, but on financial topics and their ramifications into economic and political affairs he was incisive and insightful. He was a good listener as well as a forceful talker, and on this first evening together he and Bohn transformed what had been a passing business contact into a relationship with mutual appeal and spectacular consequences.

Nothing happened overnight. It took more than a year of persuasive conversations to reach the point where Stoddard's "idea of what he'd like to do" became a plan of action, and then three more years to transform that plan into Michigan National Bank. On the bank's 25th anniversary Stoddard described the Bohn-Stoddard arrangement to the Detroit *Free Press* business editor: "We agreed that if he would do the financing, I would do the work."

The plan was simple: combine Bohn money and Stoddard know-how to acquire controlling interest in several strategically situated out-state banks and then reorganize them into a unified branch-banking operation. The banks to be sought must give access to substantial financial markets—places like Battle Creek, Flint, Grand Rapids, Kalamazoo, Jackson, Ann Arbor, Lansing and Saginaw. And the banks must be acquirable—either because stockholders desired to dispose of their holdings or because they could be interested in the Bohn-Stoddard project. Banks reorganized or newly organized under R.F.C. auspices were logical prospects, because of depositors who became reluctant stockholders in the recapitalization process. Since the policy of paying off the small depositors in full, as the big Detroit receiverships had done, was not general in the out-state reorganizations, some banks had small shareholders who were more anxious to recover their money than to be in the banking business.

The attractions for Bohn were the challenge of a new entrepreneurial field and the opportunity to get a lot of leverage out of his investment if the new banks proved as profitable as Stoddard projected. Except for Detroit's three big new banks, none of the Michigan banks had large capitalization, and in some banks formed since the holiday part of the capital was non-voting preferred stock in the hands of R.F.C. Bohn expressed his viewpoint succinctly to an inquirer later on: "If you could buy a bank for $40,000, wouldn't you?"

The attractions for Stoddard were both idealistic and practical. He had long been an advocate of branch banking as a method of combining the loaning capabilities of a big bank with the consumer orientation of a small bank. A.P. Giannini's Bank of America was in some respects his model. The giant California branch banking operation had had a few liquidity problems in the early 1930s, but it had come through and was moving forward strongly in the New Deal banking environment. To Stoddard this was the direction for Michigan to go, profiting from the lessons of the panic not by retreating into super-cautious conservatism but by testing the potential of the changing economic and political world. The federal and state banking legislation of 1933 created the possibility for a Bank of America in Michigan, and even though the legislature in 1937 prohibited conventional state-wide branching, the legal option of purchasing and consolidating existing banks remained. This approach was quite compatible with Stoddard's concept of branch banking, in which each unit would have roots in its community and would function with a degree of autonomy.

From a practical standpoint, the plan would put Stoddard back into banking at the management level. As the Bohn-Stoddard group obtained a majority of the stock in each bank, Stoddard would go onto the board of directors and the executive committee, and at some point along the line he would become president of a major unit and then of the consolidated bank. Options to re-purchase some of the stock which he initially acquired for Bohn would permit him in time to achieve a substantial ownership interest.

By the end of 1936 the collaborators had reached substantial agreement in principle, and in 1937 the scenario began to unfold. The story of each acquisition is different in particulars, but all six banks were well known to Stoddard from his R.F.C. days.

On February 18, 1937, Stoddard sent this telegram to Bohn at his winter home in Miami:

> I would appreciate an hours visit with you . . . relative to another Michigan bank stock purchase that has been offered me. Stop. Despite opinions of your eastern friends I believe you will regard this one as exceptionally attractive as it can be handled for a moderate amount and is the key to a larger development. Stop. Inasmuch as decision must be made in a few days kindly wire me. . . .

Obviously Stoddard had been shopping, and just as obviously Bohn had been influenced by other advisers in rejecting earlier proposals. This one he approved in a telephone conversation on February 22, and two weeks later enough stock was under option to give "working control."

First National Trust and Savings Bank of Port Huron was the first link in the Michigan National chain. It had been imperiled by the closing of another Port Huron bank in 1933, but an R.F.C. recapitalization loan and purchase of preferred stock, plus the joint efforts of Stoddard, President

Stephen A. Graham, and several of the directors pulled the bank through. Thereafter Stoddard kept in touch with Graham and periodically received copies of the bank's statements and examiners reports. Sometimes in 1936 the subject of bringing the bank under new control was confidentially broached. Graham, Vice President Frank J. McCabe, Director (and Port Huron *Times Herald* publisher) Louis A. Weil, and possibly other directors were favorable, because there was division in the board about past practices and future policies.

This approach to people within a bank was used by Stoddard whenever feasible. As Waldo Stoddard observed years later: "Of course it is easier to purchase stock and acquire control of a situation if you have the cooperation of the officers in the organization. Stockholders often ask officers, should they sell, and if they are for you, it is much easier."

Once Bohn agreed to proceed, events necessarily took on a "cloak and dagger" aspect. There had been so little trading in bank stocks since the crisis years that any unusual activity would almost certainly drive up prices and might generate sales resistance or even preclusive buying by other directors. Stoddard therefore formalized his arrangements with Bohn along the lines suggested in his March 9 "option" letter:

1. He would acquire at least 2,000 shares, or 50 percent of the common stock, if possible, at an average price not to exceed $60 per share.

2. He would purchase the stock in his own name, endorse it in blank and deliver it to Bohn.

3. He would become a director of the bank and a member of its executive committee as soon as working control was obtained.

4. He would receive an option to purchase within three years 25 percent of the stock bought for Bohn, at the original price plus 5 percent interest.

A comparable agreement covered each of the five other acquisitions which went into the original Michigan National Bank. To take up the purchase options required Stoddard to go rather heavily into debt during his first years as a bank president, but he and his family ultimately became the largest stockholders in M.N.B.

A Bohn-Stoddard stock interest sufficient to secure Stoddard's election to the board and executive committee was obtained immediately with the purchase, in Stoddard's name, of 1000 shares from Military Investment Company, the affiliate which had taken over some of the bank's slower assets at the time of reorganization. Graham arranged this sale, and on the basis of his banking know-how and his helpfulness in 1933, Stoddard was welcomed to the board. In June he became chairman of the executive committee, and thereafter he and Graham were in effective control of the bank's loaning and investment policies. Jennie remembers that he took many trips to Port Huron during those hectic days when his dream was beginning to materialize.

Since Stoddard was still devoting most of his time to Guardian Depositors Corporation business, the work of rounding up additional stock was carried on by Graham, McCabe and Ralph Free. Graham and McCabe apparently received a small commission on shares they obtained for Bohn-Stoddard, with the further option to convert their own shares into stock in the larger bank of which First National Trust and Savings would one day become a part. Free, no longer busy locating Guardian National stockholders for assessments, sought out small stockholders of the Port Huron bank and, with a little latitude in negotiating price, tried to make them offers which they would not resist. As was the fashion with take-over ventures in those days, he did not disclose whom he represented. A note addressed to a hotel manager in Saginaw but left in Stoddard's keeping suggests what must have been a standard operating procedure in this operation: "In the event of an accident or for any reason whereby the writer is incapacitated, this will be your authority to turn over to the bearer, Mr. Howard J. Stoddard, . . . any cash or securities that I may have left in your vaults for safe-keeping."

As Stoddard's interest in other out-state banks became public knowledge, some resistance to his policy direction developed in the Port Huron board, and early in 1939 some of his personnel recommendations for the bank were voted down. Stoddard elected to be patient until a majority of the stock was in hand and a stockholders meeting could install what he described to the Detroit R.F.C. agency manager as "more effective and constructive management." Not until mid-summer did the annual meeting select a Bohn-Stoddard board. Stoddard continued as chairman of the executive committe, with Graham, McCabe and Russell T. Jackson in charge of bank operations. By then Stoddard and his silent partner were involved with five other banks and a mortgage company, and Guardian Development Corporation was a receding memory.

When Stoddard's first telegram about the Port Huron opportunity spoke about its being "the key to a larger development," it had reference to Saginaw and the trade territory around Saginaw Bay. A key man at Saginaw State Bank was interested in the Bohn-Stoddard project, provided that the industrialist was actually ready to invest. James M. Shackleton, the executive vice president, was an acquaintance of Stoddard's from the R.F.C. days. The understanding between them now was that Shackleton would receive shares in the proposed recapitalized bank on the basis of the number and price of existing shares which he purchased for Bohn. On July 14, 1937, the first block of shares was transmitted through Stoddard.

By the end of the year about 25 percent of the Saginaw State Bank stock had been acquired. "In order to allay the suspicion of a director. . . , which if aroused might lead to some minor competition," Stoddard reported to Bohn that he was making some purchases through a Grosse Pointe agent, who registered the purchases in his own name and then endorsed them in blank for transfer to Bohn. Gladys MacGregor, through whom much of his business was conducted, remembers this man once saying of Stoddard, "String along with him, and you'll wear diamonds." Stoddard had also arranged to buy enough shares from the president, F.E. McWhirter, to "practically control the bank." McWhirter announced his retirement on January 11, 1938, and the stockholders elected Shackleton in his stead. Stoddard became a director. (Rechartering of the institution as Saginaw National Bank was approved in 1940.)

During the early stages of the Saginaw project, Stoddard wrote about possibilities in nearby communities, including the Dow Chemical Company town of Midland. None of these materialized, but the purchase of Saginaw State Bank stock continued until a majority position was obtained early in 1939. Ralph Free made some of the purchases and at least two Detroit investment brokerage firms shopped for shares on a commission basis. Stock acquisitions on all Bohn-Stoddard fronts eventually reached the point where a confidential agent was no longer required, and in October 1939 Stoddard recommended Free "without reservation" to one of the brokerage houses as an employee whose "past services have been most satisfactory."

An important consequence of the Saginaw venture was the beginning of a close business and social relationship between Stoddard, Bohn and Henry Randall Wickes. A director of the bank, Wickes was the grandson of the founder of Wickes Company, one of whose furnaces Stoddard had stoked at the lumber mill back in Oregon. At 49 he was moving toward the peak of a career which would see Wickes Corporation one of the world's largest merchandisers of lumber and building supplies. Once he became acquainted with the Bohn-Stoddard plan, Randall Wickes approved it whole-heartedly. He participated actively in the formation of Michigan National Bank, and he was a director for many years and a substantial investor in some of the banks subsequently added to the group. In the 1940s Stoddard became a member of the Wickes Corporation board, a position which he held until his death.

City National Bank of Battle Creek presented a particularly complex challenge. Prior to reorganization under R.F.C. auspices it had been a member of the Guardian Group, and the key to control now was a block of stock in the hands of the widow of the former president. Negotiations to purchase began in November 1937, with President George J. Genebach and Vice President

Glenn O. Hoffhines both supportive of the undertaking. A Bohn loan to the bank's trust affiliate, City National Company, made possible the purchase of Mrs. Ella Green's stock, but before recapitalization and reorganization could take place, formidable competition appeared. Alex Groesbeck, once the Guardian Group receiver and now head of a bank in nearby Kalamazoo, was also interested in acquiring City National Bank, and he brought suit to block the Bohn-Stoddard take-over. To avoid litigation, Stoddard arranged to match the Groesbeck proposal by securing a Reconstruction Finance Corporation commitment to increase its investment in the bank's preferred stock and adding a $100,000 capital pledge from Bohn. The case was then dismissed in June 1938, and the reorganization was completed before the end of the year. At that time Waldo Stoddard left Battle Creek's Security National Bank to become a City National Bank vice president and director.

Waldo immediately became involved in the on-going project to acquire two small banks in nearby Marshall, merge them and make the resulting bank a branch of City National. Howard had already obtained an option on a majority of the shares in Commercial Savings Bank from officers of the company, and tenders were being made to purchase shares in First National Bank of Marshall. To counter local resistance—the local Junior Chamber of Commerce tried unsuccessfully to find local purchasers to block the invasion by outsiders—the letter from Stoddard to stockholders contained the following reassurances and inducements:

> The Directors of the Bank were also told . . . that the new stock ownership contemplated no change in the local management. It was also stated that if sufficient shareholders dispose of their stock, the writer intends to work out arrangements so that the unpaid principal balance of the impounded deposits—resulting from the reorganization of the Bank a few years ago—will be paid to the depositors.

In the Marshall purchases Stoddard was acting for Roe Endicott, rather than Charles Bohn. His option to buy back 25 percent of the stock followed the previous pattern. The two acquisitions were completed early in 1939, and when the state banking commissioner and the U.S. Comptroller approved the merger, First National purchased Commercial National and Glenn Hoffhines and Waldo Stoddard went onto the board of directors. J. D. Wright, who had approved the acquisitions and merger, continued as president of the enlarged bank. The Comptroller of the Currency never did approve its becoming a branch of City National, so the interlocking directorate was the primary instrument of policy coordination until both banks came into Michigan National.

A base in Grand Rapids, the manufacturing and commercial center of western Michigan, was essential to the realization of the Bohn-Stoddard plan. That the subject had been much discussed is clear from a letter Stoddard wrote on January 4, 1939: "I do not want to appear insistent on the Grand Rapids situation, but feel that the proper time has arrived to make a deal there if we intend to do it. . . ." The proposal was to purchase at least 5000 shares of stock in Grand Rapids National Bank, which was only 20 percent of the total but would give "complete working control, as the balance of the stock is scattered among approximately 3200 shareholders."

The key figure in this project was Joseph H. Brewer, the president of both the bank and Grand Rapids Trust Company. Born in 1875 near the village of Grand Rapids, he was refused permission to graduate from high school because he had not studied algebra. (At the time he was supporting invalid parents and his income of $100 per month was more than the school principal's salary.) He moved into the public utilities field, forming his own company at the age of 37 and then selling it to Samuel Insull twelve years later for over $3 million. He then moved into the banking field, first meeting Howard Stoddard during the R.F.C. period, when Stoddard almost became president of a competitor institution in Grand Rapids. (Brewer became an active participant in the formation of Michigan National Bank, and he was vice chairman of its board of directors until his death in 1943. Stoddard later talked with Senator Vandenberg about merging People's National Bank with Michigan National, but nothing came of the exploration.)

With Bohn's approval, stock acquisitions for Bohn and Endicott proceeded rapidly. Under an arrangement similar to that with Graham in Port Huron and Shackleton in Saginaw, Brewer purchased additional shares in his own name and endorsed his holdings in blank for transmittal through Stoddard to Bohn or his son-in-law. Meanwhile Ralph Free worked among the smaller shareholders; his purchases were recorded in Stoddard's name and also delivered to the men whose resources were funding the venture. By August a majority position was obtained, and the board then authorized the merging of the bank, the trust company and Grand Rapids Affiliated Corporation, the owner of the Grand Rapids Trust Building. To the national bank examiner who had to approve the transactions, Brewer wrote:

> The proposed locations on Monroe Avenue are excellent and will afford the Bank an opportunity to successfully compete with the Old Kent Bank which has offices in approximately the same business centers. It is the opinion of every member of the Board that the equity in the Trust Company property was well worth the price agreed upon

> and that the Bank, without any cost whatever, was acquiring an established trust business which otherwise could only be built over a long period of time and at very considerable expense.

The mergers, relocation and reorganizations were completed early in 1940, with Joseph Brewer as president of the new National Bank of Grand Rapids and head of its trust department.

Last of the original six Michigan National banks to be obtained was Lansing National, one of the new banks for which Howard Stoddard had helped to arrange R.F.C. funding. Its predecessor was Capital National Bank, which had taken over City National Bank in 1931 and then gone into receivership in 1933. Its president prior to closure was Ransom E. Olds, the automobile pioneer and founder of Lansing's major industry, Reo Motor Car Company. Its home was the Olds Tower Building, the tallest building in Michigan outside Detroit when it was completed after the stock market crash. In 1936 the bank purchased Peoples Bank of Lansing.

Like the auto makers in Detroit, Reo Motors became a reluctant bank stock owner in the post-bank holiday reorganization. This was the stock that the Bohn-Stoddard partnership acquired early in 1939, in the face of the unconcealed resistance of some of the directors and the two chief officers of the bank, President Ray Potter and Vice President Eugene M. Wanger. Stoddard went on the board of directors, and on January 9, 1940, a reconstituted board elected him president. Potter sold his interest and resigned before the stockholders meeting. Wanger offered to do the same, but Stoddard had been favorably impressed by his work and asked him to stay as senior vice president. He quickly became a strong member of the Bohn-Stoddard management team.

The first night after Stoddard's election, he and Jennie went roller skating. As they moved together across the floor, he said, "I'll bet I'm the first bank president to roller skate at this rink." Just then his feet shot out from under him. Jennie's comforting comment was, "And I'll bet you're the first bank president to sit down that hard on this floor."

Stoddard left Guardian Depositors Corporation about the time he became a Saginaw State Bank director. He moved into an office in the Lafayette Building, which was owned by Charles Bohn and housed some of his other business interests. Here he became better acquainted with some of Bohn's associates, including Simon D. Den Uyl, the secretary-treasurer of the aluminum and brass corporation and eventually a director of Michigan National. Here Gladys MacGregor came to work for him again in August 1938.

The functions of the small operation in 1432 Lafayette Building were to select and manage the Detroit mortgages which the Bohn-Stoddard banks were being urged to purchase and to direct the stock acquisition program, then moving into high gear.

Stoddard made all of the major decisions in consultation with Charles Bohn. Discussions were often by phone, because the Bohns spent most of the winter months traveling or in Florida. Jennie and Howard were frequent visitors to the Bohns' palatial home on one of the Miami Beach islands, and Charles and Elizabeth first introduced them to Palm Beach society. Jennie remembers the afternoons at the Hialeah and Gulf Stream tracks, where Bohn regularly bet $20 per race, on the nose, and she put $2 on the same horse to place, or across the board. Apparently no one went home broke.

The price of the pleasant and profitable friendship, according to Jennie, was that "Mr. Bohn's desires always came first with Howard." Trips were interrupted and social engagements were cancelled as required. But the relationships within the foursome were warm and comfortable, and Charles Bohn was not peremptory. Shortly before Bohn's death the two couples went to Hawaii together, and Charles had a great time getting acquainted with the islands' Mormons.

A by-product of one Palm Beach visit was Howard's first meeting with A.P. Giannini. The president of Bank of America had apparently heard of the Bohn-Stoddard project; so when he encountered Stoddard in a hotel elevator he introduced himself and suggested that they chat in his room. Stoddard was dressed for dinner, but he had Jennie make excuses and he spent a stimulating hour talking branch banking and other subjects with Giannini. A friendly relationship was maintained until the California banker died.

Stoddard spent much of his time from 1937 to 1939 in the cities where partnership interests were maturing—cultivating major stockholders and key bank officials and attending board of directors and executive committee meetings. He also traveled frequently to Washington to negotiate with government agencies which had to approve changes in the banks' status—Comptroller of the Currency, Federal Reserve Board and Reconstruction Finance Corporation. The contacts made by "Mister R.F.C." were helpful now, especially since the federal offices were generally more favorable toward bank consolidations and the concept of state-wide branch banking than were the authorities in Lansing.

Technically Stoddard's secretary, Gladys, was actually in charge of the office, handling mortgage payments, correspondence, accounts and whatever tasks the rather impromptu business required. Both Stoddard and Bohn trusted her implicitly, with money and the most confidential partnership matters. Her first assignment, she remembers, was to buy whatever equipment she needed and to find a rug which matched the one in Stoddard's office. She also recalls that during those first days in the Lafayette Building "Mr. Stoddard had the happy habit of whistling when things were going well." He preferred bits from the classics or Broadway musicals, and when he suddenly stopped, "that meant he was thinking hard and making a decision." Even when they moved to Lansing, "he still whistled when we were working alone evenings, and it created a homey atmosphere."

Gladys handled the advances, often in cash, to the buying agents, and she kept score as the stock acquisitions moved toward the magic 51 percent ownership—first for three banks, then four, five and six. She also serviced the growing file of mortgages until this activity was assigned to a separate mortgage company.

Howard Stoddard recognized the implications of the New Deal revolution in home financing at a time when most bankers were still shying away from mortgages because of their recent bitter experiences. As noted earlier, his R.F.C. and receivership observations had convinced him that most home-owners will keep up their house payments as long as they can scrape together the money to do so. The problem with mortgages as bank investments had been that hard times could—and did—put a large number of mortgagees in such straits that they absolutely could not hold on to their homes. Hence the thousands of foreclosures in the Detroit area in the months before and after the bank holiday, and the bulging files of slow and delinquent mortgages in the hands of the First National and Guardian National receiverships. Many out-state banks had similar experiences. In Detroit both the receiverships and the successor banks were interested in disposing of mortgages, and Reconstruction Finance Corporation and Home Owners Loan Corporation also had such contracts for sale.

It was Stoddard's strong opinion that with H.O.L.C. and its 1938 successor, Federal National Mortgage Association, guaranteeing a market for mortgages, and with Federal Housing Administration insuring loans for the construction of new homes and the rehabilitation of old ones, mortgages were no longer high risk investments for banks. On the contrary, F.H.A. contracts were not only safe, but they could attract business to commercial banks which had previously gone to postal savings offices and other thrift institutions. Further, they were installment loans, producing a regular cash flow for reinvestment. They could be a key to liquidity.

Even before Stoddard became a member of the Port Huron bank board, his views may have influenced Stephen Graham and others, for the bank began to purchase F.H.A. mortgages, and it became the first bank in Michigan to make F.H.A. rehabilitation loans. When Stoddard joined the board in 1937, the bank began buying Detroit mortgages, which were available at a discount from Manufacturers National Bank and also obtainable from R.F.C. Stoddard negotiated these purchases, usually inspecting the properties beforehand. Waldo Stoddard, representing the Battle Creek bank, sometimes accompanied him on these "horseback appraisals." Frank McCabe was another key participant in the program. According to Waldo, the Battle Creek bank also pioneered F.H.A. new home financing, working with a construction firm in Kalamazoo.

As working control of other banks was obtained, the same investment policy was pursued. On October 10, 1939, Stoddard wrote to Joseph Brewer:

> The banks in which we are interested have acquired F.H.A. mortgages in the Detroit area totalling $3,500,000.00. . . . We have had about 1½ years experience in servicing of more than half of the above mortgages, and it has worked out quite satisfactorily because so many problems were handled directly by Miss MacGregor in Detroit. . . .

At first the system for handling the real estate contracts was quite simple. Stoddard was the middle-man between the Detroit suppliers and the out-state banks which adopted his program. Since the properties were in the Detroit area, he accepted the responsibility for receiving installment payments, mostly cash brought in by homeowners. This meant setting up a system to record receipts and make remittances to the banks concerned.

Since the typical home mortgage in those days was less than $5,000, the volume of traffic into the office was steady and the human problems were sometimes intense. Once a Turkish immigrant, in broken English, accused Gladys of having stolen his money because the principal reduction of his loan had lowered his mortgage insurance and instead of changing the amount charged—seven cents on each of two payments—she had credited the overage to his tax escrow. When he finally understood, there were profuse apologies. Later Stoddard, who had overheard it all, came out of his office and said, "You have certainly earned your salary today." As for the Turkish homeowner, Gladys adds, "his wife made all payments from that day on, because, as she said, 'He likes you too much.' "

The volume of business soon outgrew the fourteenth floor suite, so a separate servicing agency, Lafayette Mortgage Corporation, was chartered by

Charles Bohn early in 1939. It was located on the first floor of the Lafayette Building and staffed by people Gladys recruited from the mortgage department of the First National receivership. Waldo Stoddard and Frank McCabe developed the records and operational procedures for the corporation. Howard managed the new facility, with Gladys' help.

With offices now on two widely-separated floors, a communications problem naturally developed. Stoddard at first rejected the idea of an elaborate intercom system, declaring that he was not going to be like a Washington executive, intimidating visitors with banks of flashing lights and frequent telephone interruptions. After uncounted elevator trips, he reluctantly accepted an electronic system. A period of communications snafus followed, which Gladys enjoys recalling. "In Lansing," she adds, "the button system was simpler, and it took him only two months to master it."

Lafayette Mortgage Corporation continued to service Detroit mortgages until Michigan National Bank was formed and each of the branches took over the management of its own home loans. After Stoddard and Gladys moved to Lansing, Ralph Free was for a time in charge of the office, which continued to handle collections and to assemble packages of contracts for the out-state banks. Gladys has not forgotten the harrowing occasion when she picked up $400,000 worth of mortgages at the Lafayette Building for delivery to the bank offices in the Olds Tower and ran out of gas in downtown Lansing at 11 p.m. The next morning "Mr. Stoddard accepted the fact that the mortgages were there with the same ease as if I had carried one file across the street."

By mid-summer 1939 it was becoming clear that Lansing was the logical center for the Bohn-Stoddard banking network, and that it should become Stoddard's home base. Jennie suspected this when the partnership took an office on the ninth floor of the Olds Tower and Stoddard began to spend an increasing amount of time there. When the Lansing National Bank presidency became a real prospect and he finally suggested a move, she countered with the suggestion that he continue to commute—at least for a while. After all, the home in Grosse Pointe had recently been redecorated, the children were established in schools, Boy Scout and Girl Scout troops, and neighborhood relationships, and they had such wonderful friends in Detroit. Completely unenthused, he issued an ultimatum: "There's no other way. I'm not going without you, and we'll just have to quit the bank." Only it really was not an ultimatum, as Jennie well recalls. "There really was no other way. If we were going to do it in January, we had to move up right then. So he just called the moving van, and away we came. . . ."

Actually it was not quite that precipitate. Shopping for housing began in September, as did the round of farewell parties. In the midst of the actual move, Stoddard's mother died, November 9, 1939. So Gladys was asked to supervise Howard Jr., Virginia and Bud in the recently rented house on East Lansing's Grand River Avenue, while Howard and Jennie flew to Salt Lake City for Ellen Stoddard's funeral. When they returned, it was to celebrate Thanksgiving in a new home in a new city.

Stoddard had much to be thankful for. With a new job and six banks to work with, he had reached "the end of the beginning." Plans could become performance. Ambition could now be transformed into solid banking accomplishments.

He was thirty-eight years old.

CHAPTER 10

# Birth of Michigan National

The Howard Stoddards moved to Lansing as the city, the state and the nation were entering a new phase of their history. German and Russian armies were devastating and dividing Poland and the United States was belatedly expanding its military and naval power. Although some of the outspoken isolationists—like Senator Vandenberg and Father Coughlin—were from Michigan, defense spending began to funnel contracts for tanks and airplanes to the state's automakers, and the economy quickly moved out of the doldrums. Lansing's Reo Motor Car Company became a major producer of Army trucks, and the influx of laborers and dollars meant new business for bankers. Stoddard often acknowledged the tie between the early growth of his Michigan banks and the tragedy-based prosperity of World War II.

In November 1939, however, most Americans believed that the war would stay on the other side of the ocean, and they concentrated on tasks closer to home. For Stoddard there were three—to establish his family in a new home, church, school and community environment, to manage a $10 million bank, and to meld that institution with five others into the state-spanning network which he and Charles Bohn had begun discussing four years before.

Much of the first responsibility was left to Jennie. From the beginning of their marriage she and Howard had subscribed to the traditional division of roles: He provided the livelihood and she managed the home. The children were a shared delight and concern, but building a banking empire was no forty-hour-week affair, and so the three young Stoddards saw quite a bit more of their mother than their father. The house at 1107 Grand River Avenue, with its unique undulating roof line, was rented because it was available and close to good schools. That it continued to be the Stoddard residence for seven years was a by-product of the war. East Lansing was chosen because it was the preferred residential suburb of the Michigan state capital. The bank offices in the Olds Tower were about four miles and twenty minutes away.

Howard Jr., Virginia and Bud were 12, 10 and 8 when they experienced the coincident traumas of losing their grandmother and moving into a new world. Ellen Stoddard they had known well from their annual trips to Utah and her occasional visits to Detroit, and they loved her. This was their first real encounter with death, and if distance cushioned the impact, the hasty departure of their parents made the feeling of loss very real. School, church and the resilience of youth helped the exchange of old friends for new ones, and they sensed from their father's dedication to his new work that they would probably be in East Lansing for a long time.

Getting acquainted was easier because Stoddard had business acquaintances of several years standing, some of whom now became family friends. Jennie remembers one chain of episodes vividly:

> Howard had gone back to the office to work, and I had gone upstairs to press the children's clothes. It was a rainy night. Papers were strewn around, the house was in disarray, the children were in pajamas and the dog was barking when the doorbell rang. It was Mr. and Mrs. Olds and their daughter. . . . I invited them in, and explained that this was part of the confusion of getting the children to bed. Mr. Olds wanted to show them his watch, which had an alarm. I immediately called Howard and he came home. The maid put the children to bed, and we had our first visit with this charming family.
>
> When Christmas came, Mr. and Mrs. Olds invited us to join them Christmas eve. We explained that we could not leave the children, but they said that everyone brings their children to Woldenroe. So Howard and I took the three children and spent an unforgettable evening. . . . There was a big tree in the hall, gifts for all, a table spread with delicious food and friends to make us feel very much at home on our first Lansing Christmas.

The relationship with the Olds family continued cordial, and Gladys Olds Anderson became one of Jennie Stoddard's good friends.

If Howard Stoddard was already known to some of the leaders of Lansing National Bank and its community, he had yet to make an impression upon the bank's personnel and day-to-day operations. Shortly after he was elected president, one of the typists was heard to say, "I don't know what I'm doing, but it is for that young man upstairs."

Lansing National was a rather typical small city bank in 1940. It had about forty employees, and all operations were confined to the ornate main floor and two balconies. (The balance of the twenty-three story building was rented to various tenants, and some office space was still vacant.) According to Gladys MacGregor, who divided her time between Lafayette Mortgage Corporation and the bank before settling in as Stoddard's secretary in February 1940, "the whole place had a family atmosphere, and some of the customs were delightful." Wearers of new dresses or new suits were promenaded before their fellow employees, and the women sometimes posed on counter tops while the men whistled. The tellers—all male—gathered in the vault each morning before bringing out the cash, and sang a familiar song. The resonance in a bank vault surpassses that in a shower, and Gladys reports that "hearing that music coming up the marble stairway set the tone for the day.")

Birthdays and other special occasions were sometimes observed with after-hours parties. Howard approved an ice cream social on one occasion when a board meeting was scheduled, with the specific understanding that the festivities would be over before the directors arrived. Late customers delayed the starting, and so the board members came into a lobby filled with celebrants. Knowing most of the employees, they joined in the party, and one later observed: "It is a sign of a fine organization spirit when officers and employees join in a celebration like this."

The family of bank employees discovered that the young bank president was not only handsome but bashful when one of the "girls"—on an impulse or a dare—kissed him on the cheek when he passed beneath a sprig of holiday mistletoe. Blushing, he crossed the lobby without a word, retreated into his office, and did not emerge for several hours. There were no penalties —but there was no repetition.

Female employees were only stenographers and clerks in those days, and since marriage automatically terminated employment, it was conventional to speak of them all as "girls." Their pay was low—even lower than the standard for male bank employees—and Stoddard did not immediately implement a revolution here. His ideas of fair compensation were linked to incentives and productivity, and it took him a few years to develop the profit-sharing program which became a trademark of Michigan National and a key to its growth.

Vice Presidents Eugene Wanger, Miles D. Grant and John B. Nelligan quickly adapted to Stoddard's operational style and investment policies. The bank, already profitable, continued to reduce its R.F.C. loans, increase its F.H.A. mortgage holdings, and build its earnings. A supportive board of directors—half bank officers and half executives of Lansing-based businesses—found Stoddard's strong but quiet leadership agreeable. He listened more than he talked, but when he spoke, everybody listened. The downtown bank and its two suburban branches were soon functioning to the new executive's satisfaction, and he was able to devote his primary attention to the larger Bohn-Stoddard enterprise.

To consolidate the banks in Battle Creek, Grand Rapids, Lansing, Marshall, Port Huron and Saginaw into a state-wide branch banking business required standardizing the procedures and policies of each, securing the approval of the directors and holders of two-thirds of the stock, obtaining whatever federal and state approvals were required, and fending off the opposition which rapidly formed as competitors became aware of the plan. All of these were successfully accomplished in 1940.

Since Stoddard had for some time been attending the board and executive committee meetings of the six banks, first representing "working control" and then majority ownership, he knew the people and they knew his approach to the business. The take-overs had produced a few personnel changes, but generally the same officers and directors carried on, persuaded that the actions proposed by the confident young representative of the Bohn-Stoddard investor group were in the best interests of the institutions concerned. The establishing of social ties began. Jennie, who once described her role as "ambassador to the families" of Howard's associates, accompanied him on some of his trips and was gracious hostess when couples and groups came to Lansing. Entertaining friends and acquaintances from the Irving Trust, National Copper and Reconstruction Finance Corporation days was another activity in which she was an invaluable help to her socially reticent husband.

That Stoddard already had a well-defined concept of sound banking is attested by a letter which he wrote to Charles Bohn on February 1, 1938, just after he had moved onto the boards of the first two banks. Its substance and style make it worth reproducing:

Dear Mr. Bohn:

As a result of my banking experiences during the past ten years I have definitely concluded to pursue the following general investment and operating policy with those banks which we now control as well as any we may subsequently acquire. The earning figures are based upon present interest rates and the present cost of doing business if all expenses are reduced to a minimum.

The total resources of each bank will be segregated within the following approximate classifications as rapidly as conditions permit.

| | | | | |
|---|---|---|---|---|
| Cash | 20% | -o- | av. yield | |
| United States Bonds | 20% | 2.2 | " | |
| Other Bonds | 20% | 4.0 | " | |
| Loans and Discounts | 20% | 5.5 | " | |
| Real Estate Mortgages | 20% | 5.5 | " | |
| | 100% | 3.4 | " | |
| Misc. service charges | | .2 | | 3.6% |
| Less: | | | | |
| Average cost of deposits with 2% on savings and no interest on commercial | 1.0% | | | |
| Cost of doing business, including salaries, rent, insurance, advertising, general expenses and depreciation | 1.6% | | | 2.6% |
| Net earning on total resources prior to charge-offs for losses and exclusive of any non-operating profits | | | | 1.0% |

Under standard banking practice the ratio of deposits to capital funds is usually 10 to 1. If a bank is capable of earning 1% on its total resources this would be translated into 10% on its capital funds. In the event a portion of the capital funds consists of 3% preferred stock [R.F.C. shares] the earnings leverage for the common equity would thus be proportionately increased. . . .

The cash reserves of the banks in which we are interested will be maintained with the Federal Reserve Bank, the National Bank of Detroit, the Manufacturers Bank of Detroit, one selected New York City bank and one in Chicago.

The holdings of United States securities will be staggered over 5 to 15 year maturities unless certain special conditions require holding a portion in 1 to 5 year treasury notes.

> The other securities will include municipals, industrials, public utilities, railroads and financial with ratings of "A" and better and maturities in most cases not in excess of 15 years. Unless the present bank portfolio account is already developed extreme care will be exercised in new investments under prevailing conditions.
>
> Loans and Discounts will generally be local in nature and include a wide diversification with strict credit supervision.
>
> The real estate mortgages with few exceptions will be on a monthly amortized basis, largely on homes. The mortgage, unless insured by the FHA will not exceed 60% of the appraised value of the property.
>
> During January I became a Director and Chairman of the Executive Committee of the First National Bank of Port Huron and the Saginaw State Bank. Through this position it is possible to closely control the banks' affairs. During the coming year I hope to round out their asset portfolios as outlined and bring their operating figures within the percentages forecast.

The lessons which Stoddard had learned from his R.F.C. and receivership experiences are clear here. Liquidity is important, but it is to be guaranteed not by holding large amounts of cash but by investing in readily negotiable securities and guaranteed or carefully selected loans. Both securities and loans should produce a steady cash flow, so that in times of stress loan volume can be reduced simply by not reinvesting money as it comes in from installment accounts and maturing bonds. Stoddard was particularly leery of the kinds of speculative lump-sum loans which had produced such troubles for the Detroit banks, and he was almost a fanatic on "strict credit supervision." His experience with the strengths and weaknesses of bank credit departments began with Irving Trust in New York, and he had a "feel" for loans which his colleagues and subordinates came to respect.

By 1940 the Bohn-Stoddard banks were moving along parallel lines. To bring them together meant taking care of the mechanical arrangements and securing the necessary approvals. Both went on concurrently.

Stoddard had begun to alert some of his friends in Washington to the long-range plan as he corresponded and visited with them about the recapitalizations and personnel changes which attended each separate acquisition. This was prudent, because the 1933 Detroit fiasco had left many at the Comptroller's office, Federal Reserve Board and R.F.C. cautious about bank consolidations. By 1940 the key people were generally supportive. It cannot have hurt the project that two very strategically situated people, Jesse Jones and Marriner Eccles, held Howard Stoddard in high regard.

Stoddard, Bohn, Endicott, Brewer, Graham and others who early consulted on the consolidation plans agreed that Lansing should be the center because it was geographically convenient to the six banks and Detroit and was the seat of the state government. Michigan State College, just beginning its spectacular growth under President John Hannah, was an added attraction, both as a potential market for banking services and a cultural resource for the bank's personnel. (Brewer initially made a strong appeal for Grand Rapids, but Stoddard's recommendation prevailed.)

The name first proposed for the consolidation was First National Bank of Michigan. The Comptroller of the Currency disapproved this rather pretentious designation but accepted a title which ultimately proved much better for advertising and image-building purposes—Michigan National Bank.

To handle the voluminous legal work connected with the consolidation, a battery of attorneys was employed, including Byron L. Ballard, of Lansing, William H. Gallagher and Leo M. Butzel, of Detroit, and Eugene L. Garey, of New York. The ties with Ballard and Garey continued for many years. Described by himself and several associates as "the lawyer's best friend," Stoddard came to know many attorneys well. He picked up so much insight into the principles and techniques of litigation that his R.F.C. friend, James Alley, later thought of him as having had legal training. The plans to study law at New York University were, it has been noted earlier, wiped out by Oregon financial problems after a brief night school enrollment.)

For the complex task of developing an accounting system for the combined banks, Stoddard turned to Russell Fairles. The choice was a happy one. No Michigan National Bank officer except Waldo Stoddard was closer to Howard than "Russ" Fairles during the next thirty years.

Fairles was a Canadian, experienced with the branch banking systems of that country before he came to work for the Guardian Group in Detroit and then joined Joseph Brewer's bank in Grand Rapids in 1931. Their first encounter, as described by Fairles, produced a cryptic five-minute interview in which he affirmed that he knew something about branch banking, wanted $300 per month, and could come to work in two weeks. When he returned, Brewer's first reaction was: "You here already? I haven't fired the other guy yet." As Fairles thanked his stars that he was still single and had job options available back in Detroit, the crusty self-made millionaire continued: "You go out and come back after lunch and I'll have him fired."

So began a relationship in which Fairles helped with the reorganization of Grand Rapids National Bank in 1933 and then worked with the new National Bank of Grand Rapids and the receivership. He was auditor and credit manager for the bank when Brewer recommended him to Stoddard in 1940 as a man who could take charge of the accounting phase of the consolidation.

As he impressed most people on first contact, Howard Stoddard struck Russell Fairles as "rather reserved." "It seemed that rather than me sizing him up, he was sizing me up." Apparently both were satisfied, for an agreement on salary was quickly struck and Fairles was given virtual *carte blanche* to do what was needful. (Although he was less than a year younger and the two men became very close, Fairles never called Howard by his first name. Only a few of the bank officers ever did.)

Harry E. Ingram, from Port Huron, and Raymond L. Bundy, of the Battle Creek bank, were recruited for the Central Office staff. With Fairles they developed the procedures by which the Foote accrual system of accounting employed in the branches could be used to produce a consolidated daily balance sheet and profit and loss statement for the combined operations—something which would be essential if general policy guidelines were to be applied to a number of relatively independent operating units.

Stoddard soon came to refer to "Russ," Harry and "Speed" as the "whizkids." Fairles gathered accounting forms from Royal Bank of Canada, Security First National Bank of Los Angeles, and Bank of America, all of which had numerous branches. Those from Bank of America were particularly helpful as a complete set of Michigan National banking documents was produced during the months immediately following the consolidation. (Stickers carrying the name of the new bank were applied to checks and other papers until the new forms were printed.) The auditors in the six offices were ready for a quick changeover when Fairles gave them the word.

The delicate task of negotiating the exchange of shares in the six banks for stock in Michigan National was performed primarily by Stoddard himself. The manner in which the controlling interest in each bank had been obtained meant that most of the remaining investors, including R.F.C., had relatively sizeable holdings. The R.F.C. held non-voting preferred stock, and agency concurrence in the pending unification and recapitalization presented no problems.

With the common stock holders it was another matter. Since the law required two-thirds of the ownership to approve the mergers, and the Bohn-Stoddard group held only a majority interest in most cases, the success of these negotiations was critical. There being no established public market in such bank shares, the prices which Stoddard's agents had paid became the basis for discussion with the boards of directors and those who represented minority shareholdings. The performance of the banks under Stoddard leadership was such that most of the directors were willing to go along, but he had to barter with each bank individually and at the same time try to keep everyone happy with the varying exchange terms. Actual exchanges waited until the new bank was in operation.

Most of the reminiscences about M.N.B. beginnings mention the director who adamantly opposed the consolidation and resigned when his colleagues voted in favor. Later he reconsidered and wanted to withdraw his resignation, but Stoddard—who was stubborn, too—refused. When the consolidation was completed, the truculent man refused to send in his Saginaw National Bank stock for conversion. Even the withholding of cash and stock dividends failed to sway him. Years passed before he appeared in Lansing, "pockets bulging with envelopes," and asked for Stoddard. A cordial exchange of greetings occurred and the shares were quickly exchanged. Later when someone offered to buy some of his M.N.B. holdings he was heard to say: "Can you tell me any place in the world I can reinvest this money where it will earn as much or have as good prospects?"

Howard Stoddard's image as a maverick banker took form at this time, and it has endured in Michigan financial circles to this day. What he was doing was unprecedented and challenging—and the resentment at his refusal to conform was as strong as the resistance to his competitive drive. As noted earlier, community resistance to "outsiders" appeared in several of the Bohn-Stoddard cities as the local banks were purchased. Now, as the magnitude of the project dawned on the press and other bankers, opposition spanned the region and reached out to the state and federal governments for help.

Large Detroit and Chicago banks immediately recognized that the merging of the six banks would mean that many of the needs of business and industry in those communities could be met locally. Previously no out-state bank could make single loans in excess of $500,000, because none had more than $50,000 capital and the law fixed the maximum loan-to-capital ratio at 10 to 1. Now a bank with resources to sustain multi-million dollar loans was entering the market in cities which were already feeling the defense-generated economic revival.

Small banks around the state reacted negatively for other reasons. Where two or more conservatively managed banks shared a trade area without competing too aggressively with one another, the prospect of one being purchased by a bank which would bring in big city competition was enough to produce nightmares in some of the finest homes. Where a single bank enjoyed a local monopoly the danger was only a little less formidable, for shopping habits were being revolutionized by the automobile and who knew when it would do for the family-owned country bank what it was doing to the corner grocery and the independent gas station. The popular alarm about the "chain store octopus" was a political resource which the country banks—and Michigan Bankers Association, their spokesman—could use in their efforts to block Michigan National before it breeched the walls of the *status quo*.

Some of the opponents of the Bohn-Stoddard project thought that the legal walls were already impregnable. The 1933 Michigan law which followed federal legislation in authorizing state-wide branch banking had fallen before anti-branching sentiment four years later, as previously noted. The 1937 state law restricted branches to a 25-mile radius of the home office, and the exception covering acquisition through purchase and reorganization was probably intended to cover special situations where a local bank was in trouble and purchase by an outside bank could save it from closing. This, at least, was the interpretation of the state commissioner of banking, Frederick B. Elliott, Jr., and early in 1940 he asked the state attorney general to institute a suit to block the proposed mergers.

The question was a delicate one, fraught with politics in a state where virtually no issue of consequence was immune to political considerations. Elliott's position was that since the federal legislation permitting national banks to establish branches was limited by what state laws permitted to state banks, state banking authorities had the right to judge whether branching by national banks conformed to state laws. Michigan Attorney General Thomas Read disagreed, ruling on June 6—six days after Saginaw State Bank became Saginaw National Bank—that "there is nothing in the state laws to interfere":

> It is my opinion that a national banking institution, duly and legally chartered by federal authority, may establish and operate as branches within the state of Michigan, existing state or national banks legally acquired by purchase or consolidation and subject to the approval of the federal comptroller of the currency.

Asked by the Associated Press to comment on the ruling, Howard Stoddard attributed much of the opposition to jealousy. He regretted that there had been "a great deal of misinformation concerning our plans," and he offered this explanation:

> For the sake of economy and efficiency in management, we are attempting to merge these banks under a single board of directors that would give equal representation to all of the cities involved. This board would have in its membership some of the strong men, financially, morally and mentally, in Michigan.

This was no scheme to impose on the public, he pointed out. "We do not plan to sell stock in this enterprise. But with a single board operating these banks, and with a unity of purpose, we would be in a position to employ some of the best talent available. . . ." The plan would strengthen an already strong group of banks.

Now it was up to the federal authorities. On August 4 United States Attorney General Robert H. Jackson advised Comptroller Preston Delano that he had legal authority to approve the proposed purchase of the six banks by the new Michigan National Bank and the operation of five as branches of the Lansing-based firm. (In 1941 a new Michigan Attorney General instituted proceedings in the state courts to undo the merger and strip M.N.B. of the trust operations which it had assumed under the prior charters of its Battle Creek, Grand Rapids and Port Huron branches. The Michigan Supreme Court rejected the suit on the same grounds that Read and Jackson had earlier found persuasive. 298 Michigan Reports 417.)

With the go-ahead from Washington, the tempo of preparations increased. Stoddard now turned to the crucial directors meetings scheduled in the six cities. Discussion was protracted in some cases, and voting was not always unanimous. However, the necessary two-thirds majorities were obtained. The action of the Grand Rapids First National Bank and Trust Company board produced state-wide headlines. SIX MICHIGAN BANKS JOIN IN MERGER PLAN was the Grand Rapids *Herald* headline on November 20, and the Lansing *State Journal* of the same date added a community-interest emphasis: BANKING CHAIN WITH OFFICES HERE PLANNED. Stoddard's picture accompanied the story, and his face soon became familiar to the readers of what was already his "home town newspaper."

To Howard Stoddard this was only the beginning. Detroit and another eight or ten out-state trade centers were in the plan. The six banks came first because they were available. The largest was Port Huron, with assets of over $14 million at the time of merging. Next in order came Grand Rapids ($13 million), Lansing ($10 million), Battle Creek ($8.8 million), Saginaw ($8.3 million), and Marshall ($2.8 million). Preferred stock held by Reconstruction Finance Corporation was part of the capitalization of all banks, constituting 50 percent of the capital funds for Port Huron and Battle Creek, about 25 percent for Saginaw and Marshall, and 15 percent for Grand Rapids and Lansing. When Michigan National Bank was chartered by the Comptroller of the Currency, almost exactly one-third of its $5.1 million in capital funds was R.F.C. stock—which explains why so many of Howard Stoddard's 1939-1940 trips to Washington included stops at Jesse Jones' agency.

M.N.B. people long believed that theirs was the first simultaneous merger of six national banks. A letter from Elizabeth Rauld, a representative of the Comptroller of the Currency, July 18, 1978, advises that a 1935 combination of South Dakota banks has that distinction. She adds: "Therefore, the merger in 1941 which resulted in your bank was one of the two largest mergers of national banks to date in the history of the United States."

With the way cleared, instructions for the transition went to six different destinations. Fairles and the other "whizkids" designated the records which must be transferred to Lansing and mapped out a central accounting office on the north mezzanine of the Olds Tower. Gladys MacGregor prepared notarized copies of minutes and multiple copies of applications for Washington, and Stoddard made several trips to insure that everything was in readiness in the Comptroller's office. A final round of board meetings was scheduled for the days after Christmas, to approve the changes planned to take place on the first working day of the new year.

On Saturday, December 28, 1940, a telegram was sent to Deputy Comptroller E. H. Gough: "Shareholders of six national banks have given almost unanimous ratification to consolidation agreements." Monday Stoddard and Ballard flew to Washington to insure that the documents were safely delivered and to touch bases with the key people one more time. They returned to Lansing late.

Now there was nothing to do but wait. According to the plans, the Comptroller would send approval by telegram if the application was complete and in order. Only a last minute injunction by foes of the merger could stop it now, and there were rumors that such an action might occur. At 2:15 p.m., December 31, the message from Washington arrived. The next fifteen minutes, according to Gladys, "Mr. Stoddard walked the floor, telegram firmly clasped in his hand and his eyes on the clock. A guard stood poised and promptly at 2:30 the doors were locked. *We were in business*!"

CHAPTER 11

# The War Years

"Being in the right place at the right time" was, Howard Stoddard often said, an important element in business success. Michigan National Bank would not have been conceived if he had not been in the state during the bank holiday. Now the circumstances of its birth were favored by circumstances beyond his planning or control. With the expansion of the national defense effort and the adoption of the Lend-Lease Act after the election of 1940, the American economy expanded rapidly and the industries and financial institutions of Michigan were primary beneficiaries. In its first five years the Bohn-Stoddard branch banking enterprise trebled its resources, from $57 million to $187 million, increased its capital funds from $5.1 million to $6.7 million, and expanded its annual income after taxes from $518,000 to $817,000. By the time World War II ended in 1945, M.N.B. ranked 103rd among the national banks of the United States.

In announcing to the stockholders at the close of 1944—as he did with monotonous regularity for the next quarter century—that "the bank has had another good year," Stoddard cautioned that "these gains have resulted almost entirely from conditions imposed by the war and the wartime financing of the Federal Government." This modest reminder that the growth "is not something that we as bankers can properly regard as an individual or collective achievement" drew favorable editorial comment in *The American Banker*, an indication that Michigan National's president was already becoming a man to watch on the national financial scene.

What made Howard Stoddard a man to watch, however, was not his modesty, but the vigor with which he managed and promoted his new company and the impact which he had—from the very outset—on banking in Michigan.

On January 1, 1941, Stoddard confronted four tasks. First, the technical phases of consolidating the six constitutent banks into branches had to be completed quickly and with a minimum of confusion. Second, general policies had to be defined so that operational autonomy could be safely lodged in the branch officers. Third, customers and the public in the affected cities had to be reassured, lest they be swayed by critics of the consolidation. Fourth, strenuous efforts to check the further expansion of Michigan National Bank by state legislation had to be resisted.

In the circumstances, Howard and Jennie did not join the Bohns in Florida to celebrate the advent of a new year and the fulfilment of a shared dream. Instead, Stoddard saw more of Russ Fairles, Gladys MacGregor and several other key bank people than he did of his wife and children during the forty-three hours between the closing of Lansing National Bank on December 31 and the opening of Michigan National on January 2. Young Howard, Virginia and Bud shared the excitement, however, for dinner table conversations between their father and mother had long since caused them to anticipate this big event.

Loosely organized chaos prevailed at the Olds Tower. Calls went to all the offices advising them officially of Washington's approval, and tellers, accountants and managers from Port Huron to Grand Rapids worked far into the night putting their year-end reports into the standard form which had been devised to simplify the consolidation of accounts. Papers were shuttled to Lansing, fortunately without collision with New Year's Eve celebrants. At Central Office, as the rear balcony overlooking the bank lobby was already christened, boxes and files were stacked informally. There Fairles, Harry Ingram and "Speed" Bundy put the data together for Stoddard's inspection. (For the first two weeks the final report was ruled up by hand because the new printed forms were late arriving.)

So many small details needed to be looked after. A bank has its name on checks and check cancelling machines, clocks and calendars, deposit slips and display ads, notices of business hours and name plates for departments, savings account books and statements of many kinds. When the doors opened Thursday morning, customers must be left with no doubt that they were in a new bank, and every effort must be made to make that realization reassuring. Where improvisation was necessary, it must not be shoddy-looking. Not in Howard Stoddard's bank!

Coordination of these activities in the six branches was by men with familiar faces and new titles. George J. Genebach, Glenn O. Hoffhines and Waldo I. Stoddard were the key figures at Battle Creek. Genebach, who was also president of United Steel and Wire Company, was named senior vice president in recognition of his stock ownership position and his role in engineering the Battle Creek acquisition. Hoffhines and Waldo both bore the title of senior vice president, which designated the chief operating officer of a bank; Hoffhines was the executive head, while Waldo's assignments left him some flexibility to work with Howard on special system-wide projects.

The official organization meeting of Michigan National Bank was held on January 15, 1941. Joseph H. Brewer, who continued as chief operating officer in charge of Grand Rapids, changed his designation from bank president to chairman of the board of directors. He continued in this capacity until his death in 1943 when Waldo I. Stoddard became executive head of Grand Rapids office. Stephen A. Graham, head of Port Huron office, was named vice chairman of the board, in recognition of his contribution to the total operation. Upon his retirement at age 70, the position was abolished. Frank J. McCabe, who had been his chief aide, was named senior vice president in charge of Port Huron operations. J. D. Wright changed his title from president to senior vice president and kept on running the Marshall office, as did James M. Shackleton in Saginaw.

Michigan National Bank inherited the trust company charter from Brewer's Grand Rapids bank, and the new M.N.B. Trust Department was set up there with Brewer presiding and James R. Hooper as senior vice president. Trusts arranged by all of the branches were to be managed here; the value of trusts in hand when the department opened exceeded $25 million. Waldo took charge of this operation also in 1943.

The creation of Central Office in Lansing necessitated some personnel rearrangements there. Charles B. Bohn, who had the most stock in Michigan National, was quite content to let Howard Stoddard run the show. (After Mr. Brewer's death in 1943, Mr. Bohn accepted the chairmanship of the board of directors, and continued in that capacity until his death in 1952.) Stoddard became president of the consolidated bank, with Fairles as comptroller, Miles D. Grant as vice president and cashier, and Gladys MacGregor as secretary. For a year or so Stoddard also headed the Lansing branch, with Eugene M. Wanger and John B. Nelligan as vice presidents. The dual role in time proved unwieldy, as well as unsymmetrical, and Wanger was designated senior vice president in charge. He still enjoyed the mixed advantage over his colleagues in the other branches of being more constantly under Stoddard's watchful eye.

The exchange of bank stock certificates began immediately, the previously-negotiated terms being different for each of the units. For the six kinds of preferred stock held by the Reconstruction Finance Corporation, certificates with a par value of $10 and a guaranteed dividend of 3 percent were substituted. Common stock, in shares with a par value of $10, aggregated $1.5 million. Between them Bohn and Stoddard had a majority interest, although

Stoddard was still paying for most of his shares under the buy-back arrangement established with Bohn during the years when the banks were being collected.

The letter which went to all customers of the six branches and the news releases and display ads which appeared at the same time stressed that the new bank "is owned by Michigan capital, operated by Michigan directors, and designed to meet the modern banking needs of one of the nation's most progressive states. . . ." Without sacrificing the strengths of the constituent banks, the consolidation provides "all the facilities and advantages enjoyed by the larger metropolitan banks."

All the early publicity emphasized the theme of "local control." Here Stoddard's concept of branch banking differed from his Bank of America model. He spelled out the difference in a policy statement to all officers: "The bank functions thru the coordination of several large banking offices rather than the centralized direction of a myriad of small offices." In another context he spoke critically of chain banking in which "a branch manager does his business out of a black book of regulations." One of the senior officers described Michigan National as more like a multi-bank holding company than a conventional branch bank.

Since the branches of Michigan National had been annexed rather than established new, Stoddard had pragmatic as well as theoretical reasons for leaving a degree of autonomy in each. As the letter to customers declared, "Local control of the making and supervising of loans . . . will be under the direction of resident directors and officers, and the banking operations will be carried on by the present staff of officers and employees." The local boards of directors now became advisory boards. They had generally been reduced in size when Bohn-Stoddard control was instituted, and now they continued with few personnel changes.

Overall control of Michigan National Bank was, of course, vested in its central board of directors. The composition of the initial board reflected the realities of stock ownership. Bohn was the only representative of his stockholder group until Simon Den Uyl and Roe Endicott filled two vacancies in 1943. Randall Wickes, of Saginaw, held a large block of stock. Brewer, Genebach, Graham, Shackleton and Waldo Stoddard were substantial shareholders as well as operating officers. Attorney Byron Ballard was there as a reminder that the new bank was moving out into a legal and political minefield. The balance of the 25 directors were key men from the local advisory boards. Mervin F. Cotes, of Lansing's Motor Wheel Corporation; Congressman Fred L. Crawford, of Saginaw; James M. MacTaggart, of St. Clair

County Abstract Company, Port Huron; and John M. Maynard, of Lansing's J.C. Penney Company, were still on the board when the bank celebrated its tenth anniversary.

Within a few years the board took on a more symmetrical aspect, as Fred Lavery, J.D. Wright, Frank McCabe and Eugene Wanger, the senior vice presidents for Flint, Marshall, Port Huron and Lansing were added. The senior vice presidents, plus Fairles and Grant, then functioned as the executive committee, with Howard Stoddard as chairman. This general pattern was retained during the thirty years that Stoddard was at the helm. The executive committee was the group within which policies, innovations and problems were most thoroughly explored, with the board of directors serving primarily as a ratifying body. For years the board met on the second Friday of each month and the executive committee met on the fourth Friday.

Each office, according to the 1941 policy statement, "functions under the direct control and supervision of its designated presiding officer. He is responsible to the President, Executive Committee and the Board for the proper organization of the office and the activities of its staff." He was expected to follow M.N.B. policies and use prescribed forms and procedures, but he was definitely the man in charge. Only routine communications went from his branch to Central Office without his screening. Stoddard was scrupulous about working with the branch executives on all problems involving local operations. When they came to him for advice, a favorite tactic was to hear them out and then ask, "What would you do?" When an innovative idea or a proposed solution did not immediately satisfy him, he often used the debate-avoidance formula: "Let me sleep on it." Reflection might persuade him; argument rarely did once he had made up his mind.

In time a singular brand of loyalty developed between the president and the senior vice presidents. They were aware of his public reputation as "a very cold individual"—one had even heard him described as having "ice water in his veins"—but contact disclosed that consideration, even compassion, tempered his dominating personality. The blend of admiration, awe and affection with which the M.N.B. officers came to regard "Mr. Stoddard" is uncommon in superior-subordinate relationships. A customer who observed M.N.B. operations for many years once remarked to Gladys: "I tell you, Miss MacGregor, you'd charge hell with a bucket of water for a man like that."

Although they lacked ultimate control over branch officers and policies, the local advisory boards performed many of the traditional board of directors functions. Loans of consequence required their approval and they counseled with the officers on problems and changes. Stoddard had regularly attended the board and executive committee meetings when the six branches were independent, and he now faithfully attended the monthly meetings of the six advisory groups. There is a widespread impression among bank "old-timers" that he never missed a board meeting in any of the M.N.B. cities until his illness in 1967, and that very few meetings were rescheduled or cancelled to meet his convenience. He planned vacations, surgeries and other non-business interruptions around these appointments, and winter storms which were not strong enough to prevent meetings were not severe enough to keep Stoddard away.

A crucial task at the outset was to indoctrinate advisory boards, board of directors and key bank officers in the Howard Stoddard loan philosophy. The conviction that had led Stoddard to seek experience in the Irving Trust credit department in the prosperous Twenties had been confirmed by his work with National Copper, R.F.C. and the Detroit receiverships in the Thirties. He expressed it in an early memorandum to all M.N.B. officers: "The ability to successfully loan bank funds . . . is the very heart of banking, and it is a skill which every officer should master in order to further his progress in the organization."

More cautious bankers, drawing different conclusions from their depression experiences, chose to sacrifice income for the "liquidity"—and safety—represented by vaults full of cash, government and corporate bonds and short term commercial paper. Not Stoddard. The best expression of his view, perhaps, is in the 1946 stockholders report, but it guided Michigan National from its first day of business:

> A bank is a public utility. We feel a measure of pride in reporting that our loan volume is one of the largest in the State, and our income from that source in relation to our total income, is most gratifying. We believe it is one of our prime functions to extend credit to all worthy borrowers, and no request, whether it be for $50 or for $500,000, fails to receive our earnest and sympathetic attention. We have a capable and efficient staff, serving every phase of personal, installment, mortgage, industrial and commercial loans.

The lesson from the bank crisis was to avoid unsound, open-end, speculative loans, but to take full advantage of the new ground rules and guarantees which had come with the New Deal and the opportunities which were now coming with the war. The cardinal test to be applied to every loan application, he wrote, is "*Can it be repaid in accordance with the agreement?*" If the answer, based upon "careful analysis, sound judgment and considerable experience," is affirmative, the loan should be approved. Otherwise it should be declined, "irrespective of any other consideration."

Illustrative of the approach was a call for help from the president of a small manufacturing firm in Battle Creek. His loan with another bank had been called and he was unable to raise enough money to pay it in full. Stoddard sent two M.N.B. officers to investigate. They found a corporation with good management and prospects, but a shortage of cash to meet the current obligation and tool up for the defense business which it was capable of handling. The bank loaned what was needed and also helped arrange a government contract. Within a few months the company repaid the loan and was operating profitably. The image—and earnings—of the Michigan National branch also benefitted.

Although he was convinced that character is the most important single ingredient in a good-risk borrower, Stoddard rarely loaned on the basis of an intuitive feeling about an applicant, and he did not wish bank executives to operate on that basis. "As a matter of sound procedure, there should be a daily 9:00 o'clock meeting of all officers" to consider loan applications and credit problems. "This mutual discussion . . . is of great value, and should be faithfully observed," the memo continued. As a further safeguard, the loaning limit for each branch was $100,000 (Marshall $50,000) for a single line of credit. Loans in excess of that amount required the approval of the central executive committee or board of directors.

Noting that federal bank examiners classify loans into four categories—secure, high risk, probable losers, and uncollectible—Stoddard admonished the bank officers, "insofar as is humanly possible," to manage their loan portfolios so that all paper fitted the first category. Information in the credit file "should always be current and complete," and every loan should be reviewed at least quarterly. On a closely related subject Stoddard's zeal approached fanaticism:

> It should be borne in mind that with the exception of the bank buildings, approximately all the resources of this bank are represented by papers which could be placed in a medium size trunk. Our work, from its very nature, is largely paper work, and therefore there is little excuse for not having all documents and supporting data in proper form at all times.

An additional challenge which confronted Stoddard when he took over M.N.B. leadership was to realign assets to fit the scheme he had outlined to Bohn three years before, or to readjust the blueprint on the basis of experience.

The optimum distribution, he had written, was an even five-way split of resources. What the first consolidated statement of condition, January 1, 1941, showed was this:

| | |
|---|---|
| Cash | 26 percent |
| U.S. government securities | 28 " |
| Other securities | 6 " |
| Loans and discounts | 16 " |
| Real estate mortgages | 21 " |

The disparity was more pronounced among the individual branches. The closing balance sheets of those which had been longest under Bohn-Stoddard direction presented a dramatic contrast to the most recent acquisitions, Grand Rapids and Lansing. Both of these had approximately 70 percent in cash and federal securities and about 10 percent in real estate loans, while Port Huron, Battle Creek, Saginaw and Marshall were close to the Stoddard formula in cash and U.S. governments, but their real estate loans, from 26 to 32 percent, reflected the enthusiasm for F.H.A. mortgages which Howard had brought from the bank liquidation experiences of the early 1930s. None of the branches had more than 8 percent in municipal and corporate securities.

Before much could be done to homogenize the branch portfolios, the war injected a whole series of new influences. Defense contracts generated commercial deposits and loans for plant construction and equipment in most M.N.B. cities, while rising payrolls increased savings deposits and, for a while, housing loans. After Pearl Harbor housing construction was curtailed and the F.H.A. mortgage market shrank. Finally, war financing injected billions of dollars worth of government bonds into the financial system of the nation, some bought by individual savers and more purchased by banks which converted them into new deposits.

In the circumstances Stoddard soon abandoned the 1937 formula and directed the bank's investment policies toward full support of the war effort. At the conflict's end two-thirds of M.N.B. resources were U.S. government securities. Advertising stressed the patriotic and economic arguments for buying war bonds, and later both the bank and its president were cited by the Treasury Department for their service to the bond campaigns. Ration banking also involved Michigan National in the complex process by which tires, gasoline, tobacco and most foodstuffs were allocated to a population flush with money after the lean years of the Great Depression.

In general Stoddard approved of the way Washington handled the financial side of the war. In speeches to civic groups and communications to bank clients, he noted that the federal government spent more money in 1943 than in the previous 150 years of American history. In the 1944 report to stockholders he wrote:

> The one outstanding accomplishment to date, in which the government and the public can take great satisfaction, is the effective manner in which our price structure through the imposition of ceilings and rationing, has been held in line despite the enormous inflationary pressure created by expanded deposits and currency in circulation. The overall increase in the cost of living since 1939 has not exceeded 30%, a record far better than in World War I.
>
> The greatest contribution that can be made by the home front in the war effort is to cheerfully accept all sound restrictions which have as their objective the maintenance of stabilized purchasing power by the American dollar. In this endeavor we should be ever vigilant, and public opinion must support governmental policy or the economic and social consequences would indeed be tragic.

Eyewitness memories of the German inflation of the 1920s underlie these words, but they also reflect that fundamental optimism about the soundness and resilience of American economic and political institutions which Howard never lost. When the conflict ends, he wrote in the 1943 annual report, "We will then turn to the problems of peacetime readjustment, and with the innate good judgment and fairness of the American people, carry the responsibility for world leadership which has been thrust upon us."

Howard Stoddard's participation in the war effort actually began within weeks of his move to Lansing in 1939. The Michigan state capital was the home of an automobile enterprise then widely regarded as moribund. Reo Motor Car Company had been one of the pioneers, but it had come on hard times in the late 1920s and had never recovered. Stoddard had first become acquainted with this major Lansing employer during his R.F.C. visits. Now, even as he and Jennie were becoming socially acquainted with the founder, R.E. Olds and his family, one of the current Reo executives came to ask Lansing National Bank for help. A "dismal afternoon" at the plant left Stoddard at a loss, but a few days later he talked to Charles Bohn. As he later told a group of Reo employees, Bohn said, "You know, Howard, Hitler marched into Poland a few days ago. I was in Europe this summer. There's a war coming on." And he continued, "I think Reo can build trucks. Now why don't we get ourselves in shape, get the right men, and get ready for it." The upshot was that Henry Hund was sent to Washington to look for contracts while Bohn, Stoddard and others put together five million dollars in new capital for equipment. Reo became a spectacularly successful manufacturer of army trucks, reaching a production peak of 23,000 vehicles in 1947.

Two considerations linked Howard Stoddard, Michigan National and Reo Motors thereafter. One was the vulnerability of the truck making company because of its dependence on national defense spending. The other was Stoddard's conviction that a bank has a responsibility for the economic health and general welfare of the areas it serves. The display ads which carried the annual reports to M.N.B. cities during these early years carried the banner: BANKING THAT IS BUILDING MICHIGAN . . . AS IT IS BUILDING THIS COMMUNITY.

The path of service did not prove unprofitable. During the five war years Michigan National's net earnings, after paying $1 million in rising federal taxes, were $3.2 million. As a percentage of return on capital funds, net income rose from 9.3 percent in the start-up year 1941 to 12.2 percent in 1945. (In 1937 Stoddard had defined 10 percent as a desirable return on capital, and he consistently exceeded it from 1943 to 1969.)

Since undercapitalization was frowned upon by bank examiners and would certainly impede U.S. Comptroller approval of new acquisitions, Stoddard and Bohn came early to an agreement on how new capital should be generated. To offer new capital stock on the public market was to risk dilution of control. To plow back earnings into stock dividends was to expand capitalization without that risk. From the first year cash dividends were restricted to one dollar per share—a practice which has continued to the present day. During the war years more than a third of the preferred stock was bought back, reducing to $1 million the Reconstruction Finance Corporation interest. Additional earnings permitted a 33-⅓ percent stock dividend in 1944 and an additional 25 percent dividend at the start of 1946. The bank entered the post-war era with seven branches, $187 million in resources, and $6.7 million in capital funds, of which $2.5 million represented 250,000 shares of common stock with a par value of $10.

The real value was over $25 per share, but stock in Michigan National Bank was not for public sale.

CHAPTER 12

# Problems With State Legislation

The war years were marked by a strenuous and finally unsuccessful effort to defeat legislative proposals aimed at Michigan National Bank by opponents of state-wide branch banking. The controversy over whether branching was in the public interest raged nationwide from the middle 1930s, with about two-thirds of the states adopting one form of restriction or another in response to the same kinds of pressure which restricted chain stores and price discounting in many sectors of business. The battle in Michigan placed Howard Stoddard's bank at odds with Michigan Bankers Association, though a formal break did not come until a tenuous relationship had been maintained for a quarter century.

Until Charles Bohn and Howard Stoddard moved into the middle of the Michigan banking picture, two essentially conservative viewpoints prevailed. Detroit banking was dominated by the three big institutions which came out of the debacle of 1933—National Bank of Detroit, Manufacturers National Bank and Detroit Bank & Trust. The first two were still controlled by General Motors and Ford, respectively, and all three were primarily banks for business, traditional in style and cautious in policies. Out-state banking was in the hands of about 450 unit banks, most of them with capital resources under $100,000. Small towns typically were served by a single bank, and patterns of marketing were not aggressive. No Michigan bank had offices outside a single trade territory.

Michigan Bankers Association, like its counterparts in many states, was dominated by the country bankers, with the Detroit banks participating amiably on the basis of a shared "don't rock the boat" philosophy. When the Michigan General Banking Act of 1933 followed the federal emergency legislation of the same year in opening the door to unrestricted branch banking, no Michigan institution moved far from its home base, although several in Detroit and the larger out-state cities branched into adjoining suburbs. In 1937 a proposed new codification of state banking and credit statutes, the Michigan Financial Institutions Act, was amended at M.B.A. initiative to limit the establishment of branches to the home county or territory within 25 miles of the parent bank. As previously noted, the act exempted branches acquired by the purchase of the assets and liabilities of existing banks, and this proviso made possible the Bohn-Stoddard project.

Despite the fears of some that Michigan National intended to put a branch at every crossroads, Howard Stoddard and his financial backer did not change their original objectives. They wanted units in the most promising out-state trade areas, and they aimed to move into the Detroit market at the first feasible opportunity. Country banks, especially in the sparsely-populated northern half of the state, did not interest them, and they passed up several offers from small firms whose owner-presidents wanted to retire or move into other activities. (The head of one such bank became one of Michigan National's most outspoken critics when his offer to join the group was rejected.)

Suggestive of the tone and rationale of those who fought branching in general and M.N.B. in particular are these excerpts from a letter sent on April 26, 1940, to "Independent Bankers of Michigan" from the Independent Bankers Association of Minnesota:

> We understand that Charles B. Bohn and Howard Stoddard have quietly been securing control of a number of banks. . . . It is also reported that they intend to acquire a bank in every city of Michigan of any consequence and that these banks will be conducted as branches of some central institution.
>
> We understand that these men are well connected, that Mr. Stoddard is a first cousin of Marriner Eccles, Chairman of the Federal Reserve Board. Mr. Stoddard evidently sees eye to eye with Mr. Eccles on branch banking as the Chairman of the Federal Reserve Board is an avowed advocate of bank centralization.
>
> There is no popular demand for this type of banking in Michigan or they would not have had to move quietly. In securing control of different institutions they have operated surreptitiously. . . . It is reported that Stoddard and Bohn are inclined to be ruthless. . . .
>
> You bankers in Michigan are in a dangerous position. There is no telling how far this branch banking movement will go, where the lightning will strike or its effect upon unit banking. . . . You must exert

> yourselves in your own behalf. Don't let Bohn and Stoddard be the Gianninis of Michigan!

It is not surprising that Howard Stoddard found himself enmeshed in controversy. Michigan Bankers Association, at its 1940 meeting, adopted a resolution calling for legislation to make the 25-mile limit absolute, and it reaffirmed that position annually for the next five years. In 1941 an "anti-branch banking bill" which was drafted by M.B.A. and sponsored by Representative D. Hale Brake passed the legislature but was vetoed by Governor Murray D. Wagoner. In 1943—Michigan's legislature met biennially then—Governor Harry Kelly was prepared to sign a similar bill, but it failed in the senate to win the ⅔ vote which the state constitution required for financial legislation. In 1945 the measure passed handily and was signed into law.

Twenty-five years would elapse before the door to state-wide banking opened again in Michigan.

In the face of this opposition, the architects of Michigan National Bank made every effort to expand their base. During the fall of 1941 they were narrowly outbid when the stock of First National Bank & Trust Company of Kalamazoo was placed on sale by the Guardian Group receiver, Alex Groesbeck. In 1943 there was talk at the M.B.A. meeting that Bohn and Stoddard had made an offer for Ann Arbor Savings Bank, but the only result was that the head of the Ann Arbor bank, who was also president-elect of the bankers' association, reportedly pledged to the nominating committee that he would resign as M.B.A. head if his bank were sold to Michigan National. (The same Detroit *Times* story noted that Stoddard was present at the Mackinac Island meeting, along with "his charming wife" and his brother Waldo and Winifred. In an atmosphere so laden with hostility, Jennie's capacity to be charming was severely tested.)

National Bank of Flint turned out to be the only out-state company which met the M.N.B. criteria of desirability and availability during the war years. It was a bank which "Mister R.F.C." had helped to form in 1933, in order to free the impounded deposits of Union Industrial Trust & Savings Bank and First National Bank & Trust Company. The key man in the 1942 acquisition was Fred A. Lavery, a Flint trust company officer when Stoddard came to know and respect him during the banking crisis. As the Bohn-Stoddard group was being put together, Lavery sounded out the Flint bank owners but found them uninterested. So he moved to Boston to market mortgages for Manufacturers National Bank of Detroit and was there when the war began. On a visit to Flint at Christmas 1941, he found the bank people somewhat concerned about the possible impact of wartime restrictions upon the Flint auto industry and so interested in receiving a Michigan National offer. Within two months an agreement was reached.

When the directors, on March 12, 1942, voted to dissolve the bank and sell its assets to M.N.B., the Flint bank had $8.5 million in resources and capital funds of $1.1 million, none of it R.F.C. preferred stock. Three-fourths of its assets were cash and federal securities and its F.H.A. mortgage portfolio came to less than $200,000. Under the retiring president, Robert T. Longway, the bank had been conservatively but profitably managed, and the news release announcing the sale quoted Stoddard as "being highly complimentary" toward the outgoing executive. Lavery was appointed senior vice president for the Flint branch, and the board of directors became an advisory board with few changes.

The advertising blitz which accompanied the purchase sought to reassure current and prospective customers:

ANNOUNCING: ADDED BANKING STRENGTH
FOR EVERY FLINT CITIZEN . . . .
FOR EVERY FLINT BUSINESS . . . .

Themes from the public relations campaign of a year ago reappeared. Michigan National is owned by Michigan capital; its Flint branch will offer an expanded range of services; there will be "local control in the making of loans"; and "all operations will be carried on by the Flint officers and employees." The state banking commissioner gave quick approval and the transition was uneventful. The war boom made Lavery's branch a very profitable Michigan National operation.

The purchase of the assets and liabilities of Lansing's Industrial Bank in 1945 was prompted by a quite different set of considerations. This small consumer credit institution, with resources slightly under $1 million and capital stock priced at $312,000, held a 99-year lease on a one-story building on the southeast corner of Allegan and South Capitol streets, immediately south of the Olds Tower. Its location, rather than its business, was the primary attraction when Stoddard learned that the majority stockholders desired to retire from the banking business. Acquisition would eliminate the possibility of a more aggressive competitor buying the business and would provide needed space for expanding M.N.B. operations.

Since the merger was quite compatible with the pending 25-mile restraint, the state banking commissioner did not object. The merger was announced on February 18, 1945, and the personnel and accounts of the

Industrial Bank were moved immediately into the M.N.B. offices. After the vacated building was remodeled, the president's office, the central accounting operation and the supply department moved across the street, but the administrative separation proved unsatisfactory and Stoddard, Fairles and their support people soon moved into new offices on the third floor of the Olds Tower. Various uses were made of the old Industrial Bank facility until it was razed in 1958 to make room for the new Stoddard Building. Some of the Industrial Bank cash was used to buy out its stockholders and the remaining assets balanced the deposit liabilities, so the addition cost Michigan National almost nothing.

As each acquisition and annual report increased the ardor of Michigan National's opponents, Howard Stoddard defended his bank and his concept of branch banking vigorously. He disliked politics in general and was unfamiliar with the labyrinthine ways of Lansing lawmaking, so he left the one-on-one lobbying to others and concentrated on producing satisfied customers and a favorable public image for the bank. Not until 1945 did he appear before a legislative committee to oppose the ban on state-wide banking, and by then circumstances had doomed his cause.

The statement which he made to the Private Corporations Committee of the Michigan House of Representatives on March 7, 1945, seems persuasive from the perspective of a later generation. He asked: "Has the state-wide branch banking law which was enacted . . . in 1933, following the bank troubles of that period, proven unsound and against public interest . . . ?" He denied that branch banking had produced the crisis, since it was illegal in the state until 1933, and he pointed out that several banks were rescued from bankruptcy by being taken over thereafter. In a tactical concession, he praised the 1937 statutory provision "that if a bank in one city established an office in another city, it would have to do so by taking over another bank, and could not do so by putting in a new branch as additional competition. . . ." He charged that "the individuals now desirous of changing the law cannot bring forth one valid claim that it has operated to the detriment of any citizen, village or city in the state of Michigan. As a matter of fact, more than 75% of all banking customers in Michigan today are served by banks engaging in branch banking."

As evidence of enthusiastic public acceptance of the M.N.B. approach, Stoddard declared:

> Despite the charges and criticisms leveled against the bank by its competitors—attacks which have never been made against any other

> financial institution in the history of the state—the bank has enjoyed an almost unparalleled growth. Beginning with total resources of some 57 million dollars in 1941, the bank now has resources in excess of 165 million dollars. During the past four years it has probably rendered more public service in the form of loans made to individuals of moderate means, than any other bank in Michigan, regardless of size. In one phase of its work alone, namely the Personal Loan Department, the bank has made more than 125,000 separate loans of less than $1,000 each, and at rates of interest less than ¼ that being charged by most personal finance companies. The bank, through its officers and directors, has entered into the very life and activities of every community which we serve. Its common stock is wholly owned by Michigan residents, and operated by Michigan men. . . . It has as its motto the simple statement, "Banking That Is Building Michigan."

Because Michigan National was "a bank of metropolitan size, with capital funds and deposits . . . sufficient to compete with the banks in New York, Chicago and Detroit for business," the opposition of the big city banks was understandable. What Stoddard described as a fallacy was the belief that the proposed legislation would protect the small unit banks, since 80% of them were within 25 miles of a bank in one of the larger cities. He again offered the compromise which pro-M.N.B. legislators had proposed in 1941 and 1943—a ban on branch banking in communities under 25,000 or 30,000 in population. But this restriction would have left the Bohn-Stoddard target cities open to possible future penetration, and again it was rejected.

The production of a hundred copies of this statement for the legislators produced two memorable vignettes. One is of a holiday during which the cost-conscious Stoddard spent most of the time answering various bank phones so that Miss MacGregor and a helper would not be interrupted as they typed a hundred letters of transmittal. (The next holiday there was a telephone operator on duty.) The other is of three young Stoddards and their father trudging around a bank counter on a Sunday afternoon collating letters and enclosures. The atmosphere, according to Gladys, was "very sad."

What assured the passage of the 1945 anti-branch banking bill was one of those lamentable episodes that periodically mar the lawmaking process. It involved the traditional party and regional rivalries of Michigan politics, lobbyists for and against the banking bill and several other pieces of controversial legislation, and lawmakers willing to augment their constitutionally-fixed compensation of $3 per day. A journalistic exposé led the 1943 legislature to appoint a one-man grand jury to investigate. Indictments and convictions for bribery or illegal conspiracy quickly followed in connection with the other matters, amid considerable publicity.

When Stoddard made his effort to have the 1945 branch banking bill considered on its merits, he knew that the on-going grand jury inquiry made it expedient for lawmakers to put some distance between themselves and his bank, whatever their thoughts about financial systems in general. And so they did.

The trouble started with allegations that Byron Ballard, who was one of Governor Van Wagoner's legal advisers in 1941 as well as counsel for Michigan National, influenced the 1941 veto of the Brake bill. This was probably true, but it was neither illegal nor unethical, merely exasperating to proponents of the measure.

The charges of bribery and conspiracy were another matter. That one or more people who lobbied for the bank in the fight against the Brake bill offered or responded to solicitations for bribes seems certain, though it was never proved. That bank personnel were directly involved in the illegal transactions is uncertain, though it was freely alleged when the grand jury was in session. That Howard Stoddard himself knew of illicit goings-on in the corridors of the capitol during those hectic months in early 1941 when he was working day and night across the street in the Olds Tower is unanimously denied by those best acquainted with his character. He was nevertheless engulfed in the consequences.

Election-related interruptions, legal maneuvers and legislative controversies prolonged the investigation for more than two years. On July 20, 1946, indictments on charges of conspiracy to commit bribery were issued against nineteen present and former legislators and five bank officials. Stoddard's response was categorical: "I don't know of a single improper thing that was ever done. I emphatically deny the whole thing." The preliminary judicial hearing was repeatedly postponed because of the refusal of a key witness to testify, either under a grant of immunity or a conviction for contempt of court. After a ruling by the Michigan Supreme Court that the defendants were entitled to a speedy trial, all charges were dropped on April 19, 1948. (320 Michigan Reports 477)

To Howard Stoddard the experience was very painful. For all his competitive toughness and willingness to test the technical limits of banking codes and regulations, he was a moral Puritan. His stoic temperament and ability to take life a day at a time helped him to concentrate on present tasks, but the allegations and headlines found their way into his personal life. "Of course they affected us," Jennie recalls. "We weren't made of steel." These were the high school and college years for Howard Jr., Virginia and Stanford; only Charles, born on February 25, 1945, was blissfully unaware of their father's problems. Among the remembered impressions are these: "We were sure that he was an absolutely moral and honest person. . . . " "There was never any question in our minds that they were someone else's mistakes. . . . " "He was generally philosophical about it."

The shadow which this affair cast on his own reputation and that of his bank was something Stoddard always regretted. Yet he remained convinced that the 25-mile law was bad public policy, and that it stemmed from fear of the competitive challenge of an upstart banker from the West. He often quoted Senator Carter Glass:

> The plea against branch banking comes from bankers and not from the people who transact business with them; not from the people who want to borrow money, not from the people who want to buy credit or service. It comes from bankers who want to exclude from their particular communities anyone else who wants to sell credit and banking service.

Over the next twenty years more than six hundred branches appeared in Michigan, and more than a fifth of these were products of mergers or purchases of existing banks. If the 25-mile restriction was meant to keep country banks inviolate, it clearly failed. If it was meant to check Michigan National—and everyone acknowledged this to be the primary goal—it had only limited success, as events would show.

That Howard Stoddard's plans, persistence and success inspired some adverse criticism and downright dislike bothered him little. "I'm not living my life," he once said to Jennie, "to win a popularity contest."

CHAPTER 13

# One of the Top Hundred

No American banker came out of World War II more bullish about prospects for the nation than Howard Stoddard. He displayed that confidence by investing Michigan National Bank resources heavily in United States securities and insisting that these were substantially risk free. He also sounded an optimistic note in the talks which he frequently gave to service clubs and business organizations. As early as January 1944 he predicted that "the energies we have used to destroy men, if properly harnessed, will raise the standard of living here and all over the world. . . ."

He was more a traditionalist in his economic and political ideas than he was in his banking policies. Inflation was always his number one concern, but he believed the war years demonstrated that sound governmental policy and public cooperation could control that threat. His immediate fear as victory neared was a demobilization-based depression. "We are going to have to discard a lot of old-fashioned ideas about 'going back,' " he told one group. "We have the tools. We should use them . . . to eliminate poverty in the United States." In the midst of the Roosevelt-Dewey campaign he remarked, "This nation will not go to the dogs or to the celestial kingdom if we elect one of two men to the Presidency." As 1945 brought cut-backs in military procurement, he was quoted in the Ingham County *Times* of June 7:

> Americans should not become alarmed about the 300 billion dollar national debt. . . . Neither should Americans permit their thinking to become clouded by the scrapping of Willow Run and other war plants. They should be crossed off just like the cost of a battle or the sinking of a battleship. . . . .

"The lag in production at the close of the war will be taken up by the construction of new homes, house furnishings, automobiles, clothing, recreation and food," was Stoddard's prophecy, and M.N.B. policies in the post-war years were oriented toward maintaining purchasing power through new approaches to consumer services and credit.

Stoddard regretted the 40 percent rise in the consumer price index between 1945 and 1948, which he attributed to the abrupt lifting of price and wage controls. But this was a transient phenomenon, and he continued to argue against the voices of reaction. "If we return to the 1940 price levels," he told a credit men's group in 1949, "there will be more human misery and trouble than if they remain at the present levels." As for alarms about the persistent national debt, "If we tried to pay off that 250 billion dollar debt quickly, we'd bring on a depression."

Nothing was more challenging to his business audiences than the persuasive way in which he accommodated recent changes to his basic faith in the free enterprise system. Collective bargaining had no terrors for him. "You wouldn't want to go back to the conditions you had in those automobile plants before unionization," he declared. The progressive income tax, which he often described as "socialization of income," made it "impossible for anyone to get embarrassingly rich or embarrassingly poor." Competition was no longer conducted as in the era of rugged individualism, but the commitment to the free market remained. "Ours is the only country in the world to have engaged in free enterprise," he insisted. "Others who boast of free enterprise have business controlled by cartels, monopolies, and syndicates." Despite the recent legislative restraints imposed upon his bank, there was nothing cynical in his affirmation about Americans in general: "We like to compete on a fair basis, in business as well as sports."

Being hemmed in by the new anti-branch banking act, Michigan National made only one bank acquisition during the post-war period—Central National Bank of Battle Creek. A closely held company with $18.4 million in assets and $1.6 million in capital funds, Central was acquired by negotiation and merged with the Battle Creek branch on August 30, 1947. Stoddard, Bohn and several other M.N.B. stockholders purchased the ownership interest of the retiring president, Donald Ordway, and members of his family and then bought the balance of the stock through a public offering. Some of the Central stockholders took advantage of the opportunity to buy shares in Michigan National, and two or three of the directors went on the Battle Creek branch advisory board. Branches in nearby Bellevue and Nashville had to be sold to another Battle Creek bank, since they were more than 25 miles from the M.N.B. home office in Lansing. Central's main office was simply consolidated with Glen Hoffhines' branch, an operation which required a squad of armored cars and the removal of an elevator in the M.N.B. building to permit a Central safe to be lowered into the basement vault. After a hectic Labor Day week-end, the expanded branch was ready for business.

Public relations and real estate problems remained. Philip H. Ordway, who soon succeeded his father, Earl, on the advisory board and many years later became Charles Stoddard's father-in-law, remembers that anti-branch banking sentiment was strong among the customers of M.N.B.'s competitors. "We're worse off now than we were," was the reaction of many at this time when grand jury charges were still pending against key Michigan National people. Opinion changed, however, when almost all Central employees kept their jobs, no loans were recalled, and the extension of banking hours quieted fears that the consolidation meant curtailment of service.

The real estate problem was the Battle Creek office building bought by Charles Bohn as part of the Central National Bank merger. Its bank space was now vacant and a tenant or buyer did not immediately appear. Efforts were made to interest various insurance companies, and Howard even had Howard Jr., then a student at the University of Utah, ask doctors whether such a facility might fit the needs of a medical clinic. (Young Howard's report was negative.)

Finally the solution was found in a set of interrelated transactions which grew out of a golf course conversation. John H. Carton, the president of Lansing's Wolverine Insurance Company, asked Stoddard if M.N.B. people might like to buy some available stock. Stoddard knew that property insurance was a necessary adjunct of the bank's new mobile home financing program. He also knew that Wolverine needed more space. So in 1950 several of the Bohn-Stoddard group went into the insurance business, and two years later Wolverine bought the Central National building at an attractive price and moved its entire office to Battle Creek.

Carton never forgot some advice which came with these changes. "John," said Stoddard, "your new board members know nothing about the insurance business, and I don't want you to start letting the board make insurance decisions. And as long as you are coming on the board of Michigan National Bank, I might add that the same thing applies to you. We will be glad to have your counsel, but we have been in the banking business and know what decisions should be made."

One of the most comprehensive statements of Howard Stoddard's approach to business came a little later, at a conference sponsored by First National Bank of Philadelphia in April 1955. His major address bears the imprecise title, "Banking Problems Inherent in the Merger Movement and the Expanding Community." It contains an account of Michigan National's growth in the post-war era and Stoddard's diagnosis of the problems and challenges confronting American banking. Excerpts are used elsewhere in this chapter. Stoddard's central philosophy is set forth in these paragraphs:

> To my mind, as a student of life, the greatest document ever written, outside of the Ten Commandments and the Sermon on the Mount, is the Constitution of the United States as it was written here in Philadelphia. There, for the first time, the God-given principle of free agency was granted to an entire nation, . . . and there the dignity of man was firmly implanted. No particular group has yet been able to vitiate the fundamental idea of the free agency and the dignity of the individual man.
>
> I think that when that principle is applied in our banking business, as it must be applied in every American organization, we will continue to grow and develop. But whether it be a corporation, whether it be a labor union, whether it be a church, or any kind of an institution made by man, if it vitiates the principle of free agency and the free enterprise system, then it will be a sorry day for this country. As long as our growth and development in business, in religion, in corporate and social life, has the basic concept of the free enterprise of man, then I think we can adapt our economy within that framework, and whatever we do will succeed.

That Howard Stoddard's bank was succeeding could hardly be disputed. In its seventh year it entered the prestigious list of the one hundred largest commercial banks. Its resources were three times 1941 and its rate of earnings was among the highest in the country.

Innovative practices and efficient management combined to produce and sustain this growth. With the federal government no longer generating new bank deposits by selling securities to cover huge wartime deficits, both deposits and loans had to be sought in new markets. The solution, as Stoddard later told the Pennsylvania bankers, was simple. "If you wish to make money in the banking business . . . all you have to do is engage in retail banking."

On the deposit side of the business, this meant competing not only with other banks, but with savings and loan companies and other thrift institutions. Rising wages and incomes meant more savings, and Stoddard did his best to see that they did not go into "the wrong channels." (The competition from thrift institutions operating under different governmental regulations became a life-long preoccupation.)

Taking advantage of the federal rules on time deposits, Michigan National abandoned a 1 percent interest rate on all savings accounts for a schedule which encouraged people to leave their money in the bank. By paying 1½ percent on regular passbook accounts, 2 percent on certificates with 90 days' withdrawal notice, and 2½ percent on six month certificates, as some other progressive banks around the country began to do at the end of the war, Howard doubled savings deposits in only seven years. By 1955, when the passbook rate had been raised to 2 percent and time certificates adjusted accordingly, M.N.B. savings deposits stood at almost $200 million and surpassed the volume of commercial deposits for the first time.

In addition to attracting customers by paying what he liked to call a "living wage" on their savings, Howard Stoddard courted their business by making his banks as inviting and accessible as possible. During the war the refurbishing of facilities was hindered by material shortages and controls, but the removal of old-fashioned teller cages and the streamlining of internal operations began. As it became available, up-to-date accounting equipment was acquired. Lobbies, offices and building facades were modernized in the late 1940s. To a forward-looking banker in a state whose economy was built around the automobile, the next step was obvious:

> Once you get a customer that can come to you, most of the transactions are simple. There is no selection, really, in banking—a man gives you a paper and you give him a paper back. Why should a citizen have to go downtown, fight the traffic, get a place to park, get out and walk to the bank, then go in, just to exchange a piece of paper with a teller?

By the time Stoddard asked that rhetorical question to the Philadelphia audience, half of all the M.N.B. tellers' business came through drive-in facilities. The drive-in window at the branch which opened in a Quonset hut on Lansing's south side in June 1948 was a first for Michigan. James Shackleton, one of the most innovative among the original Bohn-Stoddard participants, then proposed to convert this novelty into a drive-in bank, and so produce in Saginaw the nation's first sheltered-care facility for motorized bank patrons. Even Shackleton had not anticipated that one of the first vehicles to try the money tunnel in 1949 would be a gasoline truck with a trailer. Visions of a basement vault awash and then aflame fortunately did not materialize, and soon the drive-in was a standard feature of the American banking scene.

Even as competitors began using the push-out drawer which director Randall Wickes' company developed for Michigan National, Stoddard's attorneys were challenged to prove that his bank could legally provide this kind of service. Since the drive-in booth at the Flint branch was 500 feet away from the bank building which served it through a pneumatic tube system, was it not a branch of a branch and therefore illegal under state statutes which had been specifically designed to hold Howard Stoddard in check? It was judicially determined in 1952 that a physical connection satisfied the terms of the law, but since there were practical limits to pneumatic distribution systems, only the main M.N.B. office in Lansing could establish branches with drive-in facilities near the homes of its suburban customers.

Nothing contributed more to the popularity of Michigan National among its customers than the shift to longer banking hours. "It added a little cost to our payroll and a few early gray hairs to our personnel manager," Stoddard reported in 1955, "but the way it paid off was astounding. . . . We do more business on Saturday than any two days in the week."

A schedule of 9:30 a.m. to 4:00 p.m. on weekdays and 9:30 to noon on Saturdays was instituted in 1946, and the revolutionary shift to all-day operations on Saturdays came a year later. It was precipitated by complaints of inadequate Saturday service in Battle Creek after the Central Bank was purchased and its accounts were transferred to the existing M.N.B. branch office. Fairles was sent to investigate. He found the lobby of the Battle Creek branch jammed, and when the doors were locked at noon several dozen patrons were still waiting to be served and several harried tellers and clerks were chafing to get away. The problem had occasionally occurred in the Lansing office, but never on this scale.

The Michigan National president had read about a bank in Portland that stayed open Saturday afternoons; so he and Fairles flew out to see how it was done. The technical problems proved quite manageable; many of the firms represented on the bank's board of directors used staggered work schedules. However, the psychological problems were enormous. To extend the hours of business from 28 to 42 (9:30 a.m. to 4:30 p.m. six days a week) was to defy one of the hoariest traditions of banking.

As was his custom with important policy changes, Stoddard stated his case to the board of directors and each of the branch advisory boards, then invited reactions. Sometimes, they knew, he could be persuaded to defer action for further study. On rare occasions he even changed his mind. But not this time. Resistance was expressed in terms of perils to accounting accuracy, employee morale, managerial composure, profits and even the banking image itself. Stoddard heard them out and then told each group in substance: "I've considered all the arguments, and we're doing it."

The bank staffs at all branches then began working five-day 40-hour weeks, with staggered days off. "We had a little more trouble with the officers,"

Stoddard recalled. It was worked out by offering them every other Saturday off and then simply overriding their objections. "When the officers began to see what profit sharing and other things were meaning in their futures, any criticism they might have had vanished."

Opposition to the long Saturday hours outlived Howard Stoddard, and he and many associates believed it was the main factor in the bank's unpopularity among competitors. A feature in the Detroit *Free Press* on the bank's 25th anniversary noted that Stoddard was "still frowned upon for keeping banking hours all day Saturday and for employing other techniques that break with tradition." A proposal to amend the Michigan Financial Institutions Act to declare Saturday a legal holiday for banks appeared in a 1958 bulletin of the Michigan Bankers Association legislative committee, but nothing came of the idea. Gradually many banks extended their hours of business, and then some city banks began to curtail Saturday operations in their downtown offices while keeping their drive-in branches open. Anxious to preserve its competitive advantage, Michigan National questioned the legality of this irregular scheduling, but in 1969 the state attorney general approved it. Since then there has been some variance in M.N.B. scheduling, but the extended hours remain a trademark.

Retail banking also provided the most profitable investment fields. For the sake of immediate liquidity, the bank kept about half its funds in cash and federal securities in the post-war period. The remaining funds were vigorously merchandised to the public. "Any man can pay any debt if the monthly payment is small enough," Howard Stoddard assured the Pennsylvania bankers. "There is nothing like amortization; it is the key to our future." His experience with refinancing mortgages in Detroit during the depths of the depression left him with this conviction:

> The average man is honest. He will pay his debts, and if he can't his wife will help him. If not, his oldest daughter will go to work, and that family unit will demonstrate its ability. . . . When you get a debt within the capacity of a man to pay, it is a sound debt.

It was Stoddard's boast in 1955 that more than 80 percent of Michigan National's loans were on an amortizing basis. They produced excellent earnings and a constant cash flow for reinvestment. Many of them were secured by governmentally insured home mortgages carrying around 5 percent interest. Others earned more but were not quite so risk-free—installment loans to finance business equipment and facilities, automobiles and homes with wheels. Michigan National pioneered mobile home financing in 1949, and it later

*George and Ellen Stoddard and their family in front of their La Grande, Oregon home. 1908.*

*Michigan National Bank, Lansing. Remodeled lobby with low box cages. March, 1941.*

*First drive-up bank window Lansing. June. 1948.*

*Dr. Martha Longstreet, first depositor at first enclosed drive-in bank in the United States, Michigan National Bank, Saginaw. March 2, 1949.*

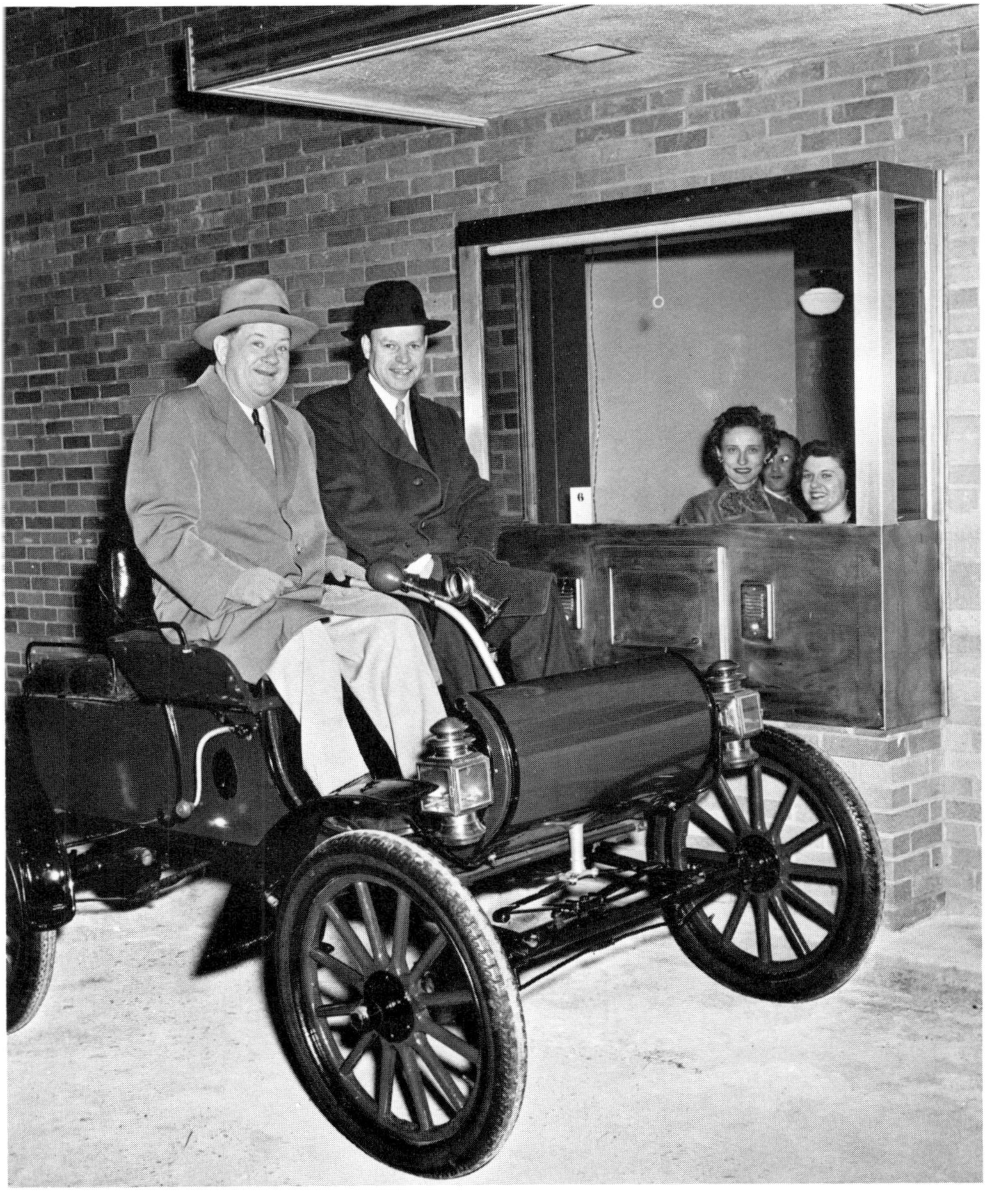

*Stoddard and Eugene M. Wanger at opening of drive-up window, Capitol Avenue and Washtenaw St., Lansing. January, 1952.*

*Stoddard signing contract with John Coleman, President of Burroughs Corporation January 6, 1958.*

*Stoddard in his Michigan National Tower office, 1959.*

*Michigan National Tower and Stoddard Building. Lansing, 1979.*

*Eight Stoddard brothers.*
*Standing, Left to right—Lester, David, Elmer, Earl. Seated, left to right—Waldo, Howard, Bob, John.*

*Gladys Helen MacGregor,*
*secretary to Stoddard 1934–1964.*

*Charles Benjamin Bohn,*
*one of the founders of Michigan National Bank.*

*Virginia Stoddard Peery*

*Charles Creer Stoddard*

*Jennie and Howard Stoddard*

*Four Stoddard Bankers*
*Left to right—Waldo, Stanford, Howard, Howard Jr.*

took Howard and some of his associates into the insurance business as well.

To win retail customers, advertising was an important element in Howard Stoddard's approach to competitive enterprise. According to Howard Jr., who started working with the bank in 1950, his father "had a keen mind for advertising" and took "a very personal interest" in each new promotional effort. Chicago and Detroit agencies developed ad campaigns, but Stoddard examined lay-outs in detail and often insisted upon changes. As early as 1943 a New York agency cited Michigan National for the "consistent excellence of its newspaper advertising the past 12 months."

Each new development produced its publicity releases. A picture of Stoddard and an Oldsmobile sales representative in a vintage Olds at the Lansing drive-in opening was given national distribution by the manufacturer of the special window. In such posed publicity shots Stoddard usually looked about as comfortable as Calvin Coolidge in an Indian war bonnet, but he gamely did what the game required. Branches energetically courted business with "Then and Now" exhibits, displays of real and bogus currency, drawings for savings accounts, and the other promotional devices which preceded the give-away era of savings solicitation.

An enthusiastic booster of Michigan State College from his arrival in Lansing, Stoddard was readily attracted to the idea of sponsoring Spartan football broadcasts. Beginning in 1945 when football came out of the wartime doldrums, the Spartan network carried play-by-play radio broadcasts from WJIM, Lansing, to stations serving the other M.N.B. cities. The relationship continued through the many years in which Howard Stoddard and his friend, M.S.U. President John Hannah, gave their two institutions comparably vigorous leadership.

In the relentless drive to maximize loans, no operations details were overlooked. Michigan National was one of the first banks to send all cash letters directly to Federal Reserve banks. Cash letters, consisting of checks drawn on other banks, were traditionally sent to large correspondent banks which required commensurate deposit balances to offset handling costs. By sending cash letters directly to the Federal Reserve, M.N.B. increased the amount of its deposits available for investment. To this day the bank carries minimal balances with correspondent banks.

Stoddard also adopted the practice of drawing most drafts on the Federal Reserve Bank of Detroit. As long as the drafts were outstanding, the balance in the M.N.B. reserve account was higher than required, permitting the bank to invest the excess funds. In the early days, when bank clearings were slower than they are now, this device was particularly advantageous.

Sensitive to the opposition within Michigan banking circles, Howard Stoddard worked hard to convert some of the critics and to establish an affirmative awareness of his bank and its president in the national financial community. Among the assets acquired with the Grand Rapids branch was the *Michigan Bank Directory*, a pocket-size edition of the complete information on Michigan from the national directory published annually by R.L. Polk & Company. Michigan National took over the publication with its 34th edition and distributed it yearly thereafter, free of charge, to every bank in the state and other firms requesting it.

Michigan National's annual consolidated balance sheet and earnings statement on all commercial banks in the United States was a product of Stoddard's insatiable curiosity about how his bank was doing in comparison with others. In 1945 he asked Fairles to prepare the first version, based on the voluminous reports of the Federal Deposit Insurance Corporation for the preceding decade. This statement, with a thoughtful two-page analysis of Stoddard's interpretation of the data, was sent to a limited number of bankers in and outside Michigan on September 30. It generated sufficient response so that the next year an updated set of data, with a shorter analysis, was sent to the president of every commercial bank. Within a few years the report had a circulation of 20,000 copies. The transmittal letters are an ongoing record of the matters which the president of Michigan National thought most timely to call to the attention of his peers.

The only time Gladys MacGregor remembers Stoddard getting "plain mad" at Russ Fairles was when he tried to save $400 by folding in the flaps on one of these mailings rather than sealing the envelopes. "You might as well not have sent them at all," Stoddard scolded. "I throw unsealed envelopes in the waste basket, because it means the sender does not think it is of sufficient importance to send first class."

Evidence that the letter was read ranges from a three-page response from the Federal Reserve Board chairman in 1946 to a favorable editorial citation in *American Banker* a few years later. Marriner Eccles took exception to Stoddard's assertion that average bank earnings, apart from windfall profits on the sale of war-related securities, were "certainly not an excessive amount." Eccles argued that the 8 percent rate was too high because banks took fewer risks than most other businesses; at least half of their income was from government bonds. The June 9, 1953 publication of the American Bankers Association quoted extensively from Stoddard's latest report, which featured the problems of debt management which the federal government was having. Noting that commercial banks were already the largest holders of the federal debt, Stoddard urged that they temper their depression-born preoccupation with "high liquidity" and "simply extend their own holdings" into longer term securities with staggered maturities:

> The example set by commercial banks would doubtless be followed by individuals, associations, savings banks, insurance companies and managers of pensions and trust funds. Thus, on a purely voluntary basis, and in conformity with our American way of accepting individual responsibility, the need for Federal debt management, as we have experienced it in the past, could be eliminated.
>
> *After all, this is our country, the huge Federal debt will be here for many years to come, and can't we as bankers, help solve the problem as our major contribution to the national welfare?*

Not only did Howard Stoddard follow his own advice, but for patriotic reasons he never speculated in government notes and bonds.

Additional evidence that the annual letter was read is supplied by Gladys. While on a vacation, she stopped at a small town bank in Colorado to cash a check. When the president overheard her identify herself as Howard Stoddard's secretary, he chatted with her at length, invited her to join him and his wife for dinner, and helped her with travel arrangements. Told of the episode later, Stoddard remarked, "Well, that just goes to show, I'll have to watch what I do. They're watching me, and I'll have to be careful."

Each report conveniently provided space for the recipient banker to match his own performance with the national averages. Not only did Stoddard do this, but he carefully studied the annual reports of some of the national leaders in profitability, such as Valley National (Arizona), Franklin National (New York), First Security (Utah-Idaho) and Bank of America (California). Soon he became personally acquainted with the heads of these institutions, and he frequently adopted their successful techniques. They were interested in him, too, because Michigan National was among the top half-dozen banks in rate of return on capital when it first entered the list of the hundred biggest.

Under Howard Stoddard Michigan National Bank was both paternalistic and progressive in its employee relations. In the first of an intermittent series of in-house publications, *Michigan National News*, the president declared it to be the fundamental policy of the bank "to develop a selected and trained personnel with working conditions and salaries equal to or better than those prevailing in competitive financial institutions." Careful records will be maintained, and "wherever possible every promotion in the organization will be made from members of the staff." This statement was made in July 1942, when there were fewer than four hundred employees, and the concepts did not change as the staff grew to 2,200 in the next 28 years.

*Michigan National News* was planned as a newsletter, but the first and only issue to appear tells more about the bank, its chief operating officers, its physical facilities, and the seven cities in which it operated than about employee policies and activities. An honor roll of 28 men serving in the armed forces and an appeal to each individual to be "vitally affirmative in supporting the war effort" place the publication in historic context. Wartime constraints on paper and non-essential printing were primary reasons why it did not reappear. (In-house publications under a variety of names appeared intermittently thereafter in Lansing and some of the branch cities. The last during the Howard Stoddard years bore the title *Interest Quarterly*.)

Stoddard believed that working conditions and financial incentives were more important to employee performance than basic salary. He challenged the conservative salary policy of the banking industry only at the lower levels. (His report to the Pennsylvania group that the minimum entry wage at M.N.B. was $200 per month tells something about compensation standards in the industry and the nation in 1955.) The bank responded quickly to developments in the field of fringe benefits, and as soon as its earning pattern was established and wartime controls on wage and price increases were removed, it moved in several new directions.

The only supplemental benefits mentioned in the 1942 *News* were $2500 of group life insurance for each employee and a medical plan "wherein reimbursement is obtained for at least 31 days of hospitalization and $150.00 of surgical work." By the time the first employees manual, *Information for Members of Our Staff*, appeared in 1949, both of these coverages had been extended to match the post-war inflation. Additional benefits included free checking accounts and tuition reimbursement for courses completed with the American Institute of Banking. Refunds for courses completed with other schools were made "if, in the Bank's opinion, the studies are directly beneficial to your work." Two weeks of paid vacation after one year's employment became three weeks after ten years. Intangible advantages for those who proved themselves in the three month probationary period included "pleasant associations, interesting work, and a place of esteem in the eyes of your friends."

A retirement program was instituted in 1948 to supplement social security. As described in the handbook, it was as circumscribed as most retirement programs of that era. Employees with fifteen or more years of consecutive employment could retire at 65 on a pension of one-half of the final salary, "less the individual social security benefits of the staff member, with a maximum of $6,000 per year including social security benefits." Retirement was mandatory at 70. With the passage of time the income ceiling was raised, the retirement age was lowered to 65, and provisions for both voluntary and involuntary early retirement were added.

The institution of a Christmas bonus in 1946 marked the first direct participation by the employees in the bank's earnings. The amount was 1 percent of the annual salary for each year of service up to a maximum of 10 percent. The maximum increased to 20 percent for 20 years service, and an across-the-board pay raise of 20 percent was given in 1952 in connection with the launching of a contractual profit-sharing program. This incentive-based fringe benefit was a key factor in M.N.B. staff relations and institutional growth thereafter.

The 1949 manual formalized advice and cautions which had been part of the employee-orientation program from the beginning. Subsequent revisions retained most of the concepts and much of the same language; Howard Stoddard is clearly discernible in the most recent *Welcome to Michigan National Bank* loose-leaf handbook. Because most bank work must be completed on a daily basis, the record of attendance and punctuality "is an important factor when you are considered for salary increases and promotions." Appearance and deportment are also important. "Excessive chatting, joking and idle conversation have no place. . . ." "Neat and conservative attire makes a good impression. It is a characteristic that will help you in your career." The two most important rules were declared to be:

> 1. Money, securities, documents and records of the Bank must be safeguarded with utmost care.
>
> 2. Business matters between the Bank and its customers must be treated as *strictly confidential.*

In all of these matters Howard Stoddard was exemplary. His desk was uncluttered, his day was organized, and his demeanor at business was businesslike. As he prospered the brand names in his wardrobe changed, but the suits were always dark and conservatively cut, the shirts were always white, and those who never saw him at home or at play never saw him without a tie. He was meticulous about confidentiality, once putting the subject on the agenda of an executive committee meeting when it came to his attention that the wife of an unnamed vice president had mixed bank business in with bridge club conversation.

The institutional rationale for this attention to deportment was spelled out:

> Always remember that no small part of the Bank's public relations is up to you. A careless word or act may injure a valuable relationship that others have spent years in developing. Our Bank sells courteous, careful and efficient service. *Selling it* and *keeping it sold* is a most important job for every one of us.

Yet there was more than merchandising of money and credit involved in Howard Stoddard's relations with subordinates. As he cared for the people who were in his missionary charge in Germany in the 1920s, so he cared now for those whose lives were interlocked with his bank. Gladys MacGregor remembers him once loaning money to a branch employee so he could have his teeth repaired and so qualify for a promotion. During the early years of the retirement program adjustments were sometimes made when it appeared that projected income would not meet needs; one man who was due for retirement when his bank was acquired by M.N.B. was given a pension sufficient to see his son through college. Employees who only wanted advice, whether on financial or other personal matters, found Stoddard as attentive and helpful as he was to customers. Many were surprised by timely letters of congratulation or condolence. Behavior so flagrant as to affect institutional morale or public image—philandering, drunkenness, dishonesty—was not tolerated, but unwitting mistakes and errors of judgment were not remembered if they were not repeated.

The result was a remarkable degree of loyalty and *esprit de corps*. Except for those employees—mostly young women—who manned the typewriters and tellers' cages for transient reasons, turnover at Michigan National Bank was very small.

A particularly close relationship developed between Stoddard and the senior officers in the several branches. Not only did he visit their offices twice a month, getting to know their key people and many other employees, but the chief operating officers came to Lansing for the monthly M.N.B. executive committee and board of directors meetings. Jennie frequently entertained groups at these times, and sometimes she accompanied Stoddard to the other cities. Of the officers and their wives, she remembers that "we were all very close. They were here and we were there. We met often."

When two federal examiners met with the M.N.B. board of directors on

December 15, 1950, for an informal discussion of the bank's unconventional approach to its business, one of the questions asked was why there was "no chain of management." Stoddard objected in principle to the concept of a "number 2 man." "If someone were designated as successor, he might not think as I do, and in my absence make decisions which it would be necessary for me to change. This would result in friction and confusion."

The bond with the senior officers was a blend of mutual respect, reciprocal self interest and loyalty. Their salaries were competitive, and such perquisites as country club memberships were paid by the bank. As Stoddard said in Philadelphia, "We want our men to live well and to act well . . . , and you can't put up an appearance and keep it up and hide behind shabby clothes and short cuts here and there." In the 1940s senior vice presidents were encouraged and sometimes given special opportunities to increase their stock holdings as the capitalization of the bank increased. With the establishment of profit sharing in 1952 the rewards for efficient management became substantial.

There was, however, more than a monetary connection. Because the branch heads came quickly to understand the parameters within which Stoddard expected them to operate, they continued to enjoy the substantial autonomy which was promised in the beginning. They conducted branch advisory board and executive committee meetings, while Stoddard mostly watched and listened. Sometimes he made an opening statement about how the bank was doing, and sometimes he prefaced it with a joke. (One of the vice presidents remembers that Stoddard's few attempts to be risque were not particularly successful.) Often he only asked questions. Three things were more embarrassing to a branch executive than having to admit that a loan was in difficulty. One was being unprepared for a question, the second was showing an unplanned reduction in loan volume, and the third was explaining some derelict behavior among branch personnel which adversely affected the bank image. Stoddard never used sarcasm to show displeasure, and the temper which he definitely had was rarely shown and always controlled. He accepted honest mistakes and even substantial losses as part of the game. He was sparing in verbal praise, partly because of his natural reticence and partly because he expected the best from those to whom he gave his confidence and loyalty. Their awareness that this confidence and loyalty were not lightly given was part of the bond.

With four people a special relationship developed. Waldo Stoddard, not surprisingly, was the closest approach to a confidant Howard had within the bank. "Although we didn't always agree, or see eye to eye, we never had the slightest personal difficulty," Waldo remembers. Several of the most innovative ideas—like mobile home financing and Michigan Bankcard—came initially from him, and he sometimes had to do a selling job on his older brother. More relaxed and outgoing than Howard, Waldo was a public relations asset for the bank, especially in Grand Rapids, where he headed the branch from 1943 to 1967.

Russell Fairles was, next to Howard, the best informed man about the inner workings of the bank. Stoddard prized him as a human resource and assumed that his dedication to Michigan National matched that of its president. The demands made on Fairles could not always be accommodated within bankers' hours, even as they were extended by M.N.B., but they were dependably met for thirty years. It is noteworthy that Fairles was the only bank officer Stoddard urgently pressed to carry on beyond the normal retirement age. Confronted with health problems at the very time he was pushing for legislation which would finally take the fetters off branch banking, Stoddard persuaded Fairles to help him see things through. He did.

Whoever wrote that no man is a hero to his secretary never talked to Gladys MacGregor. Until her retirement in 1964 she was a combination executive secretary and administrative assistant to Howard Stoddard and a multi-functional friend to his family. Assignments as wide-ranging as staying with the children while Howard and Jennie were out of town to helping with a pre-football game party at the Stoddard home were accepted as part of the job. Some stenographic tasks Stoddard preferred to have her do, even though other competent people were available. "You want to cut these stencils yourself, don't you?" was the gambit he sometimes used.

Gladys had an excellent memory. Stanford Stoddard recalls that his father could ask, "Miss MacGregor, what did we tell this man last year," and she would reply, "Mr. Stoddard, we told him this, and this, and this, and in a couple of minutes I'll have the letter for you." (It was always "Miss MacGregor," according to Gladys. The football party at the Stoddards was the only remembered occasion on which Howard called her by her first name, and that was once more than she ever called him by his.)

Had Gladys not been willing to place the bank at least as high in her priorities as Stoddard did, the relationship would not have survived the demands made upon it. The nearest thing to a reproach in the record stems from the incident when she broke a social engagement in order to meet him at the office one evening, and he showed up, apologetic, two hours late, having forgotten the "urgent business" and taken Jennie to the theatre.

If the conventions of banking had favored women in executive roles in the immediate post-war period, Gladys might have become an M.N.B. vice president. Instead her rewards took a variety of forms. Stoddard encouraged her to borrow money to buy an Oldsmobile, because her aging auto was neither safe nor suitable, in his opinion. Then he arranged for her to buy some stock which Charles Bohn was making available to bank officers. When illness laid seige to her parents in Ontario, he sometimes suggested on Thursday afternoon, "I think you had better go home Friday for the week-end." One year he surprised her with a $100 per month raise and the terse commendation, "You've earned it."

Jack E. Church joined the "special relationship" group in 1948, when he moved from the bookkeeping department in Lansing to the assignment as Howard Stoddard's driver. Earlier Stoddard had chauffeured himself to branch meetings and other appointments, but the possibility of making more beneficial use of the time—as many as 10 or 15 hours a week—led to the change. Jack was on call 24 hours a day to meet planes, perform courier service, transport V.I.P.'s to bank events, take Stoddard where he needed to go and wait to bring him back. From Oldsmobiles they moved up to Cadillacs as the bank prospered, but never to limousines with telephones and other "luxuries." Jack never wore a uniform for the same reason. They chatted enough so that Stoddard became well acquainted with the Church family, but most of the time he was in the back seat, going over the relevant reports so he could be thoroughly primed for the upcoming meeting. There was only one accident—a collision which produced bruises and property damage. While Jack took care of the reporting, Stoddard arranged for another car and drove to his appointment.

In two decades Jack Church missed only one day of work and was late for only one assignment. At times he worked as many as 60 hours a week, receiving compensatory time off when the schedule lightened. He spent his working days during the three years of Stoddard's illness in motels near hospitals or at the Stoddard home, available for any tasks which Howard or Jennie might require. No one thought it inappropriate that Jack and his wife, Velma, should be sent to Florida for a week's respite during this long vigil, or that Jack should serve as a pallbearer at Stoddard's funeral.

According to Gladys, she, Russ and Jack were three people whom Stoddard felt free to call on at any time. "It never seemed to cross his mind that we wouldn't, or couldn't, or would rather not do what he wanted us to do." Apparently it rarely crossed their minds, either.

The 10th annual report to M.N.B. stockholders, which appeared in January 1951, is an attractively illustrated public relations brochure as well as a conveyor of good tidings. Aerial photos and booster-type descriptions of the seven bank cities accompany the lists of officers, advisory board members and Michigan National directors. Howard Stoddard's picture appears twice, paired with Charles Bohn at the top of the letter to shareholders and presiding over the ten-man executive committee. "The public has responded to our modern type of banking service," is his decennial message:

> Our bank is now 5th in size in the State, and ranks 85th among the nation's 14,656 banks. Our resources have increased from $57,456,705 to $248,971,347 in the past decade, being a growth of 333% as compared with the national average for all banks of 105%. We now have more than 280,000 satisfied customers.

Cumulative data for the decade show gross earnings of $14.5 million, net earnings after taxes of $10.1 million, dividend payments of $2.8 million (one dollar per share per year), and retaining earnings of $7.3 million. These undistributed earnings, together with four stock dividends, brought current capital resources to $11.8 million. In other terms, anyone among the 2,200 stockholders who had owned 100 shares of Michigan National stock, each worth $15, in January 1941, now owned 266-⅔ shares, each worth more than $20, and had received $1,616.67 in dividends.

The expression on every face in the brochure is earnest. Attention appears to be on the second part of President Stoddard's pledge to the stockholders: "We anticipate the future with confidence and a determination to continue to merit the slogan, 'Banking That Is Building Michigan.' "

CHAPTER 14

# Successful Banker and Business Spokesman

The Eisenhower years were particularly congenial to Howard Stoddard's economic philosophy and business plans. The threat of warborn inflation dissipated with the Korean truce. The gross national product grew about 2½ percent and the cost of living rose by less than 2 percent per year. Unemployment increased with demobilization but passed 6 percent only in the brief recession of 1958-1959. The Republican administration did not dismantle the New Deal or restructure the banking system which had developed under the reforms of 1933 and 1935. The Federal Bank Holding Company Act of 1956 did not affect Michigan National Bank until the state passed matching legislation years later, but the gradual raising of the Treasury-imposed ceiling on interest payable on savings created a competitive opportunity which Stoddard was quick to exploit. The Cold War with Russia preoccupied the nation, and a trip which Howard and Jennie took behind the Iron Curtain in 1960 only increased his confidence that America would meet the test.

Michigan National Bank underwent a transformation in these years. Death dissolved the Bohn-Stoddard partnership in 1953. Thereafter there was no question that M.N.B. was Howard Stoddard's bank, although Roe Endicott, Randall Wickes and other initial investors continued to hold important blocks of stock. Howard Jr. and Stanford moved into the management group, and by the end of the decade journalists were talking about a Stoddard dynasty. With resources of $543 million, capital funds of over $33 million and 450,000 customers, Michigan National was the state's fourth largest and the nation's fiftieth largest commercial bank in 1960. It was still excluded from Detroit, but Stoddard and his associates found another way into the metropolis in 1955, as will be recounted in the next chapter.

Insight into the policies which produced this growth and into Stoddard's management style is provided by a talk which he gave to the officers on

February 22, 1955, after the best year in Michigan National's 14-year history. Assets had risen 12 percent in 1954, loans 13 percent, and capital funds 15 percent after a payment of the traditional $1 per share dividend. M.N.B. then stood 69th among the nation's banks in total resources. In Stoddard's judgment, it was "about the best job that any bank in the United States turned in. . . ."

The key to the future was persistence with policies which had brought good results and pioneering in new directions. There seemed no reason to change the pattern of keeping half the bank's resources in cash and U.S. government bonds, for liquidity's sake, and loaning the other half. Still restrained by the lessons of 1933, most national banks loaned less than 50 percent; Michigan National's leadership in earnings stemmed from its aggressive lending policies. On the investment side, Stoddard totally avoided corporate and municipal bonds, which had been the undoing of so many banks he looked at as "Mister R.F.C." He felt that the 1954 distribution among guaranteed home mortgages, consumer loans and nation-wide mobile home loans made a balanced and profitable portfolio. The value of amortization was by now clear: "82 percent of this 183 million dollars examines itself each month. Either the payments were made or the payments were not made." With a delinquency rate of only 1.6 percent in amount and 1.4 percent in number, the installment loan operation was "almost letter perfect." Losses were to be anticipated with this type of loan, and a loss rate of ½ percent would subject no loan officer to criticism. Stoddard said, "You can lose more money for the bank by cutting down volume than . . . by increasing volume and having losses."

The purchase of the Olds Building in 1954 gave the bank a suitably impressive headquarters, now rechristened the Michigan National Tower. Four branches with drive-in facilities in the north, east, south and west sections of Lansing gave suburban coverage, and a down-town drive-in was in operation adjacent to the old Industrial Bank building. Pending before the U.S. Circuit Court in the District of Columbia was a suit to require the Comptroller of the Currency to exempt drive-in offices from classification as branch banks. This would permit similar suburban coverage of the other M.N.B. cities. "If we get the permit," Stoddard observed, "We'll pay pretty good prices for the land, because the secret of these institutions is to have them properly placed." (The lawsuit failed, however, and the branches remained limited to connecting drive-in facilities.)

The expansion of commercial deposits was up to the officers, Stoddard believed. "You have to get up from your desk and go out and get the business."

Since most of the commercial deposits in the city of Lansing were controlled by members of the Lansing Country Club, bank officers should take advantage of the memberships provided for them. Similar perquisites were available in the branch cities. But more than golfing and socializing were required. "Get your visiting program working, so that you first make a friend of everybody in the community that controls deposits of any particular size, and then use that friendship, in a good way, to solicit and encourage business." He added, "I think a bank deposit, in the commercial sense, is like a life insurance policy. Nobody ever bought life insurance. All life insurance has to be sold."

In asking the M.N.B. officers to build their savings deposits to the level of their commercial accounts, Stoddard admitted that some of his policy decisions were intuitive. "I don't know why we like to, but we'd like to keep the two about as close together as we can." That meant cultivating such substantial time deposits as "school funds that are waiting to be changed into brick and mortar . . . , or retirement funds waiting to pay off a fiscally incurred debt." It also meant cultivating small savings accounts with the same people who made consumer loans. (In 1955 Michigan National became the first bank in the state to pay semi-annual interest on time certificates, and soon the compounding was on a quarterly basis. Electronic equipment made it possible to introduce Michigan to daily interest on savings in 1960; advertisements called it "Full Time Interest." As rapidly as federal regulations permitted, the interest rate on M.N.B. savings accounts and time certificates was raised from 2 percent to 2½ and then 3 percent during the latter part of the decade. The innovative Stoddard approach was also demonstrated in the early use of commercial teller machines with deposit receipts and the issuance of negotiable time certificates of deposit for large accounts.)

Recommendations that the officers promote the sale of mortgage insurance reflected Stoddard's own entry into the insurance field as well as a conviction that such protection was good for both the bank and the mortgagee. Warnings about the rising competition of savings and loan companies and other thrift agencies showed a concern which would become a Stoddard preoccupation by the end of the decade. The commitment to spend about $350,000 on 1955 advertising, using all the media, stemmed from the opinion that "advertising is most effective when you get to the saturation point."

Plans for increasing capitalization also came in for discussion. "I think at least once a month I used to get a letter from the Comptroller's office complaining that our capital is inadequate," Stoddard recalled. The pressure had relaxed somewhat recently because of his apparent success in persuading examiners that reserves were adequate. Cash and U.S. securities, he argued, required no capital protection because they carried no risk of loss. Nor did loans secured by government bonds and mortgages guaranteed by the Federal Housing Administration or other federal agencies. Mobile home loans were protected by their own reserve. "So it's our judgment that only 106 million of the 380 million dollars in the bank would be subject to a capital deterioration in the event of a severe economic problem." A capital fund of almost $19 million and gross annual earnings of more than $6 million were, Stoddard insisted, adequate reserves for the kind of business the bank carried on.

Nevertheless, the rate of growth in bank assets meant that constant attention must be given to capital formation. "We're going to continue to apply back 75 percent of our earnings—period." No change in the policy of $1 per share cash dividends and frequent stock dividends was contemplated. (And none has been made yet.)

Six years of mobile home financing had produced an admirable record by 1955. "It used to be called trailer financing until we decided to dress it up a little," Stoddard chuckled. "Unique," "profitable" and "worthwhile" were the adjectives he used to describe this phase of M.N.B. operations.

That Waldo Stoddard should have been the prime mover behind the bank's entry into this activity reflects his imaginative approach and his Grand Rapids location. In the post-war years mobile home manufacturing was in its infancy and Grand Rapids, already a national center of furniture and cabinet making, naturally became a center for "trailer" houses. Many forms of consumer credit being also in their infancy, the nature of the product made mobile home financing difficult to arrange. A skeptical bank examiner compared it to writing mortgages on a school of fish. The obvious difficulties of foreclosure and repossession tended to blind bankers—and bank examiners—to the fact that even houses on wheels were homes to their buyers. Amortizing home loans were proving to be relatively low risk.

John H. Belknap, of Forbes and Belknap Agency, Grand Rapids, came to Waldo with a proposal in 1949, when an arrangement he had worked out with another local bank was terminated at an early stage. Belknap's interest was property and casualty insurance, which he was selling through a number of mobile home distributors, but the simplicity and profitability of selling financing and insurance in a single package led him to seek a banking connection. Waldo was interested and took the concept to the executive committee. Howard and others were initially skeptical. Since repossession would be neither feasible nor desirable, how would losses be prevented? Waldo and Belknap developed a plan for putting part of the proceeds of each loan into a dealer reserve account, against which losses would be charged. Under this plan efforts to recover from the purchaser of a mobile home would be the problem of the dealer, not the bank. But what if the dealer's reserve proved insufficient? Waldo came back again, this time with the proposal that the bank put part of its interest earnings from all the dealer loans into a general reserve fund. This fund, like the undistributed earnings transferred to the profit sharing trust, would not be subject to federal taxation. It would need to be touched only in unusual circumstances, and it would become a part of the capital resources of the bank.

Eventually the executive committee and board of directors agreed and the plan was launched late in 1949. Joseph F. Shaw, in the Grand Rapids office, was placed in charge. (Twenty-two years later he succeeded Howard Stoddard as M.N.B. president.) The dealer reserve was set at 15 percent of each loan (10 percent after July 1951), with the understanding that a good loss record would generate rebates once an account had an adequate balance. The general reserve was based on setting aside 10 percent of interest earnings until the fund equaled 10 percent of the outstanding loans. Forbes and Belknap became the channel through which many dealers outside Michigan arranged financing, though the bank reserved the right to reject applications which seemed on their face to be high risk. The bank also worked with several Michigan manufacturers to finance their dealer sales, initially in lower Michigan, Indiana and Ohio, but later in almost all parts of the United States. Within the state some loans were made directly to mobile home buyers who could satisfy the same criteria used for automobile, airplane and other amortizing loans.

For some time the banking authorities were skeptical. On February 27, 1950, a deputy United States comptroller gave this reason for criticizing the rising volume of M.N.B. trailer loans: ". . . with housing problems easing off, consensus seems to indicate purchase of house trailers will narrow down to the nomadic individual whose employment would not necessarily be steady or of a particular pattern."

Despite such cloudy forecasting, the business flourished. Within two or three years, according to Waldo, Michigan National became the largest mobile home financing agency in the country. In 1951 Howard decided to keep a revolving fund of $20 million in such loans, with 12 to 60 month maturities, and to sell excess mortgages to other interested banks. More than $280 million worth of mobile home contracts were eventually discounted. During the early 1950s they were taken by major eastern institutions—First Pennsylvania Bank and Trust Company, Philadelphia; First National Bank, Boston; Continental Illinois National Bank, Chicago; and First National City

Bank and Chase Manhattan Bank, New York City. Later Michigan Bank National Association, Stoddard's Detroit company, became the primary buyer. Other banks in which the M.N.B. Profit Sharing Trust had an interest also took smaller shares. By June 30, 1968, $659 million had been loaned. Contracts outstanding numbered almost 27,000, with an aggregate balance of $89 million. Less than $40 million had been lost on trailer loans in 19 years, and none of that had been charged against the bank's general reserve account.

Mobile home financing was the most profitable phase of M.N.B. operations in the 1950s, but in the next decade several developments made it less attractive. In a memorandum to Stoddard, July 12, 1967, Shaw reviewed the rise of high volume, low down-payment dealerships, finance company competition, repossessions and dealer bankruptcies—all of which meant more headaches and smaller rewards. The combination of circumstances led Shaw to recommend a curtailment of trailer loans. In recent years they have been a minor part of Michigan National business.

This lending activity led Howard, Waldo, Bohn, and Wickes into the insurance field, as noted earlier. Howard's own association with the business dated back to the mid-1940s, when he became a director of Auto Owners Insurance Company and Michigan Millers National Insurance Company, two Lansing-based firms which used Michigan National services. (He retained these directorships until his death but played no active management role.) Now millions of dollars worth of mobile homes were going to need protection. As Wolverine Insurance Company President John H. Carton put it, Stoddard thought that "they might just as well control the insurance angle as the banking angle." Wolverine could have an office right in the bank and the processing of loan and insurance contracts could be streamlined. "They would be sure that the product was covered, and we would take it from there," Carton stated.

It was not difficult to sell Charles Bohn on the idea. Carton recalls the first time he met the semi-retired Detroit financier. He had sent some Wolverine statements and other documents ahead, and when he arrived Bohn said, "Carton, tell me what this whole damn thing means." This was Bohn's first introduction to Wolverine, but Carton remembers that when next they met, Bohn understood the business very well. The May 16, 1950, purchase arrangement was comparable to that used in acquiring some of the Bohn-Stodard banks. Bohn bought the largest block of stock and Stoddard and other M.N.B. directors bought enough to effect transfer of control. Carton was permitted to borrow money, on favorable interest terms, to increase his stock holding. One of the things his new associates believed in, he observed, "was in having people run companies who have a substantial interest they have had to pay for. If the company was going broke, they were going to be broke, too. It was the old incentive theory."

Hardly had Woverine moved its office from Lansing to Battle Creek and opened a mobile home division in the Grand Rapids M.N.B. branch when the Bohn-Stoddard group bought another larger firm in a different insurance line. Federal Life and Casualty Company, a family-owned Detroit firm, was available, Stoddard and Carton learned, and Stoddard proposed that the Bohn group buy it and Carton run it. The "angle" for Michigan National would be selling decreasing term life insurance in connection with mortgage loans, with premiums and loan installments combined in a single monthly payment. (The practice became common in the banking industry fifteen or twenty years later.)

Again Bohn responded quickly. Carton recalls the meeting in Stoddard's Lansing office at which the purchase agreement was made. Stoddard said:

> Mr. Bohn, I guess the easiest way to consumate this transaction is for you to write your check for it. If you'll excuse me, I'll go out and see if there's enough in your checking account to cover it. If not, I'll see that you're loaned enough on a short-term basis to pay for it. Then we'll agree on how to distribute the stock.

Roe Endicott joined the major Wolverine stockholders in this purchase. Howard, Waldo and Carton were given options to buy additional shares from Bohn later, and Carton became president of both companies.

The Detroit *Free Press* quoted Bohn on July 17, 1952, as saying, "We intend to grow as aggressively in the insurance field as we have in the banking business. Most insurance companies are operating no differently than they have for 250 years. They are going to seed, and we intend to offer some new and modern ideas." Asked why he was moving into insurance in his 70's, Charles Bohn replied in terms which John Carton never forgot:

> Well, I'll tell you something. I've got friends, and one of them runs a hobby shop. He likes to put things together, so he spends money with this shop, and he keeps busy. I can't do anything with my hands at all.
>
> Then I got interested in music, but I wasn't getting good tone at all on this thing, so I had to give that up. (Bohn was hard of hearing during all the years Howard and Jennie Stoddard knew him. Some-

times he would turn off his hearing aid when the business in M.N.B. board meetings did not particularly interest him.)

> Then I developed a famous racing stable. I'd go down to Florida to see them race, and I'd spend maybe two months, and then I'd seen all the races and had all the racing stable I wanted.
>
> Really the thing I like to do is to get something small and see it grow, and get the statement every month, and see how you young fellows get along.

By the time Bohn died a few months later, Stoddard and Carton were already getting along very well in insurance. Federal Life and Casualty moved its headquarters to the Wolverine Tower in Battle Creek, and by 1960 the 500 employees of the two companies were generating a $2 million payroll in the breakfast food city. Both companies had profit sharing plans. Wolverine provided specialized fire, casualty and property insurance. Mobile home insurance was a major underwriting until Hurricane Camille wiped out several hundred M.N.B.-financed trailers along the Gulf Coast in 1964 and cost the insurance company $4 million. (During the preceding 13 years the premiums on this type of coverage were almost $26 million and the losses were only $10 million.) Federal Life sold less premium-with-mortgage insurance than Howard had anticipated, despite a vigorous advertising campaign in financial publications, but its general business expanded rapidly. In 1960 its sales volume put it in the top 10 percent of American life insurance companies.

At Carton's suggestion Wolverine moved into direct competition with low cost, high volume property insurers like State Farm Mutual and Allstate, who had their own agents and paid lower commissions than companies who relied on independent agencies to handle collections as well as sales. In 1958 the Stoddard group bought Secured Insurance Company, an Indiana firm, and its wholly-owned subsidiary, Riverside Insurance Company. The headquarters of Riverside was moved from Little Rock, Arkansas, to Battle Creek, and operations were streamlined by computerized accounting and direct billing. As with some other innovations proposed by his associates, Stoddard was skeptical at first. The direct-selling program was slow in winning public acceptance, but before Stoddard's death Riverside had a larger premium volume than Wolverine.

Stoddard's relationship to the insurance business changed in 1960, when controlling interest in both Wolverine and Federal was sold to Channing Financial Corporation, a New York holding company specializing in mutual funds. Channing made the first overture, wishing to expand into insurance. Stoddard found some of his associates anxious to accept the profitable offer, so 51 percent of the shares were sold for about $10 million. Stoddard and Carton both kept their stock and went on the Channing board of directors, while Carton continued to run the insurance companies.

Channing moved its mutual fund operation to Battle Creek, but the effort to carry on an interlocking business in the changing financial environment of the 1960s did not work out well. There was friction. According to Carton, the Channing promoters "didn't understand operations." He remembers Stoddard saying of one of them, "You know, John, when they bury that fellow, if somebody yells 'Deal' he's going to sit right up." In 1964 Channing sold its shares in Wolverine to Trans-America Insurance Company, a Los Angeles subsidary of Transamerica Corporation. Five years later the controlling interest in Federal Life and Casualty went to American General Insurance Company, who sold the property a year later to Home Insurance Company of New York. Stoddard remained on the Wolverine and Federal boards until his death.

Another digression from the banking business involved Michigan National's president with the fate of Reo Motors at the end of the Korean conflict. With the prospective termination of miltary contracts, truck sales threatened to decline drastically and there was stockholder sentiment to liquidate the company. Sale of all assets except cash and receivables to Henney Motor Company, of Illinois, was negotiated in April 1954, but before the transaction was completed Stoddard, still a Reo director, and Simon Den Uyl, now president of Bohn Aluminum and Brass Corporation, entered the picture. As Stoddard explained to the Reo employees a few months later, the prospect that Henney might move the manufacturing operation out of Lansing led him to approach Den Uyl. In a complex set of financial transactions orchestrated by Stoddard's former R.F.C. colleague, New York attorney James B. Alley, the Bohn-funded Reo Holding Corporation acquired the Henney Contract and sold it to the new Delaware-chartered Reo Motors, Inc. Den Uyl, Alley and Waldo Stoddard became directors of the truck company and Howard remained on the board and became president and director of the holding company.

At the pep rally which introduced the new Reo Motors officers and directors to the employees on January 11, 1955, Stoddard was his usual optimistic self. "Because we're small is no reason that we cannot succeed. The elements are here and if we can put them together properly . . . we'll make Reo superior and one of the finest producers of trucks in this country."

The outcome did not entirely fulfill expectations, but Reo did remain in Lansing. Stoddard and Den Uyl had an unfortunate difference of opinion on what to do with Reo Holding Corp., and when Den Uyl sold his shares to a New York company, Stoddard lost his office and directorship. He remained on the Reo Motors board, however, and he helped to arrange the sale of the company to White Motor Company, a Cleveland truck maker, in 1957. With the organization of Diamond Reo Trucks as a White subsidiary, Stoddard left the board of directors, but he retained an active interest in the Lansing enterprise.

With the growth of Stoddard's reputation as an innovative businessman and an incisive, effective speaker came more and more invitations to appear before service clubs, conventions and other groups. In the post-war period they were limited to Michigan National territory, but in the Eisenhower years audiences in several states heard his thoughtfully up-beat messages. They combined topical information with timeless values, and they were delivered with a direct and simple style which was difficult *not* to listen to. Neither rhetoric nor levity distinguished them, but organization, clarity and conviction. The director of special courses and conferences at Michigan State College described Stoddard's platform impact in a thank you letter dated August 21, 1952:

> Seldom, in my almost daily experience of listening to speakers at banquets and elsewhere, have I heard a presentation which was more direct, challenging, optimistic, and thoroughly interesting than the one you made last night before the Economic Education Workshop dinner. Your brief address was superb.

The speeches of the 1950s stressed several themes—the nature and importance of money, the causes and control of inflation, the necessity for national defense, and the bright prospects for America.

Whether he learned how as a student at Columbia University or as a teacher around the family dinner table, Howard Stoddard was a master at explaining the mysteries of banking. Credible witnesses report that he could hold the attention of an after-lunch audience with a description of the meaning of a bank balance sheet. "The Changing Value of the Dollar" carried dozens of listener groups from the Bohemian valley which gave the name "Taler" to a coin in 1519 to the contemporary problem of stabilizing the purchasing power of American money. The international convention of the Florist Telegraph Dispatch Association, meeting in Detroit on August 17,

1960, heard a lucid explanation of how checkbook money is created and eliminated as bank loans are made and retired:

> It's a very simple process. . . . You walk into the bank and you say, "I'm going to buy a new car. Will you loan me three thousand dollars? I'll pay you back one thirty-sixth each month." He'll say, "Yes, I'll loan you the money. . . ." And the minute you sign your name to the piece of paper, and the banker accepts it, you and the banker make three thousand dollars that never existed before. . . . On his books, under "assets," he enters the loan, and under "liabilities" he credits your account with three thousand dollars. . . . Now, a strange thing happens. The money remains in existence in some form until you pay off the note. As you pay, say one thirty-sixth each month, he goes to his books, reduces his loans . . . and charges your account by the same amount. By the time the car is old and used up and gone, the three thousand dollars that was used to finance the car is extinguished. . . .

"It's the most perfect system in the world, because it's inflation-proof," Stoddard explained. "As long as the money you're creating by lending matches goods and services produced, you keep in balance."

The great disturber of the balance, as Stoddard saw it, was war, because war created credit money to purchase goods which were neither paid for nor consumed through the market process. In the same speech he described this problem:

> In the last war we couldn't raise over 35 percent of our governmental expenditures by taxation. The Treasurer had to borrow money. . . . On many occasions he would take as high as ten billion dollars at one time. He would give the banks his note, the banks would credit his account, and he could immediately start writing out checks for ten billion dollars. . . . Our money supply increased. Then when the war was over, we had nothing . . . the battleships, the airplanes and everything else were of no value, but the money supply remained. Therefore you had an imbalance brought in, and you had inflation. It's that simple. . . .

Stoddard was pleased that the inflationary pressures generated by World War II and the Korean police action had dissipated without economic disaster, and he was almost exuberant about subsequent events. "In the past ten years we have had in this country more talk of inflation than ever in our history, and in the past ten years we've had the most stable dollar that America has ever enjoyed," he said in 1960. To maintain this condition he advocated a sound monetary system, a favorable climate for investment, a balanced federal budget, wage increases geared to productivity, the gradual elimination of farm subsidies, and above all, the avoidance of war.

A tour of military bases early in 1953 reinforced his conviction that the way to maintain peace was to keep the nation militarily strong. He was one of seventy business and professional leaders invited to visit the Pentagon and several armed forces installations soon after Michigan State College President John Hannah became Assistant Secretary of Defense in the new Republican administration. Stoddard saw Korean veterans stage a mock attack at Quantico, rode a helicopter, inspected an aircraft carrier, took a short submarine cruise, watched a military aircraft demonstration, rode in an F-86 Sabrejet, and jumped 600 feet with parachute from a paratroop training tower. He was 52 at the time. "It was quite a lot of fun," he told a reporter, and it left him "thoroughly convinced now that we have what it would take to stop the Russians. . . ."

Stoddard was no emotional anti-Communist. At the height of the McCarthy hysteria, he wrote in the annual message to Michigan National stockholders, January 9, 1953: "We share in the general feeling that our National Government is in the hands of fine, capable Americans who will give a full measure of intelligent service to the trust imposed in them." He believed, however, that the principle of balance of power operates in international relations and that the United States must not permit the Soviet Union to upset the balance. He told a Battle Creek audience soon after his military tour, "As soon as that balance of power shifts to one of the countries, the other will be destroyed." Concerning the Korean conflict, in which Stanford Stoddard was an Army Quartermaster Corps officer, he said, "I for one think we have had a magnificent victory. . . . We have served notice on the Communist nations that 'once and for all you may go no farther.' " His concern about the threat of Soviet power was reflected in the frequency during the 1950s that he quoted Alexis de Toqueville's 1835 prophecy:

> There are, at the present time, two great nations in the world, which started from different points, but seem to tend towards the same end. I allude to the Russians and the Americans. Both have suddenly placed themselves in the front rank among nations and are proceeding along a path to which no limit can be perceived. The American struggles against the national obstacles which oppose him while the adversaries of the Russians are men. The conquests of the Americans are

> gained by the plowshare—those of the Russians by the sword. The American relies upon personal interest to accomplish his end and gives free scope to the unguided strength and common sense of the people. The Russian centers all authority of society in a single arm. The principle instrument of the American is freedom—of the Russian, servitude. Yet each seems marked out by Heaven to sway the destinies of half the globe.

To preserve American freedom was expensive. Stoddard reminded the florists' convention that "of every dollar that Uncle Sam is taking in, fifty cents is for the sole purpose of buying you an insurance policy for the American way of life." Yet the burden was bearable. "If we can just continue to do as well as we did in 1959 and 1960, your American dollar is safe for the foreseeable future, because there is no other factor sufficiently big to gnaw away its purchasing power." (In 1960 the United States investment in Vietnam was a handful of military advisors, and the budget of the Department of Health, Education and Welfare was $3.4 billion.)

Remarks in an address titled "The Role of the Business Executive in the Cold War" suggest that Howard Stoddard was not unaware of the power of the industrial-military complex to which Eisenhower called attention at the close of his administration. "There has now emerged a new breed known as 'industrial executive,' the directing heads of our American corporations," Stoddard said, "and whether we like it or not, our system has placed in their hands the future of the Cold War." The managerial class was no longer controlled by the stockholder-owners of enterprise, but Stoddard was sanguine about the outcome. "Freedom and dignity for the average man can be preserved without necessarily having a democratic organization. There are other checks and balances." Certainly the risks of private enterprise were better than the realities of collectivism.

Howard and Jennie Stoddard were among the first Americans to visit the Soviet Union when the barriers to tourist travel came down in the late 1950s as part of Khrushchev's de-Stalinization program. Their time in July 1960 was spent primarily with the sights of Moscow, Leningrad, Odessa, Yalta and Kiev. They spoke with few Russians besides their English-speaking guides. "You don't have any trouble traveling in Russia," Stoddard later told the Lansing Rotary Club; "you just find out what you can't do and everything works out well." But he went as a well-informed and perceptive observer, and what he saw largely confirmed his impressions. He took favorable note of the generally friendly spirit of the people, the evidences of industrialization, and the virtual abolition of illiteracy. He rhetorically asked the florists' convention: "As you educate a nation of 200 million people, are they going to be content to accept the system under which they have been brought to power?" Being convinced that the love of freedom is within every person, he frequently expressed a hopeful long-term view. The president of the Saginaw Rotary Club make this comment in a thank you letter:

> This was the first time that I have heard any speaker on Russia hold out hope for a gradual change in the attitude of the Russian people and their leaders towards spiritual values. . . . I have a feeling that this message gave a tremendous lift to everyone who was privileged to listen to you.

Howard Stoddard's travel-based talks were never travelogues. As "Impressions of Russia" were reported to a score of audiences, insights born of careful reading supplemented and even modified on-the-scene judgments. He was quick, for example, to move away from the monolithic view of Communism which dominated American public opinion in the post-Korean phase of the Cold War. "We know that there have been differences between the Russians and Chinese, based on the Chinese view that Russia hasn't been aggressive enough about Communism," he told a Battle Creek group in October 1960. It might even lead Russia to turn to the United States for cooperation in the "not too far off" future. This did not justify complacency, but it did warrant optimism.

Stoddard's outspoken faith in America's future permeated the press interviews and public addresses of the years between Korea and Vietnam. An address to a business symposium at Michigan State College, April 13, 1955, focused on this theme. Entitled "Basic Reasons For Our National Prosperity," it posed four questions:

> 1. Why does this nation, with only seven percent of the world's population, have fifty percent of the world's wealth?
>
> 2. Why does an American worker in one hour produce six times as much wealth as did his ancestors 100 years ago, and receive eight times as much income for each hour's work?
>
> 3. Why have we emerged from two world wars without asking one dollar of tribute from our defeated enemies, and yet have the highest standard of living known to man?

4. Why can we confidently expect with a national debt of 280 billion dollars to finance a defense program at an annual cost of 50 billion dollars?

The address was virtually a paean to the American political and economic systems, both founded upon the free agency of man. It did not answer the questions explicitly, but a single explanation was implicit in the extended review of the highlights in national growth. The items mentioned were miscellaneous—the Bill of Rights, the reaper, the American Federation of Labor, the electric light and the Sherman Anti-Trust Act, among others. The land grant college act of 1862 received special mention, the occasion for the symposium being the transformation of Michigan State College into Michigan State University. The period of the Great Depression was seen as "one of the most significant," because "either through the will of God or the help of man," America avoided the temptation to "abandon the God-given precepts of free enterprise" for "the mess of pottage that so many of the nations" found tempting. Tested in wars, the American system had now brought the people to a point where "we may have to get accustomed to being prosperous."

To Howard Stoddard the answer to his four questions was plain:

> When you turn a hundred sixty-five million people loose in this country, give them the right to work where they want, go where they want, speak as they want, think as they want, and live as they want, you have a power that transcends anything the atomic bomb could ever offer.

To insure the continuation of these blessings, Stoddard made several suggestions to the campus audience and those who might read the printed address:

> To make the American system work (and I would rather use that word than the capitalistic system, because our plan is not the capitalistic), we must have a progressively wider division of national income. . . . One of the soundest things we have to preserve in this country is our graduated income tax system. . . . Unless the purchasing power is kept in the hands of the masses, the American system cannot succeed.
>
> Another thing we must watch is that the individual rewards must be based primarily on work performed. We must never permit ourselves

> to get into the Socialistic premise that an individual will perform without being rewarded. I think it was Emerson who aptly said, "Man is as lazy as he dares to be."
>
> On the other hand, we can and we should see that our people have economic security and independence. As people become old and people become ill, we as a society can afford to keep them shored up so they need not worry about the vicissitudes of life which have plagued men for thousands of years. . . .
>
> Another thing that we must do is to develop the maximum natural capabilities of our people, which you are doing here today. . . .

In concluding, Stoddard took note of the apparent rise in religious activity and spiritual commitment in the nation. "If that movement continues forward, all the other problems which are facing us across the seas or at home will in due course be reconciled."

"I look forward with every bit of confidence that your children and my children will continue to live in a growing and prosperous America!" he testified. One suspects that if Howard Stoddard had lived through the 1970s he would have kept that basic faith.

CHAPTER 15

# Growth Through Profits and Technology

The 1950s were phenomenally successful years for Howard Stoddard and his banks. The growth of Michigan National was so much more rapid than most of the top hundred commercial banks, and its earnings as a percentage of capital were so much higher, that he compelled attention. Many Michigan bankers still regarded him with distrust or dislike, but at American Bankers Association and other national and regional meetings his voice began to be listened to. Trust funds from the M.N.B. profit sharing program proved an effective instrument for acquiring additional banks, and in 1955 they helped to open Detroit to Stoddard-style banking at last. The speed with which Michigan Bank National Association moved from a $20 million consumer loan institution to a $180 million commercial bank led the publisher of *Michigan Manufacturer and Financial Record* to remark in 1960: "Watch those Stoddard people . . . they are going to be much bigger in Michigan banking."

The profit sharing plan instituted on January 1, 1953, was the last major Bohn-Stoddard collaboration. The M.N.B. board chairman approved the post-war Christmas bonuses and salary adjustments, which reflected bank earnings and offset inflation. He believed, however, that a system of rewards based on the incentive system would be superior. If the bank employees, and the officers especially, had a direct stake in profits, they would work most effectively because they would be working for themselves. Howard Stoddard fully shared this view, and on November 14, 1952, the Michigan National Bank Profit Sharing Trust Agreement was approved by the board of directors.

The purpose of the plan was described in these words:

> The Michigan National Bank desires to share a portion of its profits with members of its staff in recognition of loyal, faithful and efficient service to the Bank, and desires to stimulate a keen interest among all of its staff members in the efficiency, prosperity and well-

> being of the Bank by assuring them that when they have attained three consecutive calendar years of full employment with the Bank, they will share thereafter in the profits. . . .

Stoddard put the concept in less formal terms in his 1955 talk to the bank officers. What could the bank offer to a young man of 25 who asked, "If I start in now, and I spend my career in that institution, and I get married and rear a family, and I have a home and I go through all the normal things that men can go through, where do I end up?" For the individual who rose to the top there was no problem. But what about the man who spent his career in middle management and rose to the then-comfortable salary of $12,000 and a pension of half that amount? "Well, off at the side, wholly independent of any saving he has done, there's a minimum of $100,000 waiting for him," was Stoddard's answer.

The mechanics of the plan were simple. Every year in which net earnings exceeded 10 percent of capital funds, an amount equal to 15 percent of the annual salary being paid to all participating staff members was placed in the Profit Sharing Account. Each participant accumulated units according to current salary and length of employment with the bank or one of its components, retroactive to January 1, 1941. A vested interest was acquired at the rate of 4 percent of the cumulative unit account for each year of full-time employment, with full vesting after 25 years or at retirement for age or disability. The vested portion was payable upon separation from the bank for any reason, including death, except criminal action against the bank. Military time counted toward longevity when the staff member returned to the bank promptly after discharge, a timely provision because of the on-going "police action" in Korea.

In Howard Stoddard's lifetime the number of Michigan National Bank employees participating in the profit sharing program increased from 355 to 1,017. Since earnings between 1952 and 1971 never fell below the required figure, the plan gave staff members a powerful incentive to stay with the bank. The retroactive feature meant that senior people had a substantial vested interest at the time the plan was launched, and profitable management of the Profit Sharing Account added value to the participation units from the beginning.

The management of the trust account was the responsibility of the executive committee of the bank. The plan clearly contemplated that they would invest the funds in such a manner as to promote the growth of Michigan National, an outcome which would also benefit the participants. The key to much of the bank's subsequent expansion is in this paragraph of the agreement:

> The Trustees may use the funds . . . to purchase stock of the Michigan National Bank, or of any other bank or banking association, or of any lawfully organized and existing corporation, and at their discretion to sell such stock, or to hold such funds on deposit in the Bank. The Trustees are authorized to vote the stock purchased by the trust . . . at all stockholders' meetings of such banks and corporations.

Under this agreement resources of the Profit Sharing Trust could be used to acquire a stock interest in strategically situated banks, in anticipation of future mergers or the day when the barrier against state-wide branch banking came down again. When a controlling position was obtained or trust funds were needed for another investment, directors and senior officers in the Stoddard banks were sometimes invited to buy shares of one of these affiliates from the trust portfolio. This increased the liquidity of the trust account and its serviceability as an instrument for Michigan National growth. A director who received such an invitation in 1966 expressed appreciation for "this opportunity to participate with such distinguished associates."

The plan gained Howard Stoddard entry into the Detroit market in 1955, and effective control of a number of out-state banks as well. The assets of two of Michigan's oldest banks, Eaton County Bank of Charlotte and Vermontville, and First National Bank of Charlotte, were purchased in 1959 and consolidated into a M.N.B. branch. This conversion was possible because Charlotte was within 25 miles of Lansing. In 1964 two small state banks in the nearby town of Grand Ledge were similarly acquired and transformed. Litigation by minority stockholders and the state banking commissioner held up the acquisition for two years, but the Michigan Supreme Court then ruled unanimously that the transaction was in the public interest.

An earlier effort to expand in Port Huron produced a different outcome. "We deal here with a story of high finance and less lofty subterfuge," was the court's judgment on one of the few business decisions which Stoddard looked back on with embarrassment and genuine regret. When Peoples Savings Bank, the only other bank in Port Huron, was offered for sale in 1956, the desire to prevent its falling into the hands of one of the major Detroit banks was understandable enough. But the intricate transactions by which a Kalamazoo businessman, using the resources of the Michigan National Profit Sharing Trust, did what Stoddard, years before, had done with Charles

Bohn's money, produced four years of litigation and this judicial censure. Two things had changed in the intervening decades. This time, when Stoddard appeared at the Peoples Savings board meeting with the two-thirds majority ownership necessary to authorize dissolution of the bank and sale of its assets, the directors refused to go along and went to court instead. And this time Michigan National Bank was not just a Bohn-Stoddard dream, but a half-billion dollar corporation; so the charge of monopoly could be—and was—successfully raised. The court ordered the stock to be sold (359 Michigan Reports 297), a group of Port Huron investors bought it, and all the profit sharing trust received was its money back and bad publicity.

From a purely business point of view, Stoddard had accurately diagnosed the situation and anticipated the future. When he and attorney James Alley met with the Comptroller of the Currency to explain the case, he "very frankly" stated:

> that he felt that the big three, to-wit: The National Bank of Detroit, Manufacturers National Bank and the Detroit Bank and Trust Company were changing their attitude toward branch banking and that we could look forward to them in the near future to seek a change in the Michigan law to permit it. They will not do so, however, until they have acquired the stock of enough banks around the state so that they will be in a position then to move in immediately.

The correctness of the analysis did not resolve the problem. The stubborn persistence which had carried Howard Stoddard from an Oregon box factory to a suite in the Michigan National Tower made him unwilling—or unable—to see that the thing to do when the Peoples Savings suit produced its first injunction was to cut the losses and give up the contest. He recognized this trait when he often described himself as "God's gift to the lawyers."

When the Detroit affiliate, Michigan Bank National Association, was formed, a similar profit sharing plan was instituted and its resources were used to establish bases of influence in the metropolitan area. When the U.S. Comptroller of the Currency disapproved the establishment of a new affiliate in Novi because the two profit sharing trusts would own stock in it, Stoddard objected vigorously to his friend, Secretary of the Treasury David M. Kennedy. "I write," he declared on February 24, 1970, "because, as one who has had extensive experience in overcoming substantial obstacles in nurturing the growth of a national bank, I know that the bank is vitally concerned with the interests of its employees." He defended the policy of keeping the trust funds in bank stocks by citing the record:

The Michigan National Bank Profit Sharing Trust was established in 1952 and during that period, including 1969, shows the following results:

| | |
|---|---|
| Paid to Profit Sharing Trust by the bank | $10,720,357 |
| Earnings on Trust Investments | 3,514,091 |
| Paid to staff members on termination of employment | 6,372,709 |
| Market value of stocks in 12 different banks | 17,227,369 |

The Michigan Bank NA Profit Sharing Trust was established in 1957. Since that time the results are as follows:

| | |
|---|---|
| Paid to Profit Sharing Trust by the Bank | $ 2,297,738 |
| Earnings on Trust Investments | 516,976 |
| Paid to staff members on termination of employment | 852,125 |
| Market value of stocks in 4 different banks | 5,411,006 |

At the time of Stoddard's death the twelve banks in which the M.N.B. Profit Sharing Trust held shares had aggregate resources of $2.4 billion. In addition to Michigan National itself, they were Michigan Bank N.A., Livonia National Bank, Troy National Bank, Oakland National Bank of Southfield, Central Bank of Grand Rapids, Valley National Bank of Saginaw, Security National Bank of Manistee, First National Bank of East Lansing, Central National Bank of Alma, and St. Clair Shores National Bank. Funds of the Michigan Bank N.A. trust were in the bank itself and the Livonia, Troy and Oakland affiliates, with resources of almost $1 billion.

(Since the establishment of Michigan National Corporation in 1972 the profit sharing program has been modified to incorporate a stock purchase plan and to accommodate changes in the federal pension laws. Contributions are now based in part on the performance of individual units in the rapidly expanding banking network.)

The story of Michigan Bank National Association can be traced back to the formation of Michigan National Bank itself, although the title dates from 1961, when the Detroit bank received a national charter. Neither Charles Bohn nor Howard Stoddard was content without a metropolitan foothold, so they asked permission in 1941 to start a branch there. They met their first disappointment when the Comptroller of the Currency denied the application. Two years later they tried again and went so far as to spend $20,000 on options on an available building. When Stoddard was in Washington trying to drum up support, he learned from Congressman Fred L. Crawford, a member of the Saginaw branch advisory board, that information allegedly from the grand jury investigation was being used to block M.N.B. expansion. By the time a new U.S. Comptroller got around to denying this application in July 1945, the Michigan anti-branch banking statute was operative and the possibility of establishing a new branch in Detroit was gone.

Another unfruitful approach during World War II took Stoddard to see Edsel Ford about a possible merger of Michigan National and Manufacturers National, the Guardian National Bank step-child which "Mister R.F.C." had helped to organize in 1933. Ford was cordial and agreed that a merger of the two banks had attractive possibilities. The combined bank, however, must be under the financial control of the Fords. Since there was no place for junior partnerships in the Bohn-Stoddard plan, nothing came of the meeting except a new and expensive car for the Stoddards. This is Gladys MacGregor's version of the dialogue as Howard left the Ford estate:

> Mr. Ford: "How is it you come to call on me in a General Motors car?"
>
> Mr. Stoddard: "You may not know it, but cars are scarce, and we ordinary people cannot get them."
>
> "Do you want a car?"
>
> "Of course I would like a new car."
>
> "As of this minute you have a new car."

Within a few days a black custom Lincoln sedan was delivered. According to Gladys, it had an impressive price tag and everything on it "except power steering and power brakes, which had not yet been invented." It was a joy to ride in, but as a family car it proved unwieldly. Jennie took the children on a trip to Grosse Pointe, exhausted herself trying to park, and finally stopped a passerby and asked him to do it. Virginia reported that "Mom sure was mad!"

The record does not show whether Jennie's difficulty with the Ford product or Stoddard's difficulty with the Ford bank had anything to do with the unbroken series of General Motors cars which followed. There were good reasons for preferring the home town product—Oldsmobile.

Death dissolved the Bohn-Stoddard partnership before Stoddard found the way into Detroit. Michigan Bank, a small industrial bank with an impressive real estate connection, was intermittently courted for fourteen years before an alliance with Michigan National was effected. Under Michigan law an industrial bank was restricted to savings deposits and consumer-type loans. Michigan Bank was the only such institution to survive the depression, and it had assets of about $6 million when Stoddard first tried to buy it in 1942. Financial control was in a New York trust, and offers to buy were declined then and in 1945, 1948 and 1951. According to Stanford Stoddard, pressure from Michigan influenced these decisions.

Stoddard explored the subject again during the summer of 1955, this time at the invitation of Detroit attorney John F. Langs, who was Michigan Bank's board chairman. Apparently the major stockholders were now willing to sell to Stoddard and some of his associates if the reorganized bank would lease space in the partially vacant Guardian Tower, which belonged to one of the stockholders. Stoddard was very much interested if the Detroit bank would apply for conversion of its state charter from industrial to commercial, which Langs was willing to do. Since Michigan National Bank was not a party to either purchase or lease, the anti-branch banking law was not involved. The state banking commissioner, therefore, informally agreed to approve the charter conversion, provided that Michigan Bank's capitalization were increased by $1 million, a public offering of stock were made, and directors and officers were chosen "to provide a sound policy making body and give the bank good administrative direction." According to Stanford, the commissioner also told Stoddard that he was approving the conversion with the understanding that "you will be a strong competitor and bring the public some benefits that they are not now getting from Detroit area banks." Stoddard laughed and replied, "That's exactly our plan."

On November 12, 1955, the deal was closed, and before the year's end the conversion of Michigan Bank's charter was approved and the change of stock ownership was made. When the capital transfusion was completed, Stoddard, Endicott, Wickes, Den Uyl, Langs, Gerald W. Chamberlin and Thomas Kaplan (the Guardian Tower owner) were large stockholders. The largest of all was the M.N.B. Employees Profit Sharing Trust.

John C. Hay came to the presidency of Michigan Bank from a vice presidency in the Lansing office. Twenty-five-year-old Stanford Stoddard moved from the Grand Rapids branch to an assignment as assistant vice president—the first big step on the way to the top. Langs continued as board chairman, but Stoddard was the director whose judgments prevailed. George A. Pierson, who was then a manager of one of Michigan Bank's five small branches, remembers that his first impression of Howard Stoddard "was one of rather immense awe. He had a fierce, rather foreboding appearance, I thought, but he impressed me at once as a man of great mental powers." Stoddard spoke to all the management people, telling them, according to

Pierson, that "we had the capability of becoming a forty million dollar bank in the next year. This seemed beyond comprehension to most of us, but, in fact, it did occur."

Indeed it did. Following substantially the same policies as its Lansing-based associate, and branching vigorously within a 25-mile radius of the Guardian Tower headquarters, the bank doubled its resources in each of the first two years, and then doubled them again in the next two. Responding to the constant pressure to maintain adequate capitalization, Michigan Bank paid $1 per share dividends. and reinvested most earnings. In addition to splitting shares at intervals, it began in 1958 to issue preferred stock. (M.N.B. preferred stock dated back to the R.F.C.-funded reorganizations of 1933-1934, and the last $1 million was retired in 1958.) When Pierson became president in 1970, the Detroit bank had 26 branches, resources of $760 million, and almost $38 million in capital funds. It had just entered the list of the hundred biggest commercial banks in the United States.

A profit sharing trust was organized as soon as Michigan Bank came under Stoddard control, as previously noted. Since the requisite level of earnings was achieved every year, the resources of the trust increased rapidly. They were used in the same manner as the M.N.B. trust, to acquire interest in selected banks and to provide capital for new banks in the metropolitan area. Sometimes the Lansing trust invested in the same institutions, both trusts became substantial holders of Michigan Bank preferred stock. In 1963 the Bank of Livonia, with resources of approximately $12 million, was acquired by purchase after the Comptroller of the Currency blocked efforts by some of the former owners to sell it to the only other bank in the community. By December 31, 1970, its resources had grown to $80 million and its offices had increased from three to seven. Troy National Bank and Oakland National Bank were established *de novo* in 1962 and 1965, respectively. The Troy bank had resources of $54 million and eight offices and the Oakland bank had $58 million and five offices by the end of the decade. Officers and directors of the Stoddard banks also participated in these new ventures. Gerald Chamberlin, a director of Freuhauf Corporation, became not only a substantial investor but he and his wife, Myrtle, became good friends of the Stoddard family.

From the start neither the main Michigan Bank office or any of the branch facilities was adequate for the business Stoddard envisioned in Detroit, so the refurbishing of the leased quarters in the Guardian Tower was an immediate concern of the new officers and directors. The Numidian marble which accented the vaulted lobby, the amber light fixtures from Czechoslovakia, the stained glass, the luxuriously paneled board and conference rooms—

all gave more than a touch of class to the new bank that was in so many ways the antithesis of the kind of banking which had died in this and other Detroit landmarks in 1933.

The reception of the bank was predictable. The financial editor of the Detroit *Times*, reporting Stoddard's election to the Michigan Bank board, January 18, 1956, observed that "bankers who once blanched at the thought" of M.N.B. competition in the metropolitan area had just learned that the man "whose hustle a few years back resulted in legislation throttling his program to have a Michigan National office in every key city in the state, has invaded Detroit. . . ." The same writer, James Boynton, used an interview with Stanford as a vehicle for pointing out on December 1, 1957, that "a second generation of Stoddards is on its way to become giants in Michigan banking like their father." At the time Howard Jr. was senior vice president of the M.N.B. branch in Marshall and Stanford was described as "the youngest bank officer in Detroit." When Boynton mentioned that Howard Sr. had told him in 1948 that money should be a compulsory subject in junior high school, Stanford recalled: "We grew up in an environment of banking. And when you are as close to it as we were, you want to go into it or you want to get as far away from it as you possibly can."

When Howard Sr. read the story, he sent Boynton a note of thanks and a better picture than had accompanied the story—"a glossy copy of one which the photographer tried to make as good as possible for publicity purposes."

Few things brought as much publicity to Michigan National Bank as the pioneering conversion to computerized accounting at the end of the decade. "'Electronic banking," as it was called, was the brainchild of James Shackleton, head of the Saginaw branch. His success with an electronic punch-card bookkeeping system, instituted in 1953, led the other branches to follow suit. With transistors and other improvements rapidly revolutionizing computers, it seemed to Shackleton that the logical next step for an innovative bank was to go electronic all the way.

After some initial reluctance, Stoddard appointed a committee to see if a system could be found to expedite the handling of the tons of paper which were Michigan National's primary commodity. Dubbed MINIMAC, the committee included Russell Fairles, Miles Grant, Harry Ingram, Joseph Shaw and Harold J. Phelps, with Shackleton as chairman. After visiting headquarters of International Business Machines, National Cash Register Company and Burroughs Corporation and reviewing presentations by other companies in the electronic data processing field, the committee recommended Michigan-based Burroughs. The company's proposal was submitted to the M.N.B. board on November 7, 1957, and contracts were executed the following January.

It was a new undertaking for both bank and Burroughs. Only two banks in the United States preceded Michigan National into electronic processing—Bank of America and First Pennsylvania Bank & Trust—and neither had yet adopted as comprehensive a system as Howard Stoddard wanted. Philip Ordway, who observed the unfolding experiment from the Battle Creek advisory board, saw it as an illustration of Stoddard's "great tenacity to purpose," once he made up his mind. If Burroughs said they could provide equipment, they had better do so. Development delays were accepted, generally with patience, but there could be no pulling back.

During the three years that the system was in production, personnel were being selected and trained and a myriad preparatory tasks were being taken care of. Fifteen men were selected from the several M.N.B. branches for a week's intensive briefing and screening in Lansing. Beyond technical potential, such considerations had to be taken into account as willingness to work at nights, to move to Lansing, and to face the pitfalls of an untested enterprise. The seven who came through the screening entered an extensive collaboration with the Burroughs people, while some of the other eight worked at preparing the branches for the change-over. Leonard M. Selden, a Burroughs expert, was hired by the bank to head the proposed Electronic Processing Center.

Not until 1959 did the American Bankers Association select the design for magnetically coding bank documents, without which electronic banking could not be implemented. Then Michigan National people had not only to prepare coded checks and deposit forms for the customers whom they supplied, but to assist all the business accounts to develop machine-readable forms. Couriers had to be selected to carry the magnetic tape records of each branch's daily transactions to the processing center and to bring back the updated accounting information a few hours later. Periodic press releases reminded the public that Michigan National was once again up to something new and better.

A publicity brochure, "Inside Michigan National," was issued at the time the new system went into operation. It described the Electronic Processing Center as "another historic customer service 'first' " for the bank. All commercial and savings accounts, mortgage and installment loans from all of the branches were involved. The magnetic ink imprinters, readers, sorters, printers, and the Burroughs 220 computer "form a master system which performs hitherto tedious bookkeeping operations with unbelievable speed and beyond the realm of human error."

To remind him that any mechanized process which is without human error is also without human judgment, Stoddard had Gladys preserve a note which came to the bank a couple of years after the Electronic Processing Center opened. A "Notice of Past Due Account" had been sent to an installment borrower in Okemos, Michigan. Unvarnished language called attention to the fact that the account was delinquent and admonished: "Make your payment immediately for the amount shown below. Additional charges will be paid if personal contact is necessary for collection." The amount past due was $.06. Written on the back of the notice was the following:

> If you people printed your books in such a manner that people could read them, instead of machines, perhaps your machine would not have printed things like this for people to read. I think such a firm notice from your bank over a matter of six cents is rather a machine-like way of treating a people-like customer. Enclosed please find six (6) cents. Please credit my account before your machine blows a fuse and shuts down the whole bank.

As it had adopted other Howard Stoddard policies, Michigan Bank N.A. quickly followed into electronic data processing. By 1963 a system similar to that in Lansing was on line in Detroit.

The decision for electronic banking triggered a major Michigan National building program. The equipment being leased from Burroughs required large work areas, vibration-free floors and a temperature and humidity controlled environment, none of which could be provided in the Michigan National Tower or other bank buildings. To build a no-frills structure in the suburbs for the E.P.C. would have been the economical solution, but Stoddard persuaded the board of directors to adopt a more comprehensive and community-oriented plan. In August 1958 he announced that the bank would build a ten story office building on the site of the venerable Industrial Bank building, which would be immediately razed. On the adjoining site of the drive-in bank and parking lot would be constructed a seven-level, 400-car parking ramp and a new drive-in facility. The total undertaking would cost approximately $3 million. (Although the law limited how much a bank could spend on its facilities, Stoddard was able to persuade the Comptroller of the Currency to let the bank build a ramp for the benefit of its customers. Downtown Lansing was in acute need of parking space, and part of the ramp would be available for public use.)

Concern for the future of downtown Lansing was pivotal in the decision to build an office building across Allegan Street from the bank tower. Parking problems and deteriorating buildings were producing the same urban blight in the Michigan capital as in other metropolitan areas. Howard Stoddard had not yet plunged into Michigan fiscal and political affairs—that came a year later—but he was anxious both as a businessman and as a citizen to reverse the trend. The announcement of the new construction was made at a meeting of the state office building committee, and when architects' drawings appeared in the papers a month later Stoddard stated that the plans would fit into the capitol and downtown development program which included new state and municipal buildings. The ten story bank building, the *State Journal* noted, would be the first office building constructed in downtown Lansing since the 14-story Bank of Lansing and the 23-story Olds Tower were completed in the early 1930s. The Detroit *Times* later described it as "the first general office building erected in outstate Michigan for 30 years."

In recognition of Stoddard's contributions to the bank and the city, the M.N.B. directors chose to call the new structure the Stoddard Building. The cornerstone laying ceremony on May 22, 1959, was a civic celebration, coinciding as it did with Lansing's centennial. Governor G. Mennen Williams and Mayor Ralph W. Crego made remarks and Paul A. Martin, publisher of the *State Journal*, gave a keynote address which tied the development of Michigan National Bank into the history and prospects of the city and state. Stoddard spoke briefly. "Lansing's destiny is unquestioned," he predicted. "This is only the first of many such buildings which will be erected by Lansing people." The Stoddard sons were among the honored guests; Charles was 14 at the time. Jennie and Howard troweled some mortar around the cornerstone, with Jennie the preferred target for the press photographers.

The handsome granite and glass Stoddard Building, complete with under-the-street tunnel to the Michigan National Tower, was ready for its first occupants in January 1960. Installation and testing of the Burroughs equipment took a while, so the Electronic Processing Center on the second floor did not become fully operational until early 1961. A few months later Howard Stoddard's sixtieth birthday was celebrated in a surprise party on the top floor of the new structure. For eighteen years the bank occupied the lower floors and leased the rest. In 1978, the computer operation having outgrown its quarters and moved to a former parochial school in the northwest suburbs, the building was sold to the state of Michigan to provide offices for members of the Senate. The plaque now identifying the edifice contains the note: "(Formerly the Stoddard Building)".

In accounting to the stockholders for the fact that bank earnings had dropped to only 10.4 percent on capital funds during 1960, Howard Stoddard pointed out that a lot of money had been tied up in building construction and equipment development, and that the costs of "Full Time Interest" would only be recouped as the policy attracted more loanable funds. The over-all record of the first twenty years, however, was a good one. The eighteen offices in eight cities employed over 1,300 men and women. The 3,700 stockholders, almost all residents of Michigan, were owners of a banking enterprise which had earned over $69 million since 1941, paid $29 million in federal taxes and $10 million in dividends, and retained almost $30 million as capital to support its growth. Each 100 shares in 1941 had grown to 800 in 1960 and generated $5,658.33 in dividends. In the process of building Michigan, Howard Stoddard's bank was moving some of its stockholders and profit-sharers into the upper echelons of the affluent society.

CHAPTER 16

# Citizen of Michigan

Howard Stoddard's concept of civic duty went beyond the routine contributions of time, money and prestige which go with being the leading banker in a community. These he freely gave, but an old-fashioned sense of patriotism, a feeling of gratitude, a desire for acceptance, a concern for the welfare of his bank, and a religious conviction about the importance of every individual found expression in his activities as a citizen. So many of his friends from the West—including his own wife, Jennie—retained strong sentimental ties with their origins that they had difficulty feeling permanence elsewhere. This, Stoddard thought, was unfortunate, and he set another course for himself and his family. Responding to a friendly interview in the Detroit *Times*, he wrote to the financial editor on December 2, 1957:

> The State of Michigan has been our home for a quarter of a century, and we feel our roots are deeply and permanently imbedded in its fine soil. We hope as a family we can fully merit the nice things you said about us, and that in the years to come we can continue to make our contribution to the prosperity and well being of the splendid state in which we live.

Opportunity to make a major contribution came soon. Michigan's fiscal peril brought her two most prominent Mormons—George W. Romney and Howard J. Stoddard—into a grass-roots political revolution which gave the state a new constitution.

The potential for impasse in Michigan politics had not changed since the early 1940s, when efforts to influence the course of banking legislation had produced such a traumatic outcome for Howard and his associates. The Detroit-based, union-dominated Democratic Party usually controlled the House of Representatives, while the rural and small town electorate always held the Senate under the Republican banner. Individual charisma rather than party label determined gubernatorial elections, and whoever won the executive chair found himself in trouble with the legislature. In the circumstances Stoddard made contributions to both political parties and tried to avoid partisan entanglements in Lansing. To keep friends in both parties became the Michigan National policy—as it is with most major business enterprises today. The necessity of validating most M.N.B. innovations with the state banking commissioner or the state courts kept the bank's lawyers busy, and they won some battles and lost others, as had been noted.

What brought Howard Stoddard into the political arena was the financial predicament which confronted Michigan in the late 1950s. Rising costs for expanding governmental services, coupled with a sharp decline in automobile production between 1955 and 1958 and a relatively inflexible tax system, began to produce budget deficits. These had to be met by various expedients because the 1908 constitution drastically limited state indebtedness. Democratic Governor G. Mennen Williams and the legislature were soon at loggerheads over both short-term expedients and long-range solutions, with proposals to introduce a state income tax at the heart of the controversies. An effort to force constitutional revision failed to win enough votes in 1958, and the 1959 legislature deadlocked with the current and pending state budgets both unbalanced. The House wanted a graduated income tax, the Senate wanted a sales tax boost, and neither would budge. Some state agencies ran out of money to pay bills and a state payroll was delayed before stop-gap measures produced additional revenue.

Concern that the search for expedients might discriminate against banks led Stoddard to write to Williams on March 4, 1958. "The bank has no objection to paying its fair and proper share of taxes," he stated, "but already Michigan banks through intangible taxes are paying 60% more in taxes in relation to earnings, than other business corporations." He was particularly concerned about the growing competition from savings and loan associations and credit unions—an issue which he was pursuing in national banking and lawmaking circles at the same time. Opposition to taxation which placed banks in particular and Michigan business in general at a competitive disadvantage was frequently expressed during the crisis years.

He recognized, however, that durable solutions to the state's fiscal problems required fundamental reforms. This led him to advocate a flat rate income tax on both individuals and corporations as the most equitable approach. Cutting state expenditures was not the answer, he told Battle Creek Rotarians in April 1959. "The taxes in this state amount to only $188 per capita, and I feel this is very cheap for the services I receive," he pointed out. To raise the sales tax would be regressive; to institute a graduated income tax would inhibit investment by adding to the federal income tax burden on higher incomes. "Whether we like it or not," he predicted, "a tax on our incomes is inevitable."

To bring his views and experience more effectively to bear on the tempestuous Michigan scene, Stoddard became active in two non-partisan organizations—Citizens Research Council of Michigan and Citizens for Michigan.

The first was a Detroit-based agency, financed by subscriptions from business, foundations and individuals. According to its literature, it was "dedicated to the promotion of responsible, efficient, and economical government through research, education, and cooperation with public officials and citizens' groups." Intermittently active since 1916, the council became prominent in the search for political alternatives in the late 1950s. Michigan National Bank was a contributor and Howard Stoddard was a member of the sponsoring board of trustees for some time before he became a member of the policy making board of directors. (Simon Den Uyl was also on both boards, and George Romney was a trustee.) Politically neutral and tax-exempt, the council conducted an active educational campaign. Two C.R.C.O.M. publications received statewide distribution at critical points during the constitutional reform campaign. *Michigan Constitutional Issues* (1960) and *An Analysis of the Proposed Constitution* (1962) were organized in pro-and-con form, but it is difficult to see how an open-minded reader could have read them and become a defender of the status quo. Howard Stoddard was not immediately involved in the editorial operations of the council, but it is unlikely that he would have remained on the board of directors through the 1960s if the outcomes had not been generally consistent with his own assessment of Michigan's needs and possibilities.

Citizens for Michigan and the constitutional revision movement which came out of it were major preoccupations for Stoddard between 1959 and 1961. For the balance of his life he held significant advisory posts in the new government which he helped to create.

Prime mover in Citizens for Michigan was American Motors President George Romney, whose experience with a study of Detroit's public school needs persuaded him that the structure, powers and policies of the state government needed attention. Preliminary informal discussions early in 1959 led to the convening of a public meeting in East Lansing's Kellogg Center on June 21. About 300 people attended, anxious to get involved in the current state crisis. Howard Stoddard was among them. When Citizens for Michigan was incorporated three months later, he became a member of the board of directors and financial chairman. Both appointments were natural, since he had served as a member of the high council of his church's Detroit Stake since its organization in 1952 with Romney as president; the men knew each other well.

Through the winter C.F.M. moved vigorously in three directions. One committee studied the needs and services of state government, a second worked on finance and taxation, and a third considered the basic structure of state government. Stoddard was chairman of the second committee and involved in fund raising for the major political effort which was mounted by the third. The campaign for a constitutional convention held center stage during most of 1960 and 1961, but when the new constitution was ratified, the revised fiscal and tax powers reflected the work of Stoddard's study group. "Unquestionably, Howard made a significant contribution in terms of providing for the state's fiscal requirements on a more equitable and productive basis," is Romney's retrospective judgment.

About fifty people were initially asked to serve on the state financing committee, but the heavy work was done by a steering committee of nine which held weekly meetings in Ann Arbor during the summer and fall of 1960. By then the prospect of constitutional reform was sufficiently bright to give impetus to the effort, and the blue-ribbon group looked at the Michigan tax system from top to bottom. "It has been a refreshing experience to me," Stoddard told the C.F.M. board of directors on October 15, "to find such men as Jack T. Conway [administrative assistant to United Auto Workers President Walter Reuther], Woodrow Ginsburg [U.A.W. research director], Edward L. Cushman [American Motors vice president], Robert S. McNamara [Ford Motor Company president and later Secretary of Defense], Brian T. O'Keefe [Chrysler Corporation tax consultant], Dic L. Dorney [assistant vice president, National Bank of Detroit], and Dr. Brazer who are willing to give up their Saturdays." Howard E. Brazer, tax expert from the University of Michigan, was the committee's consultant, and Stoddard chaired the meetings. John Carton, who was a member of the larger committee, remembers that McNamara was a particularly effective aid to Stoddard until he left for Washington in November.

To identify the shortcomings of the current patchwork system of taxes and earmarked funds took time, and to develop improvements which would be both fair and adequate for the state's needs required even more time. Given the composition of the committee, it is not surprising that considerable attention was given to the impact of business taxation. Stoddard told the C.F.M. board:

> It is the single greatest problem now confronting Michigan . . . to insure that the business climate is such that we can continue the growth that has marked Michigan for the past two decades. Michigan must . . . find means by which it can add approximately 100,000 new jobs a year. . . . We are going to see to it when we form recommendations that taxation in Michigan will not only be equitable but the burden borne by business, which produces our wealth, will be on a par or under that in any competitive state.

The committee, according to Stoddard, found that welfare and health costs were not out of line with other states. As for higher education, Michigan had years ago decided that no private college might be started without meeting standards set by the University of Michigan. As a result, Stoddard pointed out, "Our state is unique in the Middle West and the East in that the cost of higher education is borne largely, and in time will be borne almost entirely, by public taxation." The tax structure called upon to carry these increasing burdens was found to be very inelastic as well as unfair. "We discovered that the personal property tax is one of the most vicious taxes we have in this state," he reported. The sales tax was labeled "regressive," but, alas, indispensable. Soon after the forthcoming election the committee expected to be able to submit to the C.F.M. membership "a sound tax program for Michigan for at least the next five years."

While the committee was forming, studying, and preparing its recommendations, Stoddard found time not only to direct his banks and rearrange his insurance holdings, but to put in a good word for Michigan in *American Banker*. "BALANCED STATE BUDGET IN PROSPECT: STATE'S FISCAL WOES HELD DISTORTED," was the caption of the June 18, 1960, story, which presented the state's living standards and basic economy in positive terms. A clash of political philosophies on taxation had produced the impasse which "unfortunately resulted in national publicity, which created a false idea that the State of Michigan was verging on bankruptcy." Stoddard also conducted a five-hour seminar on state finances in Lansing for about fifty representatives of business and industry. He presented a combined income and sales tax plan which had been developed by Dr. Brazer and predicted that "in the next few years we will have a tax program satisfactory to both business and labor. . . ."

When Citizens for Michigan opted for a new state constitution rather than amendments to the old one, the Junior Chamber of Commerce and League of Women Voters had already launched a petition campaign for what came to be called the Gateway Amendment—a proposal which, if approved by the voters at the November 1960 election, would require the state legislature to submit a constitutional convention proposal to the people at a later special election. C.F.M. plunged into the campaign, with the evangelical Romney as chief spokesman. Stoddard raised more than $10,000 to bankroll the publicity blitz, with speakers bureau, newsletter, mailing lists, newspaper petition coupons, and local C.F.M. chapters throughout the state. The League of Women Voters spearheaded the collection of signatures, being experienced with this activity. Michigan Education Association and many other state organizations were represented in the coordinating committee.

Between May 21 and July 8, 1960, 237,000 additional notarized signatures were gathered—enough to put the Gateway Amendment on the ballot. During the campaign opposition developed from such groups as the Townships Association, Farm Bureau, Michigan Manufacturers Association and Michigan Bankers Association, primarily because of the threats of legislative reapportionment and changes in the restrictions on taxation. Ballyhoo and hard work by the proponents carried the day, however. The amendment passed by a margin of 353,000 votes.

The same election brought John B. Swainson, a Democrat and handicapped veteran, to the governorship. His tax recommendations were already before the legislature when Howard Stoddard submitted his committee report to the Citizens for Michigan board and the media on February 5, 1961. Both plans called for a flat rate income tax and a cutback in personal property and business taxes, but they took different approaches to the sales and other taxes. The mostly Republican legislature, however, had already relieved the immediate fiscal crisis by raising the sales tax, and it chose to take no further action pending the outcome of the constitutional revision proposal. Stoddard's appeal through the press that "now, with a little breathing space, is the time for the state to enact tax reform," was unheeded.

A flat rate tax on incomes was the only possible compromise between the demands of liberal Democrats, who wanted a graduated tax, and conservative Republicans, who wanted no income tax at all. The Citizens for Michigan plan also reflected Howard Stoddard's personal preference. He recognized that the services demanded from government at all levels required large revenues, but he believed that the steeply graduated federal income tax had become counter-productive. Speaking on "Federal Taxation" to the Lansing Rotary Club in November 1963, he took a dogmatic position:

> Karl Marx is the father of progressive taxation. And we took it and bought it in this country hook, line and sinker. In the days of war,

> where we had to share the burden unequally and where we had to hold down purchasing power, there might be a justification. . . . But not in peace. . . . It distorts all business judgment. Time after time, you sit in a business conference worrying about a solution to a particular problem, and somewhere along the line you hear those famous remarks, "Well, what difference does it make? If we lose, the government will stand half the cost." . . . There is no greater fiscal curse . . . in the United States today than the absurd limits to which this progressive taxation has gone. . . . And by the way, these people that have these heavy tax burdens are the ones who do not pay the taxes. They are able to put income in tax-exempt securities, or they are able to make donations, or they are able to do other things. Don't kid yourselves, the government is not getting the money, as Karl Marx thought it would. . . .

It was the hope of Citizens for Michigan that the legislature would draft the Con-Con (constitutional convention) referendum in non-partisan terms, but in this Romney and his associates were disappointed. Delegates were to be elected in primary and run-off elections, with all candidates identified by political party. The Democratic Party now adopted the cause, seeing reapportionment as the primary gain from a new frame of government. Republicans were divided; Howard Stoddard was a minority voice in a party dominated by its rural membership. All of the *status quo* groups united on "Protect Your Liberties: Vote No on Con-Con." In the April 3 election the proposal to elect delegates to a convention carried by only 23,000 votes out of 1,160,000 votes cast.

At this point Paul D. Bagwell, the recently defeated Republican candidate for governor, suggested that Stoddard would be a good convention delegate and offered to set up a campaign committee for him. Howard responded: "I have never run for any public office, and this is the first time any suggestion has ever been made that I should, or there has been any particular urge on my part to do so." He promised to consider the idea, but in the end he decided that his business and other responsibilities made it infeasible. He did prepare a statement, "It's Time to Act in Government," which appeared in papers throughout the state as part of a series on the importance of the primary election. "The citizens of Michigan now have an opportunity, only rarely available, to write upon a clean sheet of paper. . . . The success of this effort will depend upon the wisdom and integrity of the delegates chosen to perform this almost sacred task."

It was probably fortunate for the convention that Stoddard did not seek election. On June 21 Governor Swainson appointed him to head a 15-member Constitutional Convention Preparatory Commission, charged with providing facilities, reports on substantive issues, recommendations on procedural matters, and other consultative services for Con-Con. In his letter to members of the commission, the governor said, "The experiences of other states which have recently held constitutional conventions indicates that the success of the convention was directly related to the quality of the preconvention planning."

Funded by an $85,000 grant from the W. K. Kellogg Foundation, provided on Swainson's appeal when the legislature appropriated $5,000 instead of the $100,000 he had requested, the commission went quickly to work. (So frugal was the commission that almost $15,000 was returned to the foundation.) Michigan National Bank provided office space in the Stoddard Building. Gladys MacGregor, who served as secretary, remembers the sometimes heated discussions, and the verbosity of some of the members. In her opinion the only one who could cut to the heart of a matter as incisively as "Mr. Stoddard" was Michigan AFL-CIO President August Scholle. When he made a notably succinct summary of a tedious discussion, she asked Stoddard to have him repeat it for the record. Howard said, "Gus, Gladys says you expressed that beautifully, and she wants you to say it again." Scholle turned to her and said, "I'll hire you!"

The commission reviewed proposals from Detroit and Grand Rapids, then settled upon the Lansing Civic Center as the best place for the convention. Its executive director, Dr. William H. Combs of Michigan State University, recruited academicians, mostly from University of Michigan, Michigan State University and Wayne State University, to prepare eighteen background papers on the major constitutional issues with which the convention would have to deal. Sets were ready for the delegates when they convened. Suggested parliamentary procedures, based on rules used at conventions in other states, were also prepared.

Meanwhile Citizens for Michigan concentrated on publicizing the C.F.M. tax program and urging voters to choose forward-looking delegates. (The board officially endorsed the tax plan of Stoddard's committee in October, but it got nowhere in the next legislature.) When it appeared that Michigan's Republican politicos might take a solidly negative position on constitutional reform, Romney announced as a Republican candidate for Con-Con and resigned from the non-partisan group. Elected, he became one of the three vice-chairmen of the convention, and a year later he was elected governor of Michigan. Its primary purposes fulfilled, C.F.M. declined after the convention and disappeared after the new constitution was adopted in 1963.

When the 144 delegates—99 Republicans and 45 Democrats—met in Lansing on October 3, Howard Stoddard's work was substantially finished. His picture appeared on the front page of many newspapers, together with Swainson and a delegate to the 1908 constitutional convention. What the delegates produced was less than Stoddard and Romney had hoped for, but the constitution which was completed in mid-1962 eliminated some of the anachronisms in Michigan government, provided a more democratic system of legislative apportionment, and implicitly endorsed a flat rate income tax by prohibiting a graduated one. (The legislature did not get around to enacting such a tax until early in Governor Romney's second term. At that time Stoddard appeared before a joint hearing of the House and Senate Taxation Committees, endorsing most of the governor's plan but urging several modifications. According to the Detroit *Free Press*, March 3, 1967, one of his suggestions would grant an additional $1,000 standard deduction on each personal income tax return, "to assure that families living under federal poverty standards would pay no state income tax." In a statement reminiscent of his letter to Governor Williams nine years before, he also called a proposed increase in taxes on banks and similar institutions "unjustified.")

Charles Stoddard provides a poignant postscript to the record of his father's activities in the Con-Con movement. When the election of 1962 was over and Romney had defeated Swainson, Howard Stoddard went to see the outgoing governor. Knowing that Stoddard had supported his opponent, Swainson was surprised and touched. As Charles reconstructs the conversation, Swainson said that when important leaders in the Democratic Party wanted to make a campaign issue out of Romney's being a Mormon, he told them, "You can attack him in any other way, but I know something about his religion from my own experience, and if I'm going to be the candidate, you're just not going to bring it up."

Stoddard continued to participate in Michigan public life through the 1960s. On nomination by the Michigan Economic Development Commission, Governor Swainson appointed him "Michigan Industrial Ambassador" in May 1961. The Chamber of Commerce of Greater Lansing named him chairman of its Capitol Development Committee, in which role he worked with city and state officials in planning the $35 million "Compact Capitol Complex." Russell Fairles remembers that models of the development were for a time on the conference table in the M.N.B. board room. Stoddard participated with Governor Romney and others in the groundbreaking ceremonies in July 1964. Two years later he was elected a director of the Michigan State Chamber of Commerce, a post he held until illness forced his resignation.

When the legislature created the Michigan Higher Education Facilities Commission in 1964 to establish priorities for spending grants available for private and public institutions, Romney appointed Stoddard chairman. By the time he resigned in 1967 to accept another post, the commission had allocated approximately $50 million in federal funds. His last state position was on the TRIM (Total Research for Improvement Management) Committee, created by Romney to find ways to streamline government operations and reduce waste. Stoddard reluctantly left this activity in 1970.

When the Greater Lansing Chamber of Commerce awarded Howard Stoddard its Community Service Award on January 17, 1961, it was not primarily for his efforts on behalf of the state, but because of his contributions to the city. He had served as a division leader in campaigns for the Community Chest, the Y.M.C.A., and the United Hospital Fund. His bank had made a major contribution to the last-named drive, and Stoddard was a trustee of Sparrow Hospital. As president of the Lansing Country Club for two terms, he had cajoled and shamed the members into contributing materials and funds for a major enlarging and refurbishing of facilities, making the club a much more attractive social center for Lansing's business community. Early in the decade he had been chairman of the chamber's aviation committee, which helped promote the new Capital City Airport, and since 1956 he had been chairman of the city's Terminal Building committee and chairman and then member of the state's Airport Terminal Building board of control. (He resigned from both posts in 1965 to make time available for other public responsibilities.) The Stoddard Building and adjoining parking terrace and ramp were the most recent evidences of his commitment to his home town.

The *State Journal*, January 18, 1961 carried an engaging photo of Howard and Jennie at the award dinner. Not only is she smiling, but he is. The plaque read:

> In sincere appreciation of his keen vision and deep faith in the greatness of the future of Lansing, and for outstanding leadership, wholehearted support and unselfish giving of his time and substance for the betterment of our community at great personal sacrifice of time and energy.

When the Stoddards later built a summer place at Harbor Springs, he showed a similar concern for this small community on Lake Michigan. The record shows substantial contributions to its hospital fund and to the extension of its airport runway.

What has been previously described makes clear that Howard Stoddard's support of education went far beyond his enthusiastic attendance at Michigan State University football and basketball games. To him learning was a key not only to the success of individuals but to the wellbeing of a free society. He liked to quote Thomas Jefferson: "I know of no safe depository of the ultimate powers of the society but the people themselves, and if we think them not enlightened enough to exercise their control with a wholesome discretion, the remedy is not to take it from them, but to inform their discretion."

His commitment to education found a special focus in Michigan State, which grew from a regionally significant land grant college to one of the great American universities during the period that Michigan National Bank was following a parallel course. Charles Stoddard remembers that his father and M.S.U. President John A. Hannah had a lot in common; "both were entrepreneurs in traditional areas and visionaries in wanting to see their respective institutions grow." (The only child of Howard and Jennie to attend Michigan State, Charles was senior class president in 1965-1966.)

According to Dr. Hannah, Stoddard became interested in the school "when we were small and trying to lift ourselves by our bootstraps." The principal Michigan State account was carried at Michigan National for many years. When the university borrowed to build residence halls, Stoddard's bank set an example by buying many of the revenue bonds. During the 1959 financial crisis, when M.S.U. was threatened with payless paydays, Stoddard offered to advance $200,000 to the board of trustees. Other ways were found to meet the payroll, but the incident strengthened the tie of friendship between the presidents of the two institutions.

The broadcasting of Spartan football and baseball was an early and continuing link between bank and school. The M.N.B. football parties were another. They began with another sport and another place, when Charles Bohn began inviting the bank officers down to the Detroit Athletic Club for lunch before a baseball game. As the bank grew and the inclusion of wives enlarged the group, Bohn passed the responsibility to Howard and Jennie. The shift to Lansing—a more central location—and to football—Howard's favorite sport—followed naturally. For almost twenty years Jennie planned and reigned over these annual festivities, selecting the themes, arranging the catering, and reviewing the invitation list which was prepared at the bank. Except for the one time at the Stoddard home, already noted, the parties were held at the Lansing Country Club. Guests included university officials as well as bank officers, customers, prospective customers and their partners. Out of town groups sometimes came in chartered buses—an arrangement which simplified parking at the clubhouse and the game, and also kept the amount of after-game drop-in visiting at the house on Glenhaven Avenue within manageable proportions.

In 1958 Michigan National offered a "Pay-As-You-Learn Plan" to all Michigan students attending a college or university within the state. The plan permitted a student's family or sponsor to borrow for room, board, tuition and other fees, and repay in monthly installments over a six year period, two years beyond the normal graduation time. Advertisements noted that "an insurance policy is added as education and payment assurance." The plan was essentially an innovative packaging of a conventional consumer loan, but it opened up educational possibilities at a time when federally-guaranteed student loans were barely in the discussion stage.

Stoddard's willingness to speak to classes and conferences led to his becoming an honorary member of Beta Gamma Sigma, the M.S.U. business fraternity, in 1959. (When he talked with Jennie about retirement, Howard often expressed the hope that he might sometime teach a course on banking.) A year later the university named him Honorary Alumnus at the October homecoming banquet. He would have liked very much to be a member of the M.S.U. board of trustees, but under the old and new Michigan constitutions they were elected officials, and Stoddard had no interest in campaigning for the post. When George Romney passed up an opportunity to give him an interim appointment to a vacancy on the board, Stoddard expressed his disappointment to the governor.

John Hannah recalls that "on various occasions when we needed a little money for a needy student or a project which we could not finance with public money, I went to Howard Stoddard and it was always given quickly and without any ostentation whatever." Once he wrote to Stoddard acknowledging "your generosity last evening when you agreed to provide $400 to defray the cost of sending four Negro students to Atlanta tomorrow to attend the Martin Luther King funeral." Hannah remembers the M.N.B. president as "not only a good banker, but a good citizen and a good man."

It is not surprising that Stoddard's support should have been sought by other universities. He made contributions to several, including Stanford and Virginia's school—University of Michigan. Two Utah institutions also received his support, although he made clear that his primary commitment was to Michigan. The College of Business at the University of Utah—alma mater to Jennie and Howard Jr.—gave him its "Outstanding Achievement Award" in 1970. (Since 1975 Jennie has been a member of the university's

Alumni Council.) Stoddard accepted appointment to the National Advisory Committee of the Brigham Young University Development Program in 1958, and for a number of years he gave counsel as well as contributions to the L.D.S. Church-sponsored institution.

"The American Way," the address with which Howard Stoddard inaugurated the Executive Lecture series of the B.Y.U. School of Business, February 22, 1962, reflected his civic, business and personal philosophy as his career neared its peak. Using his observations of Russia to dramatize the differences between freedom and totalitarianism, he skillfully showed the limitations of the Soviet way while speaking warmly of the Russian people. To illustrate that "even under the Communistic system . . . people under the skin are remarkably alike," he told about Lydia, the tour guide. She was, he remembered, "a very attractive Russian, married, had one child, and she had what few Russian women had—a nice figure." She sensed that the American group "were more of a capitalistic type than many of the tourists," so she sought by arguments "to change our point of view about our way of living." Stoddard met the challenge with traditional gallantry—complimenting Lydia on her clothes, seating her at the table, opening the car door for her, and "treating her as we would a guest." So treated, "she responded just like human beings will always respond." There were tearful farewells at the airport, and in response to their sending her a recording of "My Fair Lady," she defied Intourist rules by sending Jennie an English translation of a Maxim Gorki volume, inscribed "To My Fair Lady. Lydia."

Given the phenomenal post-war recovery of Western Europe, Stoddard again expressed confidence that the examples of free enterprise "will so infect the Russian people that in due course, unless they make some mistakes beforehand, they will throw off the bondage . . . and emerge into this type of life which I think the Creator intended for all of us." Its essence, he believed, was in one of his most frequently-used quotations, "The American Creed":

> I do not choose to be a common man. It is my right to be uncommon if I can. I seek opportunity, not security. I do not wish to be a kept citizen, humbled and dulled by having the state look after me. I want to take the calculated risk, to dream, to build, to fail and to succeed. I refuse to barter incentive for a dole. I prefer the challenge of life to guaranteed existence, the thrill of fulfillment to the stale calm of Utopia. I will not trade freedom for beneficience nor my dignity for a handout. It is my heritage to think and act for myself, to enjoy the benefits of my creation, and to face the world boldly and say, "This I have done."

CHAPTER 17

# Husband, Father and Grandfather

There were three Howard Stoddards—the banker-businessman, the churchman and the husband-father-grandfather. In his system of values, family came first, church second and bank third. In the allocation of his time, however, the bank and associated activities were given what they required, and these claims usually came first. The church was given a pre-planned share, and this commitment was scrupulously kept. The family received almost all of what was left—and there were times when Jennie and the children felt that this was not enough. Capable, efficient and very hard working, Stoddard found many ways to multiply his talents, but he could not extend the day.

Howard Stoddard also had three images. Those who knew only the banker saw him as aloof, tightly organized, and sometimes formidable; that he had a concerned and charitable aspect was known to many, but it was not on display. Those who knew only the churchman saw him as reserved, disciplined, persuasive in pulpit, classroom and council chamber, and more generous with his means than with his time. Only those who knew the family man saw a warm, affectionate, unbuttoned Howard Stoddard, and it took him a long time to learn to relax with his own children. Stanford's wife, Ann, confesses that her primary reaction to her prospective father-in-law was one of awe until shortly before the marriage, when he took her on a trip to Utah to get acquainted with Stanford's kinfolks and heritage.

Relatively few people came to know the informal, loving side of Howard Stoddard because, in the first place, he was shy, and in the second place, he had no time to waste. People were his business, and those who dealt with him face to face in a working context almost always learned to respect and admire him. People were also his concern, and many who sought his counsel—associates in business and public life, employees, fellow Latter-day Saints, and social acquaintances—felt their respect mellow into affection. But people were not his diversion. Unlike the gregarious Jennie, Stoddard was not eager for social interaction; the little time which duty left unallocated he preferred to spend with a book, a radio or TV program, or a motion picture. Few people besides family members found their way into this unstructured portion of his life.

Jennie Creer Stoddard was an indispensable part of Stoddard's public and private lives. The initial division of responsibility—his for the livelihood and hers for the home—was maintained through their life together. However, in the patriarchal tradition which has persisted in Mormon culture, he had the last word—or at least the decisive word—on family matters when consensus did not naturally emerge. The analytical powers and quiet decisiveness which enabled Stoddard to dominate boards of directors generally prevailed in the family circle, too.

Howard once said to a friend: "After I married Jennie and I'd lived with her for a couple of years, I realized one thing. I was either going to have to get Jennie to cut down on her spending or I was going to have to make a lot more money, and I decided that it would be easier to make more money." But Jennie was scarcely extravagant, even by Utah Mormon standards, and he soon made enough to meet this side of her needs. What she really enjoyed was meeting people and doing things. Howard Jr. remembers the many times that business people were invited to dinner at the Stoddard homes in Grosse Pointe and East Lansing. His mother "always handled things extremely well." As the scope of entertaining increased, buffets and receptions were sometimes catered, but there were themes to be selected, menus, decorations and entertainment to be arranged, and always there was the exciting challenge of helping everyone have a good time.

Jennie was also responsible for much of Stoddard's social circulation outside the home. "If it weren't for her," Stanford recalls, "he would have spent more evenings reading or doing something like that." Stoddard once joked to Philip Ordway, "If there was a party, Jennie was going to be there." Even when Stoddard went reluctantly, however, his well-informed conversation and increasing prestige insured that he would be amiably engaged in the activities. He actually enjoyed parties, according to his family, but they all agree with Stanford that "he was not one to organize one." Especially a bridge party. One of Jennie's favorite diversions was to Stoddard rather a waste of time. When drawn into a game, he played by hunch rather than rules, and Jennie acknowledges that she did not enjoy playing with him.

Both community standing and personal inclination drew Jennie Stoddard into a variety of civic activities. She was one of the first female members of the Detroit Economic Club, and at one time or another in Lansing she served on the boards of the American Red Cross, the YWCA and the World Service Council. She shared her husband's interest in Lansing's hospital facilities and participated in many volunteer programs. (For her contributions "to the community, to the arts and to the University," she was designated an "Honorary Alumnus" of Michigan State University in 1976.)

Stoddard liked nice things, but he was too busy to pay much attention to them. The homes in Salt Lake City, Grosse Pointe and East Lansing suited his economic situation at the time they were occupied, but he had no interest later on in moving into a mansion just because he could afford it. Indeed, he afterward chided himself for having taken money out of his bank holdings to build the home on Glenhaven Avenue in 1946, because the investments were earning more than it would have cost him to build with borrowed funds. At Jennie's initiative decorative touches and a little more space were added after a while, but the home remained basically unchanged—comfortable and unostentatious—to the present. The paneling and other trim, selected and installed under Stoddard's personal supervision, recall his life-long enthusiasm for fine wood and quality workmanship; the curving banister for the entry stairway was handcrafted by an immigrant from Oberammergau. (He chose his wearing apparel and his office furnishings with the same care. His wardrobe was conservative and of excellent quality, and he made closet space for new suits by giving away old ones long before they showed wear.)

Growing up in Howard and Jennie Stoddard's family meant enjoying the material benefits of pleasant homes and a rising standard of living, the affection of very busy parents, and the example of lives organized around religious commitment.

Howard Jr., Virginia, Stanford and Charles all grew up feeling that they were financially secure but not exempt from the obligation to work. "Cut your hair and cut the lawn" is one of Howard's early recollections. All four took summer jobs at the bank at fifteen or sixteen, and they were expected to meet Michigan National performance standards. Charles, who always looked younger than his years, is the subject of an anecdote—possibly apocryphal—which his family enjoys retelling:

> A brusque and hurried businessman approached the teller's station and eyed the small and earnest-looking teen-ager on the other side of the counter.
>
> "Where's the teller, young fella?" he asked.
>
> "I'm the teller, sir."

"If you're the teller, then your Dad must be the president of this bank."

"Yes, sir. He is."

The Stoddard children came to know early both the obligations and rewards of success in the business world. Their father described them years later in a letter to Virginia:

> Our lives, for the most part, have been lived in what I would term the executive class. This is a group who have the responsibility for running business and other enterprises. Their work is never done when the offices close at night, and their minds are constantly occupied with planning, making decisions, assembling and evaluating information. In short, they live in an entirely different world than those engaged in day to day routine. Generally they have money and a higher standard of living than others. However, because of the very nature of their activities they live a stimulating existence. When one has been exposed to this atmosphere it is quite difficult to go back to the relatively carefree life of the average person.

As their mother learned, so the young Stoddards learned that for their father "the work is never done when the office closes at night." He was often out of town—meetings with boards and officers in the branch cities and Detroit, lobbying in Washington, and attending conventions and conferences all over the country. When he was in town he often worked evenings and week-ends, or brought home a briefcase full of papers for review in the privacy of his study. Howard Jr. remembers him typing his own working papers for pending meetings. Sometimes he had to pull out of social engagements, sending Jennie alone to make excuses for him. (Such occasions, the children recall, sometimes produced tension, but explosions were rare.) Several of Stoddard's close associates recall his acknowledging that "there were choices that were tough to make, in terms of family or bank." Particularly in the Detroit and early Lansing years the father role was sacrificed, "with some pain to him."

Stoddard himself was a conscientious but irregular golfer—about like the basketball player of earlier years and the tennis and badminton player in Grosse Pointe. For health's sake he tried to shoot a round weekly at the Lansing Country Club, but he had no regular foursome and often played with whoever happened to be at the club at the time he happened to be free. He enjoyed a small bet—never more than he could afford. Short vacations in Florida during the Bohn-Stoddard years saw him more regularly on the golf course, and when the children participated in these trips, they shared some of the outings.

Some of the best times of communication, from a family point of view, were the supper hours at the homes on Grand River and Glenhaven. When he was not out of town or he and Jennie were not committed to a dinner somewhere, Stoddard made a conscientious effort to take his evening meal at home, and he was often successful. Supper was punctually at six, it was always in the dining room—Stoddard took almost all of his meals in the dining room—and it provided many teaching moments. "There was much conversation about business . . . as the boys grew older," Virginia remembers, but there were other topics. "I can recall Dad saying at times how incredible he found men who cheated on their income tax who were otherwise intelligent and decent people." Apart from the regular blessing on the food, there was little dinner-time attention to the theological side of religion, but church assignments and responsibilities were frequently mentioned and the children early learned the importance which Howard Stoddard assigned to faith and Christian service.

Jennie recollects how he would use human problems which he encountered in the bank to inculcate the work ethic and a sense of *noblesse oblige*. "There's no such thing as a free lunch," he would remind the children, even for the poor or infirm. "Somebody's going to pay for it." Those fortunate people who are in a position to share must be willing. "So, it's up to you people to make money, to pay your tithing and to give to charity," was Stoddard's counsel to the youngsters around the dinner table.

Michigan National Bank was an unseen guest at many Stoddard suppers. "Banking was his life," says Jennie, "and so he would come home and talk about good loans and bad ones, incidents of people not being fair with one another, the difficulty of making judgments, and the importance of exercising care." Much of the conversation, of course, was between the parents, with the children picking up what they could. Charles remembers hearing his father talk about inflation for a long time before he learned the meaning of the word. Stoddard was tight-lipped about serious personal worries, so when he came home one day with word that a car dealer who had been foreclosed was suing the bank for $50 million, his children knew there was no cause for alarm.

Stoddard took it for granted that his sons would follow him into the bank, though he never mandated that choice. They spent a lot of time, mostly after hours and week-ends, in one or another of the M.N.B. offices at an age when, according to Stanford, "it all looked about the same to us. There were desks, files, forms to fill out, and a certain amount of machinery." He adds, "I don't think we really understood the functions until we actually started working as stock boys and then tellers." They got into the spirit of the business earlier, however, if one of Gladys' anecdotes is to be credited. After a discussion of how banks loan out the money which is in savings accounts, Stanford said to her, "If anyone comes in wanting to borrow $25, tell him this is Bud Stoddard's money and it is very important that he pay it back." When the children began working, their father encouraged them to borrow to buy bank stock, taking five, ten or fifteen years to retire the notes.

Holidays were times of happy family memories. As some of Jennie's sisters and their families settled in Michigan, the Thanksgiving get-togethers on Glenhaven Avenue took on some of the extended family characteristics which Jennie remembered from Utah and which Stoddard had never really known because of his father's early death. H. Perry Driggs, Jennie's nephew and later a Michigan National executive, recalls "Uncle Howard" as a warm and involved participant in these festivities. Christmases were conventional. Many years the entire family went to Harbor Springs, where cutting their own tree and skiing were added enjoyments. Stoddard's boyhood hobbies gave him an advantage over many fathers. According to Howard Jr., "he could handle any mechanical toy very well." The electric train which appeared one year was a source of delight to father and sons, though both Howard Jr. and Stanford remember that they did not fully share his zeal for keeping toys and tools in order. Jennie was an excellent cook, and even when she had help the holiday feasts bore her imprimatur.

During the early married years, Jennie Stoddard devoted virtually full time to homemaking and parental tasks. Later she had the assistance of live-in help, which permitted her to develop her potential as Michigan National's unofficial vice president in charge of social relations. Howard Jr., Virginia and Stanford remember Virginia Farrell—"Vergie"—well; she was with them during the later Grosse Pointe and early East Lansing years. Charles's memories are of Sue Hankins, who lived with the Stoddards until he went away to boarding school at sixteen. Jennie was also freer to accompany Stoddard on business trips and to travel with him to exotic places.

In later years Stoddard found that he had more time for his family, but by then the children were grown and the association took a different form. A very lovely summer retreat was built in 1962 at Harbor Springs, on Lake Michigan's Little Traverse Bay. Stanford's family already had a house there, and one for Virginia's family soon followed. Here three generations of

Stoddards played together and close friends shared informal, unprogrammed activities. Here Stoddard golfed and fished with the grandchildren, and drove his Chris Craft in the bay. Sometimes the family talked to a tape recorder about their memories, or blessings, and then laughed together as they listened to the playback. (In earlier years do-it-yourself recording sessions were held in Grosse Pointe and East Lansing, but neither plastic records nor tapes have survived.)

Stoddard's impatience with disorder and with illness affected his family relations to some extent. While neither corporal punishment nor financial penalties figured prominently in the disciplining of the young Stoddards, they learned early about the patterns of deportment of which he disapproved, and either precept or example kept them from the more serious forms of deviant behavior. The day-to-day disciplining by reproof or loss of privileges was largely Jennie's responsibility, since she was around when things happened and did not belong to the "wait till your father gets home" school of parenting. As for illness, Stoddard could be counted upon in health crises like Jennie's one-time ulcer. But he resented the mundane ailments which reduce productivity and upset dispositions, and so, according to Jennie, they were not much discussed. Apart from nasal polyps which required periodic and very painful excision—stoically borne—Howard had excellent health until his sixty-seventh year. When illness finally came to him—and stayed—he had difficulty coming to terms with this new reality.

Growing up as they did in "the executive class," the four young Stoddards took college for granted, but the choice of schools was not dictated by their parents. Stoddard expected academic excellence from his children, beginning in the elementary grades, and according to Jennie he may have pushed them a little too hard. Howard Jr. was drafted into the army right after high school and spent two depressing years with the United States occupation forces in Italy; then he gained his baccalaureate degree at the University of Utah, much to Jennie's delight. Virginia went for two years to Kingswood, a boarding high school in a Detroit suburb, because some of her friends were going there. Then she completed an undergraduate program in elementary education at University of Michigan. Stanford participated in R.O.T.C. while taking a banking course at U. of M., and his subsequent military stint in Korea kindled an enduring interest in Oriental—especially Japanese—art and culture.

Charles grew up practically as an only child, with a busy father who is still remembered in grandfatherly terms. He spent his last three high school years at Cranbrook, the boys' counterpart of Kingswood School, and then went to Michigan State and Harvard Business School. A Kingswood girl named Jan Ordway became his wife before the journey to Cambridge. Jennie and Howard spent Thanksgiving holidays with them there, and Howard took the opportunities to get acquainted with several Harvard business school professors. Jan and Charles also accompanied his parents on a nostalgic trip to the Northwest, visiting Howard's birthplace and the locales where his grandfather and father built the first Stoddard fortune.

Vacation travel produced some of the most pleasant memories for Jennie and the children, partly because of the interesting places visited and partly because Stoddard found it easier to share himself with them when he was out of town. All of the children traveled to Europe during or soon after college, it being their parents' view that exposure to the lands of their forebears was an important part of their education.

During the 1930s and 1940s the family traveled usually by car, and the explorations of the scenic West and the old haunts in Oregon were associated with annual visits with Jennie's family in Salt Lake City. Stoddard enjoyed the Creers, and he did not mind being known as Jennie Creer's husband among many Utahns. (With the passage of time his prominence in banking led to interviews by Salt Lake *Tribune* and *Deseret News* writers, and the reputation as a forward-looking businessman which he had begun to build at National Copper Bank gave him an independent identity in the region.) Since a month in Salt Lake City was far more time than Howard could take from Guardian Depositors Corporation, the Bohn-Stoddard project, or Michigan National, he usually made the journey one way with the family and spent a few days in Utah in connection with the trip.

As Jennie's brothers and sisters left home, there was plenty of room for all the visiting Michigan Stoddards in the John Preston Creer home on Gilmer Drive, and Howard Jr., Virginia and Bud enjoyed a particularly fine relationship with their grandparents. In time the Salt Lake City home of Jennie's brother Frank, and his wife Sara, became the central gathering place for the Creer clan, with family parties and Sunday evening open houses to keep kinship and friendship ties close. The Cottonwood Canyon home of Aunt LaReta and Uncle Richard Madsen and the Ogden residence of Aunt Lucille and Uncle Arch Webb also figure prominently in the children's memories of the annual Utah visits.

Stoddard's father, of course, was only a historical figure to the children, and Ellen Stoddard died when Howard Jr. was only twelve years old. There were visits with her in Utah and she also came to Grosse Pointe. Jennie recalls her learning to type on Stoddard's typewriter, because others took care of the housework and she had to be doing something.

Another kind of family travel reflected Howard Stoddard's resolve to spend more time with his children than his daily routine permitted. Often he took one or another of them with him to out-of-town church meetings, while Jennie remained at home with the others. The conversation on such drives was sometimes desultory, Stoddard having no special talent for communicating with teens and pre-teens, and usually there was time to kill while he was in conference with local church leaders. But he listened to the concerns and enthusiasms of his traveling companions, and all of them remember listening with pride and profit to the thoughtful, forceful, spiritual sermons which he delivered, sometimes to groups of not more than two or three dozen.

When the Stoddard youngsters were taken to a business meeting in a metropolitan area like Washington or New York, Stoddard suggested activities of family interest but left Jennie in charge of how the time was spent. Virginia remembers seeing the New York World's Fair. Charles recalls one trip on which he saw more Saks Fifth Avenue fashions than FAO Schwartz toys. A play or concert in the evening gave the children early exposure to some of the "finer things of life."

As the bank prospered the range of travel broadened. Some of it was definitely business-related—a flying trip to Venezuela in 1952 with Waldo, Howard Jr. and Eugene Wanger, and a journey to Rome with Jennie in 1962 to attend an international conference of bankers. Always Stoddard was the keen observer. Jennie recalls him saying after the trip to Moscow and Leningrad: "If I lived in Russia I would probably want to belong to the Communist Party to know what is going on." On his sixtieth birthday, when he and Jennie were en route around the world, lunch in Bangkok was taken with the resident managers of Bank of America and another financial institution. In Nigeria a Michigan State University aid project at a local university was naturally on the itinerary.

After three delightful weeks with Jennie in Japan, Stoddard wrote to his brother John in May 1957: "Once a year we take our vacation by flying to some place in the world. . . . We hope in this way, if we have the good fortune to live a few more years, to see most of the world." The plan was not fully maintained, but there were trips to the Soviet Union, southern Africa, South America and more than once to Europe and Japan. On November 1, 1961, the Stoddards were on a holiday trip around the world, and the taxi ride that evening from the airport to the Grand Hotel through the squalor of downtown Calcutta made his sixtieth birthday unforgettable. (A bank-sponsored luncheon, arranged as a surprise, brought senior bank officers, directors and family members together on the top floor of the new Stoddard Building on December 22, 1961, for a belated but memorable birthday celebration.)

It would not do to be completely out of touch with the bank, and Gladys tells of frantic efforts to contact Stoddard in Spain, on a Hawaiian cruise, and when he was touring military installations at the time Charles Bohn died. The first time the Stoddards planned to go to Europe, in 1949, Bohn became ill; so Stoddard sent Jennie, Virginia and Stanford ahead, along with Jennie's mother, and he joined them later in Paris. (Having not too long before seen Europe in uniform, Howard Jr. elected not to go.) This was a particularly memorable trip because it took Stoddard back to the scenes of his mission in Germany—now so changed by war. Years later the press of business led Stoddard to send Jennie off without him to Australia and New Zealand. When he then sent word that he could not join her, she came home. "The trip was over for me," she recalls. On most of their trips, however, he managed to content himself with daily telephone contacts with the Lansing office, and with keeping in touch with American economic conditions through visits to banks in places like Tokyo, New Delhi and Cape Town.

Bank, civic and church responsibilities brought Stoddard and Jennie into amiable social relations with many people, but relatively few couples found their way into the circle of close friends. Of Jennie's family, brother Frank and his wife, Sarah, lived in Michigan for a while, and her sisters Clara (Mrs. H. Perry Driggs) and Mary (Mrs. Aaron M. "Tink" Shaver) settled permanently in Battle Creek. Only Waldo and his wife, Winifred, among Stoddard's family, were near enough for much social interaction. The periodic golf reunions of the Stoddard brothers were usually stag affairs.

The parents of Stanford's wife, Ann, and Charles's wife, Jan were already friends of the Stoddards before they became in-laws, but the family connections strengthened the ties. Simeon and Dorothea Dietrich lived in East Lansing, where he was a hardware company executive. Philip and Martha Ordway's home was Battle Creek, where he headed Union Pump Company and served on the local Michigan National advisory board. Albert and Marian Redmond were Stoddard companions on many occasions. Al was a frequent golf partner in Stoddard's later years and both the Redmonds accompanied Jennie on the interrupted trip to Australia.

Stoddard was not a prolific social correspondent, preferring to maintain contact with Jennie and the children by phone and writing to others only when there was something specific to write about. He called Jennie almost daily when they were apart, and there were no extended separations after the R.F.C. days to generate letters. To Jennie was left the responsibility of telling absent children what family and friends were doing; Stoddard's occasional letters combined observations about happenings at the bank and in the world with fatherly counsel. (Since all the young Stoddards received allowances sufficient for their collegiate needs, as their father in his day had done, there was no need for financial appeals and admonitory responses.) When Howard Jr. and Stanford went into military service, Virginia left home after graduating from college, and Charles went to Harvard, they corresponded with the parents, but of the letters which came from their father, very few have been preserved. Howard Jr. remembers being reminded that even in an uncongenial military environment he should not forget his heritage and the moral standards he had been taught. Stanford received similar advice in Korea. Charles remembers the blessing which his father gave him after the first tough semester at Cambridge more than he recalls the content of correspondence.

From letters to Virginia come glimpses of the concerns which Howard Stoddard felt for his children. Responding to her happy report of pledging a sorority at Ann Arbor, he offered congratulations, then added:

> However, the part of your letter which we appreciate the most was the expressions of regret and sympathy for your friend who was not pledged. . . . If one learns in life to be humble and cheerful and undeterred by failure, then one has acquired real character. It is indeed an art to learn how to live properly with one's associates and yet maintain your standards and basic principles.

Among the virtues he mentioned on occasion were gratitude—"one of the finest qualities in the world, and there are so few individuals who really know what it means"—and, of course, industry:

> I am very pleased that you are again busy in a field which you enjoy. There is nothing worse than idleness. . . .
>
> . . . keep yourself busy as that is the best formula I know for happiness.
>
> Your letters indicate that you are very busy and happy. . . . The one always leads to the other, so I am glad you make full use of your time.

That the children find happiness through families of their own was a concern which Stoddard and Jennie shared. A thoughtful letter to Virginia in 1957 declares:

> Like most parents, our greatest joy will come when our own children are happily married and have established homes and careers of their own. We cannot and would not select your companions for life and eternity but we do know if they are honest, loyal, intelligent and ambitious, a wonderful future can be built upon such a foundation. Love is built upon so many different qualities that it is impossible to define. However, I do believe that over the years, your mother and I have found in each other as true a love as can come to husband and wife.

An impressive tribute to Jennie occurs elsewhere in the same letter. Having reviewed the good fortune which the Stoddard family had enjoyed in Michigan and having credited many people with contributing to this outcome, Stoddard noted:

> Mother has been extremely helpful and I know we could never have succeeded without her vital participation. She has a wonderful gift of friendship and instinctively draws people toward her. We may have had our small differences, as do all humans, especially those who live so close together, but your mother's energy and vitality have been a constant source of help and inspiration to me, especially in some of the trying days thru which we have passed.

A year later he wrote: "In the years to come we want all of you to feel that our home is your home, your problems are our problems, and that we will continue the wonderful association you have observed in your mother and her own family. . . ."

Stoddard was somewhat unconventional among Mormons in his views on the importance of his children marrying within the church fold. He wrote to Virginia in 1954 (and he gave similar counsel to his sons):

> The first thing to look for . . . is character. Then intelligence, ambition and consideration. If you can find these attributes in a young man who is a member of the Church, then by all means encourage his attentions. On the other hand, do not withdraw from consideration of other young men who have these qualifications, for with determination and patience on your part, the gospel can be brought into such lives. . . .

Howard Jr. never married. Virginia's marriage took her away from Michigan, but Stanford and Charles brought girls fom Michigan backgrounds—families known to Howard and Jennie through the bank—into the

Stoddard family and, in time, the Stoddards' church. Stoddard courted Stanford's fiance, Ann Dietrich, after the engagement, and Charles' Janet Ordway long before. Both came to love their father-in-law deeply, and as the grandchildren came along, the kind of extended family which Stoddard so much desired began to take shape. There were seven grandchildren prior to his death —Elizabeth Ann (Betsy), Stanford Dietrich and Simeon Dietrich Stoddard; Paul Stoddard, James Stoddard and Jennifer Lynn Peery; and Stephen Ordway Stoddard. Howard James II, Deborah Lynn and Philip Mark Stoddard have known only stories about their grandfather. Only the oldest of the new generation got to know their grandfather well before illness slowed him down and then took him away. They remember his affectionate concern, even if they found fishing with him at a stocked pond near Harbor Springs only moderately exciting. Virginia's sons, Paul and Jim Peery, remember that he smiled readily in the family group pictures and that he sometimes joked with them; one has observed that their grandfather had "a dumb sense of humor, like Uncle Chuck." They remember the birthday gifts of a dollar for each year of age, and the savings accounts which were opened with deposits of $100 when they were born. Subsequent saving was up to them.

The grandchildren, too, knew the three Howard Stoddards. They saw him in his bank, with its big vault and the $100 and $1000 bills which were kept in it. They saw him in church, a speaker whom even young teen-agers found easy to listen to. They saw him preside at many family gatherings—with Jennie sharing the grandparenting responsibilities—and to them he was neither aloof nor formidable.

CHAPTER 18

# Churchman

Howard Stoddard once wrote to his good Mormon friend, Henry D. Moyle: "I often speculate upon the beliefs which I may have had if not born in the Church and try to place myself in the position of my many friends."

To speculate on how different Stoddard might have been if he had not been born and reared a member of The Church of Jesus Christ of Latter-day Saints is, of course, idle now. He was so born, and there appears to have been no time in his life when he seriously questioned the basic affirmations of the Mormon faith. He believed in God the Father, His Son, Jesus Christ, and the Holy Ghost. He believed that the full gospel of Christ was restored to man in the early nineteenth century through the prophet-founder of the church, Joseph Smith. He accepted the scriptural authority of the Bible, the Book of Mormon and modern prophecies, and he believed in the continuity of divine revelation. He believed in the eternal nature of religious covenants, including the covenant of marriage. He believed that men and women are children of God, blessed with freedom of choice and capable of achieving eternal exaltation by a combination of faith and obedience. He accepted the taboos and obligations of conduct associated with being "a good Latter-day Saint." He faithfully contributed time, advice, and a tenth of his income. He acknowledged shortcomings, but he never challenged the standards by which he expected his own life to be eventually measured.

Family and Mormon friends perceived Stoddard as a believing and generally conforming member of his church. During most of his adult life he was a high priest in the lay priesthood organization, and he regularly attended Sunday morning meetings of the quorum to which he belonged. As soon as his sons reached the minimum priesthood age of twelve, he took them with him to their group meetings. The family usually attended Sunday School together, with both parents teaching classes at times. The fast and testimony meeting on the first Sunday of each month was one of Howard's favorite meetings, and he was often among the spontaneous speakers. As for the balance of the Mormon Sabbath, he followed his own father in taking a somewhat latitudinarian view. He spent occasional Sunday evenings in his office, and he was not averse to a family outing, or social event after the morning's religious duties had been attended to.

As noted earlier, religious instruction in the Stoddard home was more by example and by reinforcement of church learning than by formal indoctrination. Neither Howard nor Jennie inclined toward piousness, but at times of crisis—when Howard Jr. and Stanford were going into military service, or when one of the family was seriously ill or troubled—Stoddard would administer a father's blessing or call in other priesthood holders to help with the ordinance of anointing and blessing. Detroit Stake President and M.B.N.A. executive Edwin B. Jones remembers the importance Stoddard assigned to the several blessings that he received during his own illnesses.

Howard Stoddard believed both in the effectiveness and the appropriateness of prayer. He often called on Jones for invocations at board meetings and other gatherings of bank personnel. M.N.B. Director Robert Gerholz, himself an exponent of Christian idealism in the business community through such projects as Religious Heritage of America, Inc., recalls numerous occasions when he and Howard prayed together at the beginning or the end of some shared activity. Their relationship became particularly close during the years of Stoddard's illness. (Later Gerholz sponsored Jennie's appointment to the board of Religious Heritage of America.)

Since most of Howard and Jennie's friends and almost all of Stoddard's business associates were non-Mormon, a *modus vivendi* was developed early. Religious differences were not flaunted, and if there were impulses to proselyte, they were well controlled. Everyone who knew Stoddard at all well knew that he was a Mormon, but they also knew that he was at pains not to make them uncomfortable about that fact. John Carton recalls how surprised he was on an out-of-town business trip with Howard when, returning to the hotel after a very hard day, Stoddard said, "I think you need a drink." He readily agreed, and when he had ordered Stoddard asked for something called a "horseneck"—which turned out to be ginger ale and lemon. A non-smoker and non-drinker, Stoddard tolerated many a smoke-filled room, even when he was the man in charge, and he nursed a soft drink through many a cocktail hour.

Arnold Van Zanten, who came up through the ranks in the Battle Creek office, remembers Stoddard more as "a fine Christian man" than as a sectarian Mormon. He had a temper, but it was rarely displayed and then without pyrotechnics. He disliked swearing and very rarely indulged. George Pierson, Joseph Shaw and others recall that his tolerance had limits. He once had an employee discharged for pursuing M.N.B. women on company time. On the other hand, when another officer negotiated a loan with a particularly high rate of interest, Pierson remembers Stoddard saying: "No one should have to pay that kind of interest. We're not in the business to gouge people."

Stoddard had no scruples for or against hiring fellow-Mormons at the banks. He knew Edwin Jones as an M.S.U. graduate student and clerk of Detroit Stake before he offered him a post in the Detroit bank. However, he resisted suggestions from people that he hire them just because they were members of his church, and he had no double standard for bank customers. When one of the branch officers asked his advice on a loan, mentioning that the applicant was a Mormon, Stoddard asked if the loan would have been approved under other circumstances. Told no, he said that the judgment should stand.

When people asked Stoddard "What is your basic organizational technique?" Stanford says that his answer was usually to this effect:

> I draw from my religious teachings, because that technique is the best that's ever been shown mankind. . . . You may be talking about debits and credits rather than souls, but the principle is the same. . . . Suddenly something tells you, when something is proposed that you know is immoral, "I'm not going to do that because it's immoral." You don't ask for a memorandum on whether you can get away with it. You don't ask if it is 60-40, or 51-49. You just say to yourself that it's immoral. Let's forget about it and go on. . . .

By virtue of the Stoddard and Creer family backgrounds, his own prominence in Michigan Latter-day Saint circles, and his stature in American banking, Howard Stoddard had ready access to the leaders of his church and enjoyed close personal relations with some of them. Two church presidents whose combined tenure spanned most of Howard's adult life—Heber J. Grant and David O. McKay—knew and respected him. When the major decision was made in 1960 to withdraw the church from active institutional involvement in Utah banking, Stoddard was one of those whose advice was sought. The course ultimately taken coincided with his recommendations. (This was the same time Michigan National Bank became one of the regional depositories for church funds.)

Given the reliance of the Mormon church on lay leadership, Stoddard was a logical prospect for appointment to a position of considerable administrative responsibility. He decided early, however, that building and directing his banks was incompatible with such an assignment, and those who might have called him to be a bishop, stake president or higher official did not challenge that decision. He supported the church officers who presided over him, and he conscientiously fulfilled the callings which he held, but his institutional service was largely confined to Sundays. In addition to participation on building committees and frequent teaching and speaking assignments, he compiled the following record of church appointments:

| | |
|---|---|
| Missionary in Germany | 1920-1923 |
| President, New York City Branch | 1927-1928 |
| Alternate High Councilman, Liberty Stake | 1930-1933 |
| President, Detroit Branch | 1936-1937 |
| High Councilman, Detroit Stake | 1952-1962 |

Howard Stoddard made his primary contributions to the L.D.S. church in Michigan as builder, adviser and teacher.

From his boyhood, when his father helped LaGrande Ward to build a fine new chapel, Howard was convinced that constructing or acquiring suitable meeting houses was an important part of building the Kingdom of God on earth. He was embarrassed by some of the facilities used in Germany in the early 1920s, and he scored a notable coup as branch president in New York by renting Carnegie Hall as a Sunday morning home for the small Mormon congregation. (Howard Jr. was christened in this ornate auditorium.) Thereafter he was constantly looking for ways to build adequate chapels more economically, and he had no hesitancy about sharing his ideas with those who might be in a position to implement them. In 1944, while the small Lansing Branch was still meeting in the local Y.M.C.A., he sent Apostle Albert E. Bowen a picture of the early American chapel in Henry Ford's Greenfield Village, pointing out that the New England background of Joseph Smith and Brigham Young made this type of architecture particularly appropriate. He added:

> It has always seemed logical to me that in many cities with populations of 50,000 and over, small initial groups of fifty or more members, if provided with attractive chapels of modest size, could carry on a proselyting activity that would be more effective than our existing system. Naturally, if branches grew to sufficient size, larger churches with more facilities would be required, but the pressing need, as I see it, would be the construction of numerous small chapels having a physical beauty and appeal which would outwardly reflect, in some measure, the beauty and character of the Gospel.

In Stoddard's church-related correspondence are "thank you" messages from Willard Marriott, then president of Washington, D.C., Stake, and Paul C. Andrus, head of the Northern Far East Mission. The first acknowledges receipt of plans of the new Lansing chapel, which might be adaptable for Alexandria, Virginia. The second expresses appreciation for help from Stoddard and Henry Moyle in expediting the church building program in Tokyo. He and Moyle were in agreement on the importance of buildings to the Mormon missionary program, and they spent many hours discussing how to finance and expedite such construction.

Stoddard saw himself as part of the answer. As Stanford expresses it:

> From the moment my father came to Michigan, he felt that the housing of the church population was one of the most important aspects of helping the church to grow and develop, and every hour that he spent in the rented halls and the places without any church building, he was figuring out how we eventually could see a chapel there. . . .

He began, naturally, in Lansing. The first Mormon-built meeting house in Michigan was dedicated there in 1951, after a fund-raising drive in which Stoddard played a major part as donor and promoter. Its New England design, too, reflected his input. He strongly believed that meeting houses should reflect regional architecture and special local needs, and he frequently argued for more flexibility in adapting standard church designs to the Michigan scene. As in his contests with federal and state banking authorities, sometimes he won and sometimes he lost, but always he persisted. When headquarters criteria would not permit church sharing in the purchase of upholstered pews for the Detroit Stake Center, he paid the additional cost himself. A decade later he did the same for the lovely wood paneling in the Lansing Stake Center. At the very last, when Salt Lake authorities were reluctant to purchase an existing Protestant chapel in Petoskey to serve the small branch in the Harbor Springs area, he created a *fait accompli* by buying the building himself and then persuading the church to accept it.

Charles Stoddard vividly remembers the occasion when his father took Apostle Moyle to look at a piece of property on East Lansing's Saginaw Boulevard. It was available, and Stoddard saw it as an ideal site for a future stake center. He wanted the church to purchase it, even though such a building would not be needed for several years. As Charles describes the conversation, Stoddard argued:

> Bureaucratic procedures would require someone coming out from Salt Lake City and taking a couple of months, and he was afraid that if they didn't move quickly it would surely be gone. Brother Moyle said, "Howard, you go ahead and buy it this afternoon." And he went ahead and bought it that afternoon, and that was that.

Edwin Jones, who visited many church construction sites with Howard, provides another vignette. He recalls that Stoddard kept a cloth in his car and carefully wiped off his shoes at the end of the inspection tour.

At the heart of Howard Stoddard's monumental participation in building Mormon chapels in Michigan, however, lay a challenge program which was first worked out for the Lansing Branch. To appreciate it requires understanding the church building program, which is directed and largely funded from Salt Lake City. Where the membership is scattered and organized into missions and branches, as was Michigan until 1952, the local membership is required to raise 20 percent of the cost of a building, and the church provides the balance out of general tithes and other income. Where numbers permit stakes and wards, the formula becomes 30 percent and 70 percent. Most of the building projects in which Howard participated after 1952 fell into this category.

When Sylvan D. Wittwer, then president of the Lansing Branch and later bishop and stake president, approached Howard Stoddard in 1950 about serving with the building committee, Stoddard offered to match any amount that the rest of the local membership would raise. "He kept his word," Wittwer affirms, and he repeated the process with every chapel built in Michigan until his death. He further contributed substantially to stake centers built in Detroit, East Lansing and Grand Rapids, to the Washington, D.C., Temple, and to sundry welfare projects and other undertakings. (When his name found its way onto the mailing list of a non-Mormon congregation in Lansing, he surprised the sponsors of that building campaign with a check for $1000.)

There is a record in Howard Stoddard's own hand which bears the heading "Church Buildings." It lists payments from 1950 to 1970 and names the projects helped each year—Lansing, Saginaw, Ann Arbor, Flint, Battle Creek, Detroit, Grand Rapids, Kalamazoo, St. Joseph, Traverse City, Jackson, Roseville, Muskegon, Midland, Petosky and Washington, some in connection with more than one building. The ledger is not totaled, because Stoddard did not anticipate that the 1970 entry would be the last, and it does not include other contributions to the Church.

During his years of service on the Brigham Young University National

Advisory Development Committee, Stoddard reaffirmed his loyalty to his adopted state and region. In a letter to B.Y.U. President Ernest L. Wilkinson, March 30, 1959, he acknowledged the attraction which the West holds for many dispersed Latter-day Saints, but added: "However, many of us are developing the same feelings for the midwest and eastern communities in which we have our homes and businesses. We therefore feel the responsibility to see the same development take place in this area. . . ."

A unique witness to this commitment is the Deseret Student Living Center at Michigan State University. This residence facility is described in its promotional brochure as "for college students who desire to live in an environment of high Christian ideals." Each of the two buildings has seventeen housekeeping apartments. The one for women bears the name of Jennie Creer Stoddard, and the one for men has Howard's name. What makes them unique among the impressive housing facilities on and adjoining the M.S.U. campus is the pledge that "the standards of The Church of Jesus Christ of Latter-day Saints will be fully maintained. . . ."

Although the project was not constructed until after Howard Stoddard's death, the impetus which carried it through was his. He became convinced that it was often neither practical nor desirable for Mormon families in places like Michigan to send their children back to Utah, as his parents had done, for higher education in an L.D.S. environment. The church had long ago recognized this by establishing institutes of religion near many campuses, offering religious instruction, social fellowship and counseling services. The logical next step, it seemed to Stoddard in the 1960s, was to develop living quarters in which the deportment standards taught in the institutes would be maintained: no use of alcohol, tobacco or narcotics, separation of the sexes and strict limitations on visitation, and encouragement of church activity.

According to Edwin Jones, the church had already purchased property for an M.S.U. institute when Stoddard and he reached the conclusion that the tract would not accommodate the additional facilities Stoddard had proposed. Shopping elsewhere on South Hagadorn Road, which defines the eastern limit of the campus, they found an eight acre tract which seemed ideal. Stoddard's persuasiveness, his prestige as Lansing's leading banker, and his assurances to both Jones and the owners that he would see that money was available led to a deal. Mr. and Mrs. Kenneth A. Rumsey reduced the price as a contribution to the church and transferred the property immediately under a life annuity contract. All that then remained was to persuade the church authorities. According to Jones, Stoddard had already sounded out his friend Nathan Eldon Tanner, a counselor in the First Presidency, and won support after an initial negative reaction. Other church leaders also became enthused. The ways of bureaucracies, even ecclesiastical, being sometimes very slow, Howard Stoddard was dead before final authorization for the project was received. His family, however, worked with the church representatives and contractors to see the institute-living center concept to realization. The Stoddard financial participation was also substantial.

Stoddard's impulse to give was by no means restricted to institutional channels. A posthumous tribute to him bears the title "Let Thy Alms Be in Secret"—a reflection of a pattern which fitted his natural reticence. More than one M.S.U. student, bank employee, and prospective Mormon missionary benefitted from his generosity at critical junctures. According to Sylvan Wittwer, Stoddard's open-handedness was only tempered by the work ethic. "He did not mind helping people, but there had to be a genuine effort on their part. He didn't just hand out money to church people, though many of them expected him to."

Members of Stoddard's family found him more than helpful, especially in their retirement years. Correspondence with his brothers and sister Jeanette was not voluminous, but much of it reflects an almost patriarchal concern for their material welfare. Illustrative is the letter congratulating his older brother John on a 1957 call to serve the church on a construction mission in the South Pacific. Accompanying the letter was a check for $750 and a wrist watch.

Those who turned to Howard Stoddard for advice on church-related matters included bishops and branch presidents, stake and mission presidents, and members of the central church hierarchy. He was perceived as a valuable resource because of his deep religious commitment, his practical experience and judgment, and his willingness to speak directly to problems. Wittwer writes: "I found great satisfaction in visiting with Howard Stoddard, usually by appointment and usually in the evening at his home. . . . This continued almost monthly up until about a year prior to his death. I marvelled at his wisdom." George Romney, who observed him for a decade in the Detroit Stake High Council, describes him as "a very good High Councilman . . . a man of great wisdom and understanding and dedication to the Church. He attended regularly . . . and was a very strong member of the leadership group." Henry Moyle wrote as a member of the Council of Twelve Apostles in 1954: "I want you to know that we have not only a deep affection for you but a very great admiration, and are certain that there are few men in the Church who have succeeded to any greater degree in their chosen professions." In counsel he did not always favor the viewpoint which finally prevailed, but he sustained decisions once made and did not publicly criticize either policies or leaders. Even his family members do not recall him speaking antagonistically or derisively about such matters. His strong sense of loyalty restrained him in those limited areas where he entertained private misgivings or dissent.

The same concern for a positive Mormon image which kindled Stoddard's interest in buildings led him to play a prominent role in one of the church's pioneer mass media undertakings. He was chairman of the board of directors of Radio New York Worldwide, Inc., from its original incorporation in 1962 as International Educational Broadcasting Corporation until 1970. Thereafter he was a director until his designation as Honorary Chairman Emeritus and Director Emeritus a few weeks before his death.

I.E.B.C. was originally created to acquire five short-wave radio transmitters located near Scituate, Massachusetts, and managed in New York City under the call letters WRUL. At the time the church decided to enter the international broadcasting field, a number of prominent Mormon businessmen were invited to become directors. Stoddard's close association with Henry Moyle probably led to his designation as chairman of the group. The mission of WRUL was to broadcast L.D.S. conferences and other special events to Europe and Latin America, with the balance of its programming—largely music and public affairs—aimed at developing an international audience with an affirmative awareness of the church.

In 1964 the church organized Bonneville International Corporation to hold and operate all of its radio broadcasting properties, and I.E.B.C. became a subsidiary. Stoddard endorsed this move and thereafter lobbied energetically for enlargement of the mission and transmitting power of WRUL. He wrote to David O. McKay on November 16, 1965:

> Certainly the amount being expended to develop the short wave transmission system, which will carry the message of the Church throughout the world, is but a nominal amount when related to the overall cost of the missionary effort. At this time no one can foresee the tremendous value that will ensue if the broadcasting effort can effectively carry out its assignment.

The conversion of I.E.B.C. into Radio New York Worldwide, Inc., followed in 1966. The transmitting operation was upgraded in power and transferred from Massachusetts to New Jersey. WNYW, as it was now designated, broadcast church messages and other compatible programming worldwide. Stoddard was delighted with these developments. According to Arch L.

Madsen, current president of Bonneville International, Stoddard often visited the corporate offices in New York, and when he was in Washington on banking business "made it a point about once a month to visit with . . . our general counsel and vice president, to be updated on trends and developments."

Stoddard responded enthusiastically to the management suggestion that Radio New York acquire an FM station to project the same image to the metropolitan audience that WNYW was to the international audience. WRFM was purchased in 1966 and within four years it became the most listened-to FM station in the New York market. Madsen notes that Stoddard "was very proud of the station because of its winning many awards for programming, especially public affairs."

Unfortunately, WNYW did not do so well. Overseas audiences, to the extent that they could be estimated, remained small. As early as 1967 officers and directors began to debate whether the operation justified its cost. Stoddard resisted early proposals that the station be disposed of, and for a time President McKay supported him. To broaden financial support, Stoddard proposed in 1969 that WNYW redefine its mission "to include the presentation and fostering of the American way of life, the philosophy of the free enterprise system, and high standards and ideals." According to Madsen, the aim was "to interest substantial numbers of United States companies doing business abroad to place an appropriate budget with WNYW as institutional advertising." This was only an extension of Stoddard's earlier concern that the station project an affirmative view of America and its institutions, and he had for several years been chairman of a marketing management committee of the board of directors. "The concept was sound," Madsen notes, "but it was never saleable to the promotional and advertising directors of the corporations."

About the time that ill health compelled Stoddard to resign as board chairman, Radio New York disposed of WNYW. He maintained an active interest in the corporation's activities until his death a year later.

Howard Stoddard's talents for organization, analysis and persuasion found expression in the teaching and preaching opportunities which came frequently during his adult life. He taught the Gospel Doctrine Sunday School class for many years, and the books in his study show that he carefully studied the Bible, other L.D.S. scriptures, and the basic doctrinal commentaries in preparing these lessons. (The library also contains the *Harvard Classics, Encyclopedia Americana, Life World Library*, and a diverse collection of volumes in history, biography and the social sciences. There is almost no contemporary fiction.) He had neither time nor inclination for theological speculation and on a few occasions he expressed impatience with the intellectualization of religion. His personal philosophy encompassed eternity, but his focus was on the here and now. He frequently endorsed Dr. William Osler's concept of "living in day-tight compartments"—neither weeping about yesterday nor worrying about tomorrow.

His emphasis in teaching was on strengthening spirituality and moral living, and he had considerable skill in eliciting class discussion and directing it toward lesson goals. Virginia, who was frequent participant in his classes, writes:

> He taught Sunday School with the special gift of one who knew what he was talking about, who could clearly convey his thoughts, and who made those in class think about the lesson instead of simply listening to it. Simplicity was often the essence of his teaching. I recall a lesson on how to disarm your enemies. . . . He cited three ways to treat someone hostile to you. . . , return their hostility, ignore them, or totally disarm them by treating them with love and affection, and he proved how the last course was by far the most effective.

(To the extent that Stoddard did not achieve the third goal with some of his business adversaries, he did at least manage—generally—to ignore them.)

Because of his speaking ability, Stoddard was in considerable demand among the Mormon congregations in Michigan. Even when he was not assigned as a high councilman, he was frequently invited to speak. He was no preacher or pulpit orator in the traditional sense; only a controlled emotional dimension sometimes distinguished his Sunday style from his deportment before luncheon clubs and university audiences. To George Romney he was "a very effective speaker. He had a good appearance. He always talked to the point, and he had a message." Sylvan Wittwer corroborates this view: "I was impressed by the speaking ability of Howard Stoddard. Every word counted. There was no time for jokes and frivolities." Charles Stoddard, even as a boy, was an attentive listener:

> I just loved to hear my father speak. Not that he was theatrical about it. . . . He wasn't exciting to hear in terms of delivery, but in terms of content he was very eloquent. . . . I remember when he came back and spoke about the contrast of being a member of the Church here in this country and living in Russia, where there was no opportunity for religious beliefs. . . . I think he had a very fervent testimony of the Church. Often he would verge on becoming emotional about it,

but he never quite crossed the line. . . . You knew that it was very profound with him.

When Perry Driggs, Jennie's nephew, and a friend were called to fulfill two year L.D.S. missions, Stoddard spoke at the farewell meeting in the Birmingham, Michigan, Ward in December 1962. The talk recalled highlights of his own missionary experience in Germany, including the remarkable border crossing without passport visas. Then he used the recent round-the-world trip to illustrate the universal questioning about the basic meaning of life. According to Stoddard, Perry and his friend were setting out to carry answers to this questioning—answers revealed to a modern prophet, Joseph Smith. He concluded—as he did almost every church address—with a personal testimony:

> The church of Jesus Christ is organized in all of its fulness today. It will remain and in time will dominate the hearts of men. . . . You are a part of it, a small part. . . . But each, if he does his or her own part, will contribute to that which is intended and bring into the hearts and minds of men the answers that every thinking man and every thinking woman wants to know—
>
> "Who am I?"
>
> "Where did I come from?"
>
> "Why am I here?"
>
> "And where am I going?"
>
> And when you get the secret of life locked in your heart so firmly to the testimony of Jesus Christ that you no longer worry about it, it gives purpose to you. It gives motivation to everything that you do. It makes you into a finer person. And it will eventually bring you to the point where—As God is, man in the centuries to come may become like Him.

CHAPTER 19

# Leader in the Financial World

The completion of 25 years of notable banking accomplishments was an occasion for celebrating. Jennie and Howard Stoddard hosted a pre-game birthday luncheon at the Lansing Country Club on October 2, 1965, and then a large group of M.N.B. officers, directors and friends watched Michigan State defeat Illinois in the Spartan stadium. In December a group of Stoddard's admirers met in the M.B.N.A. board room in the Guardian Building to unveil a portrait by New Jersey artist Charles J. Fox, and the Detroit *News* carried a long feature about the "mighty maverick of the financial world." The $1.4 billion in resources of the Stoddard-controlled banks put them in a class with Manufacturers National and Detroit Bank & Trust, according to the December 12 articles, with only National Bank of Detroit larger in Michigan. Each of the Stoddard banks was described as a separate corporation, "but they have interlocking boards of directors and they cooperate in many ways, to their mutual advantage and to the disadvantage of their competitors." Stoddard was quoted as pointing out that the three big Detroit banks collectively controlled 40 percent of Michigan's banking resources. "He contends that his own group's 10 percent helps provide competitive balance, not domination."

Michigan National Bank's annual report for 1965 reviewed "25 years of vigorous and useful service to the people of the State of Michigan." An attractively printed public relations brochure, it contained a bar graph showing that the initial $57 million in resources had grown to $889 million. Pretax earnings for 1965 were almost $10 million, and after payment of federal taxes and a dividend of $1.8 million, retained earnings for the first time exceeded $4 million. Over the quarter century the bank had earned $110 million and paid $47.5 million in income taxes and $17.5 million in dividends, leaving almost $46 million of retained earnings to expand the capital structure. The 1,800,000 shares of common stock were carried in the balance sheet at their par value of $10, but each had an estimated market value of $50. Among the 4,513 shareholders, according to the report, "about 40 percent of the stock is still retained by the original owners and their families."

Howard Stoddard's philosophy of consumer-oriented banking seemed to be vindicated by cumulative losses of only $3.8 million, or .05 percent of the $7.3 billion loaned. The bank had financed more than 100,000 Michigan homes, and paid $131 million in interest to depositors. Most of the 1,617 staff members were participants in the Employees Profit Sharing Trust, which had assets with a current market value of $12.7 million.

The pencil portraits which illustrated the brochure showed that among the original group of senior executives only Howard and Waldo, Russell Fairles and Frank McCabe were still in harness. Howard was chairman of the board, as he had been since the death of Charles Bohn. Waldo had become M.N.B. president in December 1961, but he continued to head the branch and the trust department in Grand Rapids. Fairles was senior vice president in the central office, and McCabe was in charge in Port Huron. New faces among the senior vice presidents were Arnold Van Zanten, Battle Creek; William B. Otto, Charlotte; Wendell J. Cook, Flint; Joseph F. Shaw and Edwin Barnes, Grand Rapids; John B. Nelligan and Howard P. Stoddard, Lansing; E. Lear Kaye, Marshall; and Paul C. Souder, Saginaw. Howard Jr. had moved from Marshall to Lansing in 1961, to be in charge of M.N.B. public relations and advertising. Among the 25 directors, only Howard, Waldo, McCabe, Mervin F. Cotes, George M. Endicott, James M. McInerney and H. Randall Wickes had been on the board from the start.

Also sketched were the bank headquarters in the eight M.N.B. cities. All had changed to some extent over the years. Not shown were the Stoddard Building in Lansing or the pending changes in the Michigan National Tower. In 1965 the adjoining Elks Lodge Building on Allegan Street was purchased and demolished to make way for a ten-story addition to the bank, completed late in 1967. The Romanesque exterior of the Olds-built skyscraper was matched on the new structure. Except for the top two floors of the tower, the upper levels of the expanded bank building were rented. In 1962 Jennie and a Chicago architect had been given *carte blanche* to develop a board of directors conference room and a dining room on the 22nd and 23rd floors. Stoddard, naturally, had a voice in selecting the paneling and the elegant conference table. The overall result was spectacular.

To support the claim that the bank had well earned the slogan, "Banking That Is Building Michigan," the report recalled such innovations as longer hours, drive-ins, daily interest and the newly introduced Michigan Bankard. It also emphasized two ongoing concerns—the continuing resistance of Michigan to statewide branch banking and the continuing threat of inflation to the banking industry and the American economy. Efforts to reverse or evade the legislative decision of 1945 produced no tangible results in the 1960s. Meanwhile the changing economic picture forced Howard Stoddard to reconsider some of the confident assumptions on which he had based M.N.B. investment policies for two decades.

In mentioning the fifteen-fold increase in Michigan National Bank resources, the 25th Annual Report cautioned that "the 1941 dollar, largely as a result of wartime inflation, decreased in value and is worth slightly less than fifty cents today." In his public addresses Stoddard still expressed confidence that inflation could be contained, but as the Vietnam War produced bigger federal deficits and escalating prices, he called for a halt both to the demoralizing conflict and the "guns and butter" fiscal policy which accompanied it.

Stoddard's certitude that U.S. government bonds provided a sound major component for any bank's investment portfolio stemmed from general patriotism and two specific convictions. One was that Regulation Q, the instrument by which the Federal Reserve Board had controlled interest rates on commercial bank savings since 1935, would keep the interest ceiling in line with what government securities were earning. The other, which his cousin Marriner had emphasized during his days with the Federal Reserve, was that U.S. government bonds could always be used as collateral at the Fed if a bank needed to borrow cash to expand its loans or meet other obligations.

In the late 1950s competitive pressure from savings and loan companies and mutual savings banks forced commercial banks to begin raising their interest on savings, and the Fed gradually lifted the Regulation Q ceiling. Even as Stoddard spearheaded a partially successful campaign to end the income tax advantages of savings and loans and other thrift institutions, his banks raised their own interest rates on time deposits as fast as the law allowed. He also began to call for a comparable interest ceiling on all savings accounts, or for the abolition of Regulation Q altogether.

Since the earnings on federal securities did not rise proportionately, Stoddard was forced reluctantly to abandon the fifty-fifty formula which he had announced even before Michigan National Bank was organized. In 1960 approximately half of the bank's assets were still cash, U.S. securities and federally-insured loans—what Stoddard called "risk-free" assets. Ten years later these items comprised only a quarter of the bank's resources, and the book value of federal obligations had increased by less than $5 million.

Municipal bonds and notes—the *bête noir* for "Mister R.F.C."—now accounted for almost $75 million on the balance sheet. All of them came from Michigan cities, and all had relatively high interest rates and short maturities. Howard Stoddard's banks still had a larger fraction of their assets in U.S. governments than did the banking community as a whole, as reflected in the M.N.B. annual letter of January 15, 1970.

The contraction of credit which came with the Treasury Department and Federal Reserve collaboration to stem war-born inflation destroyed Stoddard's other conviction about U.S. securities. In order to curtail individual and business borrowing, which was carrying bank interest rates to spectacular highs of 9 and 10 percent, the Federal Reserve Board announced in mid-1969 that a commercial bank could no longer borrow by discounting its government securities until it had exhausted the possibilities of the Federal Funds market (borrowing from other commercial banks on an overnight basis) and the Eurodollars market (buying dollars owned abroad). The announcement, according to Waldo and Fairles, had an almost traumatic impact on Stoddard. Soon after the Nixon inauguration he wrote to the new Secretary of the Treasury, David M. Kennedy, expressing confidence that "ways will be found to stabilize the American dollar and prevent its further substantial erosion." But after Kennedy outlined the administration plans to Stoddard and 23 other bank presidents in Washington on July 16, 1969, Stoddard wrote to the secretary comparing the mood of the meeting to that which he had felt in Detroit in February 1933. "In both cases, there was a feeling of frustration and inability to cope with the problem for which they were not responsible, and yet had to bear the burden of public criticism."

Because about 80 percent of all Michigan National loans were—as they had been from the beginning—installment contracts, it was possible to adjust to the credit crunch without calling loans. Funds received in payments were simply not reloaned at the same rate. Although the volume of deposits and loans actually declined through 1969 and barely exceeded December 31, 1968, levels at the end of 1970, the bank still earned more than 10 percent on stockholder equity both years. The experience, however, left Howard Stoddard disillusioned about the liquidity of government bonds and an advocate of new federal monetary policies. His message for the 1969 stockholders report, which appeared as he was convalescing from the major surgery which finally slowed him down, ended with these words:

> We concur in the judgment of Milton Friedman, Professor of Economics at the University of Chicago, that "the Federal Reserve

> Board should allow the money supply to expand at a fairly constant rate of about 5% a year. This would be in line with the long-term growth rate of the nation's production of goods and services."

Perhaps the most significant impact which Stoddard had on national economic policy in the 1960s was as a partner with Franklin National Bank President Arthur T. Roth in the drive for equalization of taxation between commercial banks and savings and loan and mutual savings institutions. As co-chairmen of the Bankers' Committee for Tax Equality, Howard, Roth and Chicago banker L. Shirley Tark managed a lobbying campaign which achieved a degree of success in the tax reform legislation of 1962.

During the early years of Michigan National's successful consumer-oriented banking, Stoddard was unconcerned about the competition of the thrift institutions. He told a Philadelphia banking audience in 1955, "We are not worrying at all about what the savings and loans or what other people are doing." The competitive picture was already changing, however, and in the M.N.B. letter to the presidents of all commercial banks, June 10, 1960, he sounded the alarm:

> By the close of the 1960 decade, the combined assets of mutual savings banks and savings and loan associations may actually exceed those of commercial banks. The reason for this is perfectly clear. *The mutual savings banks and savings and loan associations pay virtually no Federal income taxes, and as a result can pay a higher rate of interest and dividends than commercial banks.*

Stoddard's involvement with Michigan's fiscal affairs during the preceding months had convinced him that state tax laws were also discriminatory, but an effort to challenge their validity in the courts failed. Five national banks joined Michigan National in the suit, but Michigan Bankers Association supported the state authorities in defense of the *status quo* and the case was lost.

At the 1959 meeting of the Independent Bankers Association in Denver Stoddard first met Arthur Roth. They had corresponded previously, because Franklin National, on Long Island, was one of those rapidly growing banks which Stoddard studied with particular interest. Now Roth argued that the best way for Stoddard to forward his cause on the national scene was to join the already-existent Bankers' Committee. Within a year he was co-chairman, and he held that post until January 1966. (The Stoddard-Roth personal relationship continued through the decade. Roth remembers that he sometimes called Jennie "Sparkle Plenty.")

The goal of the campaign was to secure Congressional modification of 1951 tax legislation which permitted thrift institutions to set aside tax free reserves until the total of their surplus, reserves and undivided profits equaled 12 percent of their share accounts or deposits. This provision, coupled with the lack of a limit on the rate of interest or dividend which could be paid, had the effect of substantially eliminating federal income tax liability. Commercial bank pressure led to the introduction of several tax equalization bills, and after the 1960 American Bankers Association convention, at which Stoddard was one of the speakers, the association relied primarily on the Bankers' Committee as its lobbying voice. (Stoddard returned from an A.B.A. tax conference in Washington the day before his surprise sixtieth birthday party.)

During the next several years the directors of the committee met annually to formulate strategy, but Stoddard, Roth, Tark and the committee staff did most of the work. Stoddard featured the campaign in his 1961, 1962 and 1963 letters to his fellow bankers and in the annual reports to M.N.B. stockholders. Variations of a talk, "Tax Justice Between Competing Financial Institutions," were delivered to audiences around the country. Through entree which Roth had to John F. Kennedy's father, the President was led to recommend non-discriminatory taxation to Congress on April 20, 1962. He also recommended another measure in which Stoddard had become interested—a 20 percent witholding tax on corporate dividends and taxable investment-type interest. Tax evasion was even more repugnant to Stoddard than tax inequality, and for a number of years he corresponded with House Ways and Means Committee Chairman Wilbur D. Mills and others about how the withholding principle might be applied to interest earnings without unmanageable paperwork. (No solution was found, but the current requirement that interest and dividend disbursements be reported to the Internal Revenue Service is an approach to the problem.)

Three times Howard Stoddard and Arthur Roth appeared before Congressional bodies as representatives of the Bankers' Committee. On August 10, 1961, Stoddard was the chief spokesman before the House Ways and Means Committee, urging tax equalization and also arguing that the Federal Reserve Board should raise—or eliminate—the ceiling on the interest rate which commercial banks could pay on savings deposits. "As long as our competitors have no ceiling, I don't know why it should be on the banks," he contended. (A partial equalization came when the thrift institutions were also brought under control but with a small permissible margin over the comparable commercial bank rate.)

Both Roth and Stoddard testified before the Finance Committee of the

Senate on April 11, 1962, in support of the Kennedy reform proposals. The upshot was a complex change in the income tax laws which had the effect of requiring thrift institutions to pay the regular tax rates on 40 percent of their net earnings. To Stoddard this was still an "unfair formula," but in time he came to the conclusion that further changes were unlikely. The new financial environment created by the Vietnam War and accelerating inflation also added so many variables to the financial market that the savings and loan issue diminished in importance.

Stoddard's testimony before the Ways and Means Committee on March 11, 1963, focused on banker reactions to the Kennedy proposals to cut taxes in order to stimulate economic recovery from the mild recession that the country was experiencing. A survey had found most bankers cautious about such an experiment in deficit financing. On behalf of the Bankers' Committee Stoddard suggested a two-stage reduction, the second year's cut dependent on the results of the first. His recollections of German inflation doubtless reinforced the emphasis which he placed on the bankers' concern for "a policy to return to a balanced budget." The pamphlet version of his testimony features his response to a committee question: "Would you explain what is so bad about having tremendous deficits with tax cuts?" Stoddard replied:

> When you try to balance the budget with taxes, you impose a discipline on people. When you budget with deficits, you throw the discipline out of the window. We all, as human beings, require discipline, whether we are working in corporations or in Government. The great evil of deficit financing is that you take away the discipline which people need to live together in an organized society.

Howard Stoddard actually enjoyed these opportunities to discuss national issues with Congressional committees. He was always composed, even under critical questioning, and according to Roth, his informed responses inspired confidence. He was the last scheduled witness in the 1961 Ways and Means hearing, and he began by observing, "My plane left three minutes ago. I am good for the rest of the evening." After noting that "it is like trying to pick up a piece of quick silver from a highly polished table to pin down the arguments of the savings and loan officials at this late stage," he offered his extensive statement for publication in the record and simply responded to questions. When a Congressman charged the Bankers' Committee with having shifted its support from one tax equalization measure to another, Stoddard replied, "You and I have lived long enough to know that we take a position, and when better information comes to us we sometimes change our position." Complimented, toward the close of the session, on "the way your stock has increased all the time you were paying taxes," he noted jocularly, "We have all reached the stage of life where we only get the compliments from the men now." In response to the comment, "Mr. Stoddard, you contend that you are asking only for tax equality," Howard smiled and replied, "If I may, I prefer to use the words *tax justice.*"

Stoddard was less successful in influencing Congress in a matter of concern only to Michigan National. The story is less significant in the history of the bank than as an illustration of the stubborn side of its president. As James Alley expressed it: "He had complete confidence in his own judgment, and when he thought he was right, he'd go through with it, come hell or high water." The moral absolutism which guided Howard's general deportment stood in interesting juxtaposition to the adventuresomeness with which he tested the legal limits of the banking environment. If a proposed innovation seemed to run counter to prevailing interpretations of statutes or regulations, he sought legal advice, and if an alternative interpretation was judged to have a chance, he was almost always willing to take that chance. For example, late in 1956 the Federal Reserve Bank of Chicago challenged an accounting practice of Michigan Bank N.A. which was inconsistent with Comptroller of the Currency regulations but made a better picture of earnings. The bank responded that it intended to continue the practice because it seemed to be "a fair interpretation of the law." The consequence of such episodes, as Alley later remarked, was that "the bank had almost daily problems" with one or another of the regulatory bodies. Once a legal point was settled, Stoddard complied, but he never gave up looking for ways to maximize his banks' opportunities for growth.

During the 1960s he spent a great deal of time, money and nervous energy in an effort to secure legislative reversal of a decision made at the time the bank was formed. When the six-bank merger was submitted for approval in 1940, Comptroller Preston Delano interpreted the prevailing U.S. and state statutes as precluding the consolidated bank from retaining three branch offices in Grand Rapids and one in Saginaw. Stoddard and the bank's legal advisers did not contest the decision at the time, there being more pressing organizational and legislative matters in Michigan to claim their attention. Stoddard was never reconciled to the branch closures, however, and as the competitive banks in the two cities established their own suburban branches, he decided to seek relief.

One of James Alley's major assignments as eastern legal counsel in the 1950s and 1960s was to work with Stoddard on matters involving the comptroller's office, such as acquisition of new branches and changes in capitalization and key personnel. Alley was retained for this work after illness forced

Eugene Garey to retire, and the connections which he had maintained in Washington since Reconstruction Finance Corporation days proved helpful. (The fact that Garey and Alley were two of Stoddard's closest personal friends is the more remarkable since they lost as many bouts with the regulators and lawmakers as they won.)

In time three successive comptrollers were persuaded that the Delano decision had been erroneous, but since the 1945 anti-branch-banking law had changed the ground rules in Michigan, none of them could authorize replacements for the four lost branches. At their suggestion Stoddard turned to Congress.

Bills to permit the comptroller to authorize new offices in lieu of those improperly closed were introduced in 1963, 1965 and 1967. Democratic Senator Philip Hart sponsored the last two, while Michigan's other Senator, Republican Robert Griffith, opposed the project. (Despite his nominal Republicanism, Stoddard was often more successful in working with Democrats at both the state and national level. As previously noted, he and the bank regularly contributed to both party organizations. In 1964 he paid $1000 for the privilege of shaking hands with President Lyndon Johnson at a Detroit reception.) Nothing happened to the first two bills, but a mobilization of political resources in which U.S. Chamber of Commerce President Robert Gerholz played an important part generated action on the third. After a hearing in which Stoddard testified to the damage which his bank had suffered from the lack of branches in Grand Rapids and Saginaw, the Committe on Banking and Currency reported the bill (S. 356) favorably to the Senate.

Gerholz tells how the committee hearing ended at an hour when a late winter storm and rush hour demand made taxis unavailable. While he scouted for transportation in vain, Stoddard napped in a chair in the conference room. Eventually they paid a delicatessen deliveryman to take them back to the hotel in his vintage automobile.

Few things disappointed Howard Stoddard more than the denouement of this business. When he and Gerholz next went to Washington, it was with the confident expectation of meeting with Wright Patman, chairman of the House Banking and Currency Committee. The promised appointment never materialized. To Stoddard this was more than a mortification—it was a breech of honor. That Patman may simply have been influenced by the expressed opposition of the Federal Reserve Board, Federal Deposit Insurance Corporation and Michigan Bankers Association or doing a favor for an old friend of Grand Rapids' Old Kent Bank and Trust Company—Representative Gerald Ford—is a plausible hypothesis.

The Senate passed S. 356 on July 11, 1968, shortly after Stoddard's first stroke. Subsequent efforts by bank representatives were unsuccessful in securing any committee action in the House of Representatives. Two years later, as he convalesced from major surgery, Stoddard confided to Edwin Jones that if he had it to do over again, "he would not spend as much time trying to redress all the wrongs that were done in the past."

Stoddard was no more comfortable with the political side of national government than he was with Lansing politics. Testifying about matters within his competence he found challenging, but arm twisting and favor soliciting he felt to be demeaning, and he did not do it skillfully. Gerholz, who discussed Howard Stoddard with *Time* publisher Henry Luce as a possible Secretary of the Treasury for the first Nixon Cabinet, now acknowledges that both health and temperament made the appointment inadvisable.

Another consideration which would have made a political appointment improbable with either political party was the outspoken position which Stoddard took as early as 1967 in opposition to the Vietnam War. As the inflationary consequences of the conflict became apparent, he began to call for an appropriate fiscal response. "The United States is presently in a 'war economy,'" he told Marshall Rotarians in October 1966, "but we bury our heads in the sand and refuse to admit it." A month later he told the Lansing Rotary Club that "the taxes in America should have been increased by enough to cover fully every dollar of the Vietnam expenditure," but he acknowledged that businessmen were no more enthusiastic about such a step than other taxpayers.

By 1967 the disruptive social and economic consequences persuaded Stoddard that the United States should abandon the conflict. So impressed was he by a talk which Marriner Eccles, an anti-war spokesman since 1965, gave to the San Francisco Commonwealth Club—"Vietnam: Its Effect on the Nation"—that he distributed 20,000 copies with the annual mailing to all commercial banks. Charles, then a student at Harvard, sent the Eccles talk to *Vital Speeches*, where it shortly appeared. (Stoddard wrote to Eccles, "I am of the opinion that you have already changed the mind of Governor Romney . . . on this tremendously complex problem.") "Get Out of Vietnam" is the *State Journal* headline, September 20, 1967, on a report of Howard's talk to a Battle Creek service club. "He said that the cost of the war in terms of military outlays, casualties, inflation and ill will of the world is too high." The account continued: "If taxes were to be hiked 30 percent to put the war on a pay-as-you-go basis, Stoddard added, the fighting would stop 'in 30 days.'"

The so-called "domino theory" of Communist conquest "is not valid," Stoddard insisted, reflecting impressions formed from earlier visits to Russia,

Western Europe and parts of the Third World. "The Communist threat is not a united front because we have seen divisions between Russia and China and variations of communism practiced by other nations."

Hope that the Nixon administration would extricate the nation marked Stoddard's talks early in 1969, and he was greatly disappointed at the course events took. His letter to Secretary Kennedy after the July anti-inflation meeting concluded: "There is no question that the Vietnam war is the cause of our inflation. I hope to the extent that your influence can be persuasive that the President will take immediate steps to terminate that unjustified conflict."

The banking business, of course, went on. Waldo Stoddard is generally given for credit for suggesting the most profitable innovation of the 1960s—Michigan Bankard. Although Franklin National was a pioneer with bank credit cards, Howard and the M.N.B. board turned down a staff proposal that they follow Arthur Roth's lead. But when Waldo returned from a family visit in California in the spring of 1965 with word of the success of Bank of America's new program, a study team was appointed to investigate several plans in operation. A proposal was approved and in December the plan was ready to launch. Frank A. Shumway, who had headed the study team, was placed in charge of the Lansing-based program.

Howard realized that Michigan Bankard would require seed money. Gladys MacGregor remembers that when Sales Manager James Kaufman told him that the venture would cost several million dollars to implement, he replied, "If it does, it does." What was not fully appreciated, according to Fairles and others involved, is that not everyone who pays on a home mortgage or a car loan, where foreclosure is a possibility, is a good risk for a credit card. It took three years and almost $5 million to bring the program to the break-even point. Michigan Bank N.A. affiliated with the plan early and had a comparable experience in Detroit.

To recruit merchants for what was a brand new concept in Michigan took selling. The first participant was Andreae Fashion Fabrics, a chain store with locations in three M.N.B. cities. By March 1, 1966, about 4,000 accounts were enrolled, and on that day the first authorization call came in from a merchant. For the first few days only a handful of sales had to be approved, and Shumway was seen as an optimist when he predicted that before long there would be hundreds of calls a day. (Now the computerized bank card department handles more than 7,500 approvals per normal day and nearly 20,000 at Christmas time.)

To secure statewide acceptance, an agent bank program was instituted. Given the arms-length relationship between M.N.B. and most Michigan banks, it took time to convince local bankers to align with the system, but the attractiveness of a good business opportunity in time prevailed. (Today about 125 banks with more than 500 offices participate.) To accelerate growth, a new department was established in 1967 to purchase merchants' accounts receivable. Soon all types of businesses from shoe stores and auto-dealers to dentists and doctors were signing up to have Michigan National collect their accounts for a negotiated percentage. Several large department store and discount chains came into the system in time.

A major change took place in the Bankard program during the summer of 1970, when the bank affiliated with National Bankamericard, Inc. Negotiations began in 1968 with this subsidiary of Bank of America, to facilitate the out-of-state use of the M.N.B. card and to avoid possible legal entanglements with the nationally-franchised BankAmericard plan. Michigan Bankard became a two-sided credit card, with the reverse—labeled Bank Americard—used for out-of-state and foreign purchases. (In 1977 the shift was made to Michigan Bankard Visa, shortly after Michigan National also began to handle Master Charge accounts.)

From a beginning with less than 50 employees to manage a money-losing program with sales of $13 million and about 200,000 cardholders in 1965, Michigan Bankard reached the point of profitability in September 1968, and sales of $106 million and about 600,000 cardholders in 1970. (Today sales exceed $750 million and about 1,750,000 cards are in use.)

Less successful was Michigan National's venture into international finance. With economic developments attracting or forcing banks into the world money market, Stoddard responded favorably to an invitation to join several other major regional institutions in forming an international bank to serve them all. American Overseas Banking Corporation was formed in September 1968, with headquarters in New York and Howard Stoddard as one of the directors. (Waldo Stoddard and Joseph Shaw later held the M.N.B. seat on the board.) According to the press release, the bank would "supplement and extend services now provided by member banks and conduct complete international banking services for American and foreign customers."

Robert Gerholz recalls that some of the M.N.B. directors were not enthusiastic about this venture. It would take the bank into a volatile field in which none of the officers had experience. The decision to participate was made with the understanding that the initial investment would be only $2 million. Ten other banks contributed similar sums as paid-in capital; later a few more joined. Personnel shifts and operational problems contributed to a slow start, and changing the name to Allied Bank International in 1969 did not produce an operation which fulfilled Stoddard's expectations. (Michigan National's interest was finally sold in 1978.)

By no means the least of the factors sustaining Howard Stoddard's interest in statewide banking was the continuing expansion of his Detroit operations. He succeeded John Langs as chairman of the Michigan Bank board of directors in December 1960, a few months after the bank opened its eleventh branch office—in a trailer in Dearborn. Stanford was named executive vice president, and Edwin B. Jones and Frank R. Welsher, both of whom soon became senior executives and directors, were designated vice presidents. In 1961 the bank surrendered its state charter and became Michigan Bank National Association. When the former president unexpectedly resigned the presidency to accept a post in another Detroit bank, Stoddard proposed Stanford for the vacancy. "Bud" was only 31.

Not content with a *de facto* branch in Detroit, Stoddard kept probing for ways to formalize the connection. One reason for obtaining a national charter for Michigan Bank was to bring it into the same regulatory framework as Michigan National, so that identical policies could be pursued without running into contradictory state and federal controls. Another was to take advantage of the somewhat more friendly atmosphere which Stoddard found in Washington as memories of the 1940s faded and he gained prominence in the national financial community. The same comptrollers who were sympathetic in the matter of the lost branches would have to approve any change in the Lansing-Detroit connection.

Early in 1966 conversations with the comptroller left Stoddard confident that an application to exchange Michigan Bank N.A. stock for Michigan National Bank stock would be approved. Both boards of directors readily agreed; at the time Stoddard and his family, his close associates and the M.N.B. Profit Sharing Trust owned about 27 percent of M.N.B. and 58 percent of the M.B.N.A. stock. When the formal application was made, however, the three biggest Detroit banks and Old Kent of Grand Rapids challenged the merger in the courts, alleging that the comptroller had no authority to permit one national bank to acquire the stock of another and that the proposed merger would cause plaintiffs "irreparable damage." With the battle joined, the Federal Reserve Board joined the objectors, and in May 1967 a new comptroller refused to approve the stock swap. Instead of becoming a branch of Michigan National, the Stoddard bank in Detroit continued to function as a technically independent institution until the Michigan Bank Holding Company Act of 1971 made it possible for both to come under the Michigan National Corporation umbrella. They were the fourth and sixth biggest banks in the state for most of the 1960s.

Among those extending sympathy to Stoddard at this disappointment was

Louis B. Lundborg, chairman of Bank of America. Stoddard's reply, May 31, 1967, contained a quotation from A.P. Giannini about which Lundborg had inquired: "The soundest business in the world is one that takes a little from a lot of people." Stoddard had repeated it to his associates many times, for the Giannini concept had become his own.

The break with Michigan Bankers Association finally came in 1965. The relationship between the Stoddard banks and the association had been strained since the controversies of the early 1940s, but Stoddard, his family and other M.N.B. and M.B.N.A. personnel usually attended the annual conventions, and they enjoyed being with many of the other members. Charles and Howard Jr. remember the golf games at the Mackinac Island gatherings. Jennie recalls asking one of the M.B.A. officers why Stoddard was never invited to speak and why he was refused when he asked to speak about the equal taxation issue. Stoddard remained outwardly unruffled, but it bothered him that officers from the association's second-largest dues paying banking group were rarely appointed to committees and never considered for major offices. And it angered him when M.B.A. periodically took positions on state and national banking legislation diametrically opposed to his own. Gladys heard Stoddard say that "the bankers would rather legislate against us than compete against us."

The parting of the ways came when the legislative committee of M.B.A., without consideration by the association as a whole, endorsed a proposed state law (Senate Bill 460) to limit stock ownership in Michigan banks. No individual or organization—such as a profit sharing trust—could acquire more than 15 percent of the stock of any bank. The proposal was obviously aimed at Michigan National and other groups who owned bank stock in partnerships and profit sharing trusts. This arbitrary restriction made little economic sense and Stoddard opposed it—much to the delight of small town bank owners who controlled more than 15 percent of their institutions but wanted to avoid controversy.

On the grounds that the committee's endorsement of S.B. 460 was deviously made, that the proposal was prejudicial to the participants in the profit sharing trusts, and that it "would also greatly curtail the market value and thus lower the sales of all Michigan bank stocks, particularly of smaller institutions," Stoddard wrote a letter of resignation on December 27, 1965. Its last paragraph read:

> For the past 25 years, our bank has patiently hoped to have normal relations in the Association despite our views on the soundness of

> branch banking. However, the present situation leaves this bank with no alternative but to terminate its membership. . . . Our bank cannot justify paying dues to an organization that uses its influence to the serious detriment of our employees and stockholders.

The M.B.A. executive committee reversed the action of the legislative committee, pending further study of S.B. 460, but Howard Stoddard did not reverse his decision. (To this day none of the banks controlled by Michigan National Corporation is a member of the association.)

The episode gave financial journalists another opportunity to review the Stoddard story, with emphasis on Stoddard's image as a non-conformist. Detroit *Free Press* Business Editor David C. Smith, in a story headlined "Banker Stoddard Still Goes His Own Way," began:

> Sit down with Howard J. Stoddard in the high-ceilinged, walnut-paneled boardroom of the Michigan Bank and you'd find it difficult to discern why he is widely known as the bogeyman of Michigan banking.
>
> Mild mannered, soft spoken and arrestingly articulate, Stoddard—a slim, erect 64-year-old dressed in banker's gray—comes across as a banker's banker.
>
> Yet for more than a quarter-century controversy has swirled around Stoddard.

Smith attributed Stoddard's reputation to his advocacy of "shareholder management versus management with little or no stock ownership," his profit sharing trust investments, his vigorous penetration of the Detroit market, and his continuing enthusiasm for branch banking. The article, incidentally, reported speculation that "legislation toward a return to statewide branch backing in some form may ultimately win M.B.A.'s backing."

The decade saw Stoddard speak to a widening audience. The old standby, "Our Rubber Dollar," was presented with timely adaptations. He was less than prophetic when he told a Marshall service club in 1964 that "the next decade will bring more stabilization to the dollar, barring a major holocaust. . . ." Talks based on the round-the-world tour often featured India, which Howard saw as "one of the great problems in the world today," not because of any danger of Communism but because of the magnitude of its development tasks. (Observations on this trip may have influenced him to make a substantial contribution later to a Planned Parenthood World Population campaign.) In 1962 he was one of 50 financiers invited by the American Bankers Association to take part in an international monetary conference in Rome, and the experience left him bullish about the future of Western Europe. To one group he expressed the thought "that the successful operation of the Common Market might within the next 10 years bring living standards to a comparable position with those in the U.S." Speaking to Lansing Rotarians on "Communism and the Common Market," he argued that free world productivity was the answer to the Soviet threat. If the architects of the Common Market adhered to the political principles of representative government and individual liberty, he concluded:

> A solution has been found for Communism, and if the men who are guiding the destinies of the European nations, and the men who are guiding the destinies of the nation, will combine in the movement now under way, it won't be too many years until you will see the burial of Communism.

A spin-off of Stoddard's involvement in the campaign for equal taxation was participation in A.B.A.-sponsored workshops on mortgage financing in Phoenix, Dallas, Washington and elsewhere. Always he expressed the testimony that had come to him during the years with R.F.C., the First National receivership and Guardian Depositors Corporation: "A properly made, properly serviced residential real estate mortgage is, next to a government bond, the soundest asset in this country." He opposed conservatives who argued that mortgage institutions were better able to handle this business than commercial banks, telling a Dallas audience in September 1961: "The home owner is now our basic customer. . . . We should not solicit his checking and savings accounts without offering his required loan facilities, especially the financing of his home. . . ." He found time to write an optimistic article about the automobile and Michigan's economy for *American Banker*, June 25, 1964, and he spoke on principles of money and banking to several workshops for teachers sponsored by the Michigan Council on Economic Education.

Another useful contribution to economic education was Michigan National's preparation and distribution of a chart, "The Changing Value of the Dollar, 1860-1970." Howard Stoddard would have agreed with the economic historian who said that more can be learned about American history from such a chart than from all the pictures of heroes and scoundrels that appear in the traditional textbooks.

In the latter part of the decade the Vietnam tragedy and the attendant inflation dominated Stoddard's public addresses, but he responded to such other issues of the period as civil rights, equal employment opportunities, environmental protection and the war on poverty.

Michigan National Bank experienced the militant aspect of the black employment movement at its Flint branch in August 1963. The city had a large black population, and the bank had at the time no black employees. An earlier meeting at which representatives of the National Association for the Advancement of Colored People had pressed for the employment of Negroes, particularly in non-custodial positions, had produced no results, Senior Vice President Fred Lavery being in a particular bind because the new Electronic Processing Center in Lansing had taken over several clerical tasks from the Flint branch. Thirty or more N.A.A.C.P. pickets appeared at the bank on August 19, and a peaceful but hardly tranquil three-day confrontation followed. An agreement was then reached to hire an undisclosed number of blacks within the near future, and the picketing stopped. Thereafter informal minority hiring programs were instituted at all the Stoddard banks. (Today affirmative action statements are part of the employee relations manuals and Michigan National has many blacks in management positions and on boards of directors.)

Five years later Stoddard told a Heritage Day banquet at Grand Ledge that racial problems and Vietnam were the nation's major social pollutants. "The money being poured into Vietnam," he said, "should be used to solve the black problem." He told many audiences that the 1968 election would determine the course of the nation and the world for many years to come. The Battle Creek *Enquirer*, December 5, 1967, quoted him as being confident that "law and order will reassert themselves, because they must." But this was not enough. "The problems of the slums, discrimination, employment and education can't be solved by money alone—we need guidance from the ground up to help people find better ways of life."

The standing which Howard Stoddard had achieved in the American business community by this time was reflected in his invitation to speak to the President's Luncheon series at Columbia University Graduate School of Business, October 11, 1967—forty-two years after his own graduation from that institution. About the same time he wrote to Federal Reserve Board Chairman William McChesney Martin, commenting on remarks which Martin had made about possible unification of the American banking system. Martin replied to "Dear Howard" on December 22, 1967:

> I am appreciative . . . of the confidence in the Federal Reserve inherent in your suggestion that "the American banking system . . .

> be unified in one structure under the direction of the Federal Reserve Board," with the savings and loan industry brought within the structure. However, I think you are wise in recognizing also that "traditions of the past and the emotions of men run very deep."

Events of the next two or three years shook Stoddard's confidence in the Fed to some degree, but they did not shake his basic belief that monopolistic small town banks and hodge-podge state laws were the chief impediments to effective and serviceable banking.

Two stories published in the mid-1960s also drew favorable attention to Howard Stoddard as he reached the normal time for retirement. *Michigan Manufacturer and Financial Record* featured him on the cover of its October 1964 issue and devoted three pages to a well-illustrated account. "A success story unequalled in the annals of Michigan banking" is its description of the Stoddard career. "In less than 25 years, this admitted maverick in our state's banking circles carved out a banking empire with aggregate resources well in excess of a billion dollars against the combined and militant opposition of virtually every other banking institution in Michigan." The ancedote-filled review of Stoddard's life also featured Waldo, Stanford and Howard Jr. It told about Charles at Michigan State, and after the manner of that pre-feminist era, mentioned "Mrs. Stoddard" only as the promoter of Howard's trips abroad.

The sober, even dour, picture on the magazine's cover prompted this comment from a friend in Connecticut: "I think I like the one on page 28 better." (That was of Howard and his seven golfing brothers at Sun Valley.) "On the cover page I cannot quite make up my mind as to whether you have refused a request for a loan, called one, or foreclosed the mortgage on the widow's home."

A national business audience read about "How to Succeed in Banking in Michigan" in the July 15, 1966 issue of *Fortune*. The lead paragraph described Michigan National Bank as "an aggressively unconventional institution—and a handsomely profitable one." The lengthy article continued:

> Michigan National's leadership in profitability is nothing new—in return on capital it has been No. 1 since it moved into the ranks of the fifty largest in 1963. The reasons for its high return are suggested by some other entries in FORTUNE'S bank directory. . . . Michigan National is only fiftieth in capital funds. . . , only forty-sixth in assets . . . , and only forty-fifth in deposits . . .—but it is thirty-ninth in loans. . . . Says an admiring Wall Street analyst: "Michigan Na-

> tional rejects conventional wisdom about what constitutes a proper ratio of loans to capital."

Defying the conventional wisdom had brought Howard Stoddard to the top of the banking profession. Now, at the close of the decade, he faced the prospect of winning one fight—for statewide banking—and losing another.

CHAPTER 20

# Fulfillment of a Dream

For the first 66 years of his life, Howard Stoddard enjoyed very good health. It was a fortunate thing, for the demands which he made on himself would have broken a man who did not have a sturdy body to go with his resolute will. According to Charles Stoddard, his father never planned to retire, and according to Jennie, Howard was reluctant to face the fact that he must eventually die. Associates differ as to whether he should be called a "workaholic," but he was a man with a mission, and he did not spare himself in its pursuit. After his first stroke he wrote to his cousin Marriner, who was then 78: "I thought I had inherited about the same splendid health which you have enjoyed . . . , and did not recognize that possibly I was stretching my situation a little too far."

Stoddard was of medium build and 5′10″ in height. His erect bearing suggested to some observers that he was taller. The visible signs of passing time were a receding hairline and an expanding waistline. He could do nothing about the former and his sedentary vocation, limited exercise and taste for sweets kept him from dealing effectively with the latter. Golfing vacations in Florida, California and at Harbor Springs became a larger part of his life in the 1960s, but when he was at home there was never time for a consistent physical fitness program.

The nasal polyps which periodically afflicted him were stoically endured until they required excision, and then the surgery was borne in the same manner. Dr. Oliver B. McGillicuddy, his Lansing physician for many years, reports that Howard was one of the most cooperative, courageous and uncomplaining patients he ever had. He was amazed, however, when Stoddard once insisted that the polyps be treated at the same time he was in the hospital for hernia surgery, because he "couldn't take time for two operations."

The first sign of circulatory problems came in June 1968. Jennie was recovering from surgery, and Stoddard had accompanied Charles to a doctor's office. While Charles was receiving treatment, his father fainted. He was hospitalized with what was diagnosed as a minor stroke. Recovery was rapid and almost complete; Jennie remembers that there was occasionally a little difficulty with speech and writing. Within a few weeks he was back at the banks, and on the service club speaking circuit, and in Washington advising Treasury Department officials on Vietnam and inflation, and in strategy meetings on how to get the Michigan legislature to rethink statewide banking. He talked a little about retiring—Waldo did so in September 1969—but the time was not yet right. His strength was not what it had been, and he spent a little more time on rest and recreation. However, he was still very much the man in charge of the Stoddard banks.

The next crisis came in October 1969. He and Jennie were contemplating a trip to Harbor Springs for the weekend when he felt a tremendous weakness come over his entire body. At Jennie's insistence, he was driven to Detroit where Stanford had made arrangements for his admittance to Providence Hospital. Tests there clearly indicated that he was suffering from arteriosclerosis throughout his system, and, in particular, that there was a blockage of one of the carotid arteries in his neck.

An operation was performed on November 28 by Dr. John Pfeifer, a specialist in vascular surgery who was also a convert to Mormonism and at this time a counselor to Edwin Jones in the Detroit Stake presidency. As described in the statement which Stanford released to directors and officers of the banks, the arterial blockage was removed and normal circulation was restored. The letter added hopefully, "it is now apparent that the operation was one hundred percent successful."

That the surgery prolonged Stoddard's life for another year and a half seems clear. Progressive arteriosclerosis, however, precluded full recovery, though the letters he wrote during his months of convalescence conveyed the same optimism that had helped him to meet earlier obstacles. He wrote to N. Eldon Tanner, a counselor in the L.D.S. First Presidency, on December 30: "I am now of the opinion that my life span has been extended for several years, during which it will be possible to accomplish many constructive programs which I had hoped to see fulfilled."

During part of 1970 he was able to go to the office for a few hours a day, but he attended only a few board meetings and rarely traveled except to Detroit and Harbor Springs. He was hospitalized intermittently for tests and rest. His strength happily permitted him to attend the 19th Annual International Monetary Conference at Hot Springs, Virginia, in May, and to be present when the University of Utah College of Business presented him its "Outstanding Achievement Award." Jennie, of course, accompanied him on these trips, sharing the pleasure of reunions with friends among the banking leaders of the world and the Stoddard and Creer kin in the West.

Gradually Stoddard accepted the fact that he must depend more on others. He had always been willing to give people latitude in doing assigned jobs, but he had kept closely in touch with what was going on. Now, as Stanford recalls, he started saying about major projects, "Get it done and it will be fine with me." "He possibly did more delegating in the last two years of his life than in the prior thirty." His correspondence reflected this change. To George Romney, who was now Secretary of Housing and Urban Development, he wrote in January 1970: "I do not expect to resume the same day to day direction of our banking affairs in the State, but we have quite a number of fine younger men who will take over most of my responsibilities." He had already confided to Marriner Eccles after a quiet Christmas at home: "I of course am most happy that my three sons, each with completely different personalities, are working harmoniously together and in their various fields will lend great support to the future of the banks. . . ."

In the administrative restaffing of the Stoddard banks which took shape in 1969-1970, Stanford relinquished the presidency of the Detroit banks to take the new post of vice chairman of the board of directors of both Michigan National and M.B.N.A. He and Ann continued to reside in the Detroit area, but he spent considerable time in Lansing and East Lansing, conferring with officers and briefing and receiving counsel from his father. Howard Jr. headed the Marketing Division at the Lansing office. Charles and Jan were in New York, and flying home on many week-ends. (He left his position at First National City Bank in 1973 to join the Grand Rapids M.N.B. office and then take the presidency of Michigan National Bank—Central.) Waldo continued on the Grand Rapids advisory board, and he also spent a lot of time talking banking and old times with Howard.

Joseph F. Shaw, from Grand Rapids, succeeded Waldo as president and traveled to Lansing each day. George A. Pierson succeeded Stanford in Detroit. To enlarge the advisory team which worked most closely to help Stanford prepare to step into his father's shoes, Edwin Barnes was made executive vice president, with particular oversight of the Grand Rapids and Flint branches, while Paul C. Souder was given the same title in Saginaw. (With the retirement of Shaw in 1973, Souder was elected to the M.N.B. presidency.) Frank R. Welsher and Edwin B. Jones became executive vice presidents at Michigan Bank N.A. in Detroit.

Through all the changes, and in spite of the national credit crunch, growth continued, as the December 31, 1970, reports to stockholders disclosed. This thirtieth anniversary M.N.B. report noted that fourth quarter earnings were "the finest . . . that the bank has enjoyed."

Total assets now aggregated almost $1.25 billion, and capital and reserves came to almost $70 million. Each of the 2.2 million shares of common stock still carried a par value of $10; it earned $2.91 in 1970 and in a few weeks would produce a dividend of $1, as every share had done every year from the beginning. Over the three decades of M.N.B. operations those dividends had passed $27 million, and $66 million in retained earnings had gone toward the enhancement of the Bohn-Stoddard project.

The Detroit area banks also had a good year. Michigan Bank N.A., at the end of its fifteenth year, had over $750 million in assets and capital and reserves above $37 million. Because most of its capitalization was in the form of capital notes, surplus and reserves, the earnings per share on each of the 426,000 shares of common stock was $7.91, but the forthcoming dividend would also be $1. Since its organization as a commercial bank, M.B.N.A. had paid almost $5.7 million in dividends and retained earnings in excess of $19 million. The banks in the Detroit suburbs also produced reports to delight the partially-invalided but still intensely-interested empire builder who watched it all from 736 Glenhaven Avenue.

The Stoddard home was a busy place. Jennie did her best to help Stoddard conserve his strength, and it was not easy. When he could no longer handle the stairs, his study was converted into a bedroom and then the sun porch was enclosed and made a light and spacious visiting and sleeping room. Gladys MacGregor was in and out gathering the materials on which the Howard Stoddard story would one day be based. Virginia, who was now back in East Lansing with her children, and Howard Jr. did what they could to aid Jennie in her taxing situation. Visitors were frequent—from the banks, the church and the community.

Generally Stoddard's spirits were good, and the exciting prospects for statewide banking kept him going. It was exasperating, however, to have to cope with faltering speech, deteriorating handwriting and an impairment of that ability to quickly grasp the meaning of figures at a glance which had been a key to his executive decisiveness through the years. Charles remembers that his father showed irritation and anger more, and Stanford recalls that it was easier for him to handle verbal communication—even numbers—than the printed page.

Dictation flowed to the Michigan National Tower, and letters from all over brought good wishes and news of activities in which Stoddard was interested. A Christmas note from Simon Den Uyl particularly pleased him, for it restored a relationship strained fifteen years before by a business disagreement. On February 8, 1971, he wrote to Eccles: "My mind is clear, my body is gaining strength each day and I feel that I can live a very satisfactory life for many years to come." Two weeks later he wrote: "We are hoping this year to form a holding company and put 12 banks with resources of $2¼ billion in that institution. If we succeed, then our future in this State will be a success."

This was the project to which increasing attention had been given for the past three years. Russell Fairles had been persuaded to postpone retirement because the transition would benefit from his expertese. (Fairles says that it was also because Stoddard did not want to be the only exception to the bank's mandatory retirement rule.) Stanford and the bank officers were heavily involved in lobbying and planning, and Howard and Waldo spent many hours discussing strategies and possibilities.

The movement to legalize bank holding companies developed belatedly in Michigan as part of a national trend. Michigan's prohibition on the ownership of bank stock by other corporations dated to the Great Depression, when banking disaster was widely attributed to holding company abuses. Comparable impressions and experiences led to similar bans in many states. In the post-war years, however, pressure for expansion and consolidation led many banks to seek changes in the laws or ways to organize related institutions. Branch banking was an alternative where it was permitted, and the restrictions were relaxed in some states. The multi-bank holding company was another popular device, since it permitted the corporation to engage not only in ownership of many banks, but also in a variety of more-or-less related business activities.

Where legal constraints went against the expansion trend, as in Michigan, a wide variety of strategems were employed. Howard Stoddard's use of the profit sharing trusts to acquire control of additional banks was such a device. By the late 1960s more than 200 Michigan companies owned bank stock in clear violation of the law. A Michigan Bankers Association-sponsored study by Robert F. Lanzillotti, *Banking Structure in Michigan, 1945-1963* (1966), noted that concentration was increasing in spite of the anti-holding company and anti-branching statutes. To the extent that it registered concern and proposed tentative remedies, however, the study was soon out of phase with predominant banking opinion in the state.

The multi-bank holding company gradually emerged as the favorite expansion instrument. Its creation required only the chartering of a corporation —Delaware's laws were particularly hospitable—and the exchange of that corporation's stock, on a negotiated basis, for the stock of two or more banks. Open market purchase of existing bank stocks and formation of new banks were other options open to the holding company. The advantages were coordination of policies and economies of scale in connection with such operations as internal accounting, advertising, bank credit cards and data processing. (Those who argued that Howard Stoddard had already achieved a *de facto* multi-bank holding company through the profit sharing trusts, individual ownerships, and interlocking directorates were not far from the mark.) As early as 1956 Congress permitted national banks to be owned by such companies where state banks were legally permitted to enter into similar relationships. So rapidly did the states fall into line that in 1970 a second federal statute was adopted, clarifying the responsibility of the Federal Reserve Board to regulate both one-bank and multi-bank holding companies when one or more of their subsidiaries belong to the Federal Reserve system. By then only Michigan and Vermont still prohibited such companies.

Responsive to the trend, the banks in Detroit came to feel locked in by the 25-mile branching limit, even as some of the outside bankers began to see advantages in identifying with a larger base or establishing regional groups of their own. Two considerations argued against reopening the issue of statewide branch banking. One, of course, was its long association with Howard Stoddard, who was not necessarily loved more because events were proving him right. The other was that the holding company was a more flexible instrument when the acquisition—or rescue—of existing banks, rather than the formation of new banks, was the primary approach to expansion. Very little new capital was required. All that was necessary was to satisfy the Federal Reserve Board that the consolidation would improve service to the public without adversely affecting competition.

As noted earlier, talk of a change in Michigan Bankers Association policy on branching began to be heard as early as 1965, when Howard's banks left the organization. When the 1968 M.B.A. convention endorsed the holding company concept, it was clearly only a matter of time before Michigan joined the rest of the states.

Based in both the business and political capitals of Michigan, Howard Stoddard and his associates lobbied energetically for repeal of the 1931 ban. Directors cultivated their contacts in the legislature and the banks' legislative representative, Thomas Cleary, was busier than he had been for some time. On March 31, 1969, Stoddard appeared before a joint meeting of the Senate and House Corporation Committees to give his view on three banking reform bills. He endorsed the one which proposed to recodify and update the banking code. He opposed the authorizing of one-bank holding companies, arguing: "A bank is a *creator* of money and all other businesses are *users* of money. This distinction too often is lost sight of by the promoters who use the banking function for other than its real purpose." On the multi-bank holding company proposal he showed that he also understood diplomacy:

> In my younger years I was a strong advocate of statewide branch banking. I no longer share that point of view. In my considered judgment, nothing would be more beneficial to the State of Michigan than well developed holding company operations vigorously competing against each other to serve the people better.

He emphasized that the holding company could make modern, diversified banking services available to the Upper Peninsula and other parts of Michigan which were developing under the impetus of tourism, and that past and pending federal legislation would prevent the real and alleged abuses of the past. In this connection he went on record with a revisionist viewpoint which he had earlier expressed to close associates:

> In looking back at this stage, the First National Bank of Detroit and the Guardian National Bank of Commerce, two leaders in the two holding companies, in my opinion, should never have been placed in receivership. With the same assistance as provided to other banks of similar size and importance, they could have been saved and not forced to close their doors.

So confident were Stoddard and his colleagues that the legislature would act favorably that they initiated preliminary consultations with the Federal Reserve Board even before the debate began. Russell Fairles and legal representative Ronald R. Pentecost met with Washington officials on January 30, 1969, to receive instructions on how to fill out the forms and meet the requirements which were prescribed for F.R.B. approval. The work moved ahead as the Michigan Senate approved the multi-bank bill (S. 213), and then came to an abrupt pause when the House Committee on Private Corporations turned down the measure on June 26. Apparently the pressure for approval had produced a backlash. One of the legislators who attended what the Detroit *Free Press* described as "a plush Wednesday night dinner . . . in the penthouse of the Michigan National Bank tower" complained, "They've been trying to run through too much banking legislation this session." Another expressed fear of "domination of the banking system by about six banking giants."

The next time around the groundwork was more carefully laid. Stanford and Joseph Shaw met with Governor William Milliken early in 1970, and thereafter Republican legislators were assiduously courted. Most of the state's bankers were now involved, and when the 1971 legislature met, both Milliken and the state financial institutions commissioner endorsed the holding company idea. The bill which was finally signed by the governor on April 5, 1971, (S. 12) was a simple amendment of the existing statutes for the regulation of corporations. It authorized any corporation, unless otherwise prohibited, to "guarantee, purchase, hold, sell, assign, transfer, mortgage, pledge or otherwise dispose of, the shares of the capital stock of, or any bonds, securities or evidence of indebtedness created my, any other corporation or corporations. . . ."

By the time the Holding Company Act was adopted, Howard Stoddard's physical condition precluded his attending the signing ceremony. He was pleased to receive the pen which Milliken used and to hear that Michigan National Bank stock rose $4, or about 16 percent, in the two days after the bill passed. The Detroit *Sunday News*, April 4, reported that neither Howard nor Stanford was available for comment, but Joseph Shaw was hardly guilty of overstatement when he said that the M.N.B. management was "certainly considering a holding company as soon as it is legalized." Five days later Howard Stoddard was briefly present—for the first time in six months and the last time ever—at a Michigan National board of directors meeting. It was a happy occasion.

Discussions with Federal Reserve authorities had been going on for some time and the voluminous *Application . . . by Michigan National Corporation . . . for Prior Approval of Action to Become a Bank Holding Company Pursuant to Section 3(a) (1) of the Bank Holding Company Act of 1956, as Amended* was executed and sent to Washington on June 29, 1971. Deliberation there was prolonged. The long-standing contention that the Stoddard banks were undercapitalized was raised again by the Michigan commissioner of financial institutions on behalf of several banks. Fed officials also expressed concern, and a pledge to increase capital funds by December 31, 1973, was made by the corporation. Allegations of unorthodox banking practices were countered with evidence and argument. For example, Joseph E. Lutz, regional administrator of national banks for the district which included Michigan, reviewed his experience with Michigan National in a March 3, 1972, letter, and recommended favorable action with the comment: "I have considered the bank to be a well-managed institution, and history will show [its] growth record has been outstanding. . . ."

On August 3, 1972, the application was approved. Michigan National Corporation was authorized to become a bank holding company through the acquisition of 80 percent or more of the stock in the five Stoddard banks:

Michigan National, Michigan Bank N.A., Livonia National, Troy National and Oakland National. The holding company, according to the F.R.B. statement, would thus control $2.03 billion in deposits—approximately 9.3 percent of the total held by commercial banks in Michigan—and it would become the second largest banking organization and the largest bank holding company in the state. (In terms of total assets—$2.46 billion—it ranked third.) The approval order noted that the company would also gain indirect control of the shares which the M.N.B. profit sharing trust owned in the following banks: Central Bank, Grand Rapids; Valley National Bank, Saginaw; Security National Bank, Manistee; First National Bank, Wyoming; First National Bank, East Lansing; Central National Bank, Alma; and St. Clair Shores National Bank. It found no unacceptable impact upon competition, however, and took no stand on the possible subsequent acquiring of these banks by the company. (The Grand Rapids, Saginaw and Wyoming banks are now parts of the Michigan National network.)

Stanford Stoddard was president of the new company. The other principal officers initially were Glenn J. McVeigh, vice president and treasurer, and Ronald R. Pentecost, secretary. Of the men who went on the board of directors of Michigan National Bank in 1941, only Randall Wickes and Roe Endicott became directors of Michigan National Corporation.

The man whose ideas were behind it all did not participate in this campaign for Washington approvals, nor did he direct this consolidation. A poignant addendum to the five-inch-thick sheaf of documents which went forward to the Federal Reserve Board begins with this statement:

"On June 15, 1971, Mr. Howard J. Stoddard died after a long illness."

Late in 1970 Stoddard experienced a setback and for a time death was believed imminent. "One of the great spiritual experiences I've ever had" is the way Charles remembers the family gathering in the hospital just before Thanksgiving Day, when Stoddard received a blessing under the hands of Wayne K. Berge, Bloomfield Hills bishop, and Edwin Jones. He was able to return home, but he required intermittent hospitalization thereafter and his activities were largely confined to his home and those of his children. For the first time in his life he was unable to complete his own income tax return; Fairles was asked to help. For the first time he squarely faced the necessity of planning for his estate, and an *intervires* trust was established, with Michigan National Bank and Stanford as trustees.

Stoddard was back in Providence Hospital for rest and observation when he succumbed without warning to a heart attack. His good friend Frank Welsher, comptroller of the Detroit M.N.B., had died suddenly three days before, but the news had been kept from him. Jennie, who almost lived at the hospital, went with Stanford and others to visit the Welsher family in Grosse Pointe and then spent the night with Stanford and Ann in Bloomfield Hills. Bishop Berge, aware that Stoddard would be alone that evening, spent an hour with him and found him clear in mind and composed in spirit. About 3 a.m. Stoddard suffered a coronary infarct, and by the time family members could reach the hospital, he was gone.

Newspapers in Michigan and Utah gave prominent place to Howard Stoddard's obituary, and it was noted in the major financial journals. Where there was a picture, it was not forty years different from the firm-jawed, steady-eyed photographs which first appeared in the press when Stoddard was learning how to run banks at National Copper and then learning how to take them apart and put them together as "Mister R.F.C."

Tributes came from many places. Governor Milliken, who happened to be attending the Michigan Bankers Association convention at the time, called Stoddard "a giant" in banking and in civic leadership. The Michigan State University board of trustees commended "his great help." A resolution of tribute and condolence from the two houses of the Michigan legislature reviewed Stoddard's career and found it "truly fitting and proper that there will be a living memorial"—the proposed student living center next to the M.S.U. campus—"as a lasting symbol of Mr. Stoddard's love of youth and the University, his dedication to public service, and his vigorous and principled approach to life. . . . "

The local TV station, WJIM TV, broadcast the following editorial:

> A man of the stature of Howard J. Stoddard passes our way far too seldom. His death this morning at the age of 69 is a loss to the entire commonwealth he served so long and so well.
>
> He was a man who will be remembered . . . remembered for vitality and creative energy . . . remembered as a fighter against great odds . . . remembered as a public servant, a father and as a man whose success story is unequalled in the annals of Michigan banking history.
>
> In 1940 Howard J. Stoddard headed a group of bankers and industrialists to form Michigan National Bank, the first statewide banking organization in Michigan. Today with offices in 9 Michigan cities the bank's resources have grown to over a billion dollars. But the genius of Howard Stoddard did more than revitalize the Michigan banking industry . . . throughout his career he directed his considerable energies

> to the calling of public service. An expert in the fields of insurance, taxation and education, Howard Stoddard was called upon by three Governors who sought his advice and leadership for the welfare of this state, and throughout his life he always found time to work for his church.
>
> It is most fitting that the Stoddard family announced today the establishment of a living memorial to be known as The Church of Jesus Christ of Latter Day Saints Institute Living Center. The facility will be located on a nine acre tract on Hagadorn Road in East Lansing across from the Michigan State University dormitory complex. When completed the Center will house some 200 students in a manner fitting with the moral precepts of the Church. His love of the University, of young people and of his church combine to give the project a total appropriateness.
>
> Irving S. Cobb once said 'lay my ashes at the roots of a dogwood tree at the proper planting season . . . should the tree live that will be monument enough for me.' The Institute Center that will grow and serve in East Lansing will be an always living reminder of Howard J. Stoddard.

The memorial service on June 18 brought an overflow gathering of approximately 1800 to the Lansing Stake Center, where the paneled walls were a visible reminder of Howard Stoddard's role in his church's history in Michigan. After the fashion of traditional Mormon funerals, this one focused on two themes: Stoddard's character and accomplishments and the testimony of eternal life which linked him to those whom he was now joining and those whom he had temporarily left behind. Stake President Sylvan Wittwer, who conducted, recalled his generosity and devotion to his church. Lenore Romney, Michigan's former first lady, spoke of Stoddard's family, and especially of what Jennie and Howard meant to each other. Edwin Jones, now a regional representative in the Mormon hierarchy as well as a senior officer at Michigan Bank N.A., placed Stoddard's banking career in the context of human values. "He left something more enduring than the financial empire that he created, because he left an organization that has the ability to grow and people that are a little bit taller and can climb a little higher because of him."

Stoddard's good friend N. Eldon Tanner had accepted an invitation to speak, but a death in his own family led him to ask Sterling W. Sill, assistant to the Council of the Twelve, to represent him. Sill, who knew the Creers better than the Stoddards, paid tribute to both families and placed Stoddard's life in that same context of pre-existence, mortality and immortality which Stoddard had described at Perry Driggs' missionary farewell and many other gatherings. "Home," Sill concluded, "is where you were brought up. Howard Stoddard is going home."

Prayers at the service were by Dr. John Pfeifer and J. Willard Marriott. In his prayer, Marriott described life as "a bridge over which we pass and we are not to build our dwellings upon it . . . that we may have the happiness and joy of eternal life." The graveside dedication was by Detroit Stake President I. Morris Brooks. According to his frequently-expressed wishes, Howard Stoddard was buried in Michigan—his adopted home.

When the books were closed on June 30, 1971, Michigan National Bank and Michigan Bank N.A. stood 49th and 88th among the 100 largest commercial banks in the United States. The proposal to bring Howard Stoddard's five banks, with their 47 offices in the Detroit area and 25 outstate, under the umbrella of Michigan National Corporation was already in Washington. What had started as a dream shared with Charles Bohn was now a banking empire worth almost $2.5 billion, and this was only the beginning. In the funeral eulogy, Edwin Jones recalled that Stoddard often said, "Whatever you do, whatever we do, let us do it for fifty years."

It is a safe prediction that in 1991 the precepts and example of Howard James Stoddard will still be guiding "Banking Which Is Building Michigan."

# Bibliographical Note

Howard J. Stoddard's business correspondence is voluminous and preserved at the Lansing office of his bank. His social and family correspondence is scattered and meager; he was rarely away from home for any length of time and he kept in touch by phone when he was. Two scrapbooks of clippings, largely the work of Gladys H. MacGregor, highlight the business and civic career in Michigan. Miss MacGregor was Stoddard's secretary, 1934-1935 and 1938-1964, and since his death in 1971 she has collaborated with Jennie Creer Stoddard in gathering and organizing materials for his biography. The scrapbooks, together with two small travel diaries and a collection of memorabilia and pictures are now in Mrs. Stoddard's possession.

To recapture the personality and style of the founder of Michigan National Bank has been, to a considerable extent, a project in oral history. The following family members, friends, business, church and community associates were interviewed on one or more occasions between 1976 and 1978, and almost all of the interviews were audiotaped and transcribed.

Jennie Creer Stoddard
Howard P. Stoddard
Stanford C. Stoddard
Charles C. Stoddard
Virginia Stoddard Peery
Paul S. Peery
James S. Peery
Waldo I. Stoddard
James B. Alley
Edwin Barnes
John H. Carton
Gerald W. Chamberlin
Jack E. Church
H. Peery Driggs, Jr.
Russell Fairles
Miles D. Grant
Robert P. Gerholz
John A. Hannah
Edwin B. Jones
Victor W. Klein
Fred A. Lavery
C. Lincoln Linderholm
Gladys H. MacGregor
Oliver B. McGillicudy
Philip H. Ordway
George A. Pierson
George W. Romney
Arthur T. Roth
Joseph F. Shaw
Paul C. Souder
Arnold Van Zanten
Sylvan Wittwer
Jean Wunderlich

Helpful in exploring genealogical background were the Stoddard family research by Mary Ellen Smith and the Eccles family research by Leonard J. Arrington. Insight into both father and son is provided by Howard Stoddard's biographical sketch, *George E. Stoddard: An Appreciation*, a 26-page pamphlet which was privately printed in New York City in 1924. In preparation for his father's sixtieth birthday, Stanford Stoddard gathered reminiscences from Howard's brothers, boyhood friends and long-time business associates; this scrapbook and associated documents constitute a valuable source.

Transcripts of many Stoddard talks are in the bank files. Speeches which were printed include:

"The American Way." Address to the Brigham Young University School of Business, Provo, Utah, February 22, 1962. n.p., n.d., 12 pp.

"Banking Problems Inherent in the Merger Movement and the Expanding Community." Address published in *Twelfth Annual Discussion Meeting, April 5, 1955, First National Bank of Philadelphia.* n.p., n.d., pp. 9-30.

"Basic Reasons For Our National Prosperity." Address to the Business Symposium, Michigan State College, April 13, 1955. n.p., n.d., 9 pp.

"Bonds and the Purchasing Power of the Dollar." Address to the Los Angeles Regional Conference of the American Institute of Banking. *Bulletin of the American Institute of Banking*, June 1932, pp. 407-412.

"Communism and the Common Market." Address to the Lansing Rotary Club, December 7, 1962. n.p., n.d., 9 pp.

"Howard J. Stoddard Tells Ways and Means Committee Bankers Want Taxes Reduced and Loopholes Closed. Testimony before the House Ways and Means Committee, March 11, 1963." Washington: Bankers Committee for Tax Equality, n.d., 11 pp.

"Oral Testimony of Howard J. Stoddard Before the Ways and Means Committee, August 10, 1961." Washington: Bankers Committee for Tax Equality, n.d., 10 pp.

"Tax Justice Between Competing Financial Institutions." Speech to the Thirteenth National Credit Conference, American Bankers Association, Chicago, January 23, 1961. n.p., n.d., 15 pp.

Stoddard testimony before Congressional committees may also be found in the following government documents:

Hearings before the Senate Finance Committee, 87th Congress, 2nd session, April 11, 1962, pp.

"President's 1963 Tax Message." Hearings before the Committee on Ways and Means, House of Representatives, 88th Congress, 1st session, Part III, Feb. 26, March 4, 5, 6, 7, 9, 11 and 12, 1963 pp. 1789-1816.

"Taxation of Mutual Savings Banks and Savings and Loan Institutions," Hearings before the Committee on Ways and Means, House of Representatives, 87th Congress, 1st session, August 9 and 10, 1961, pp. 389-396.

Books which provided useful background on Howard Stoddard, the Detroit banking crisis of 1933-1934, and the Michigan banking scene during the Stoddard era are:

Leonard J. Arrington. *David Eccles: Pioneer Western Industrialist.* Logan, Utah: Utah State University, 1975.

John Joseph Holland, Jr. *The Detroit Banking Collapse of 1933.* Ph.D. Dissertation, New York University Graduate School of Business Administration, 1972. Ann Arbor, Mich.: University Microfilms, 1973.

Sidney Hyman. *Marriner S. Eccles: Private Entrepreneur and Public Servant.* Stanford, Calif.: Stanford University School of Business, 1976.

Jesse H. Jones, with Edward Angly. *Fifty Billion Dollars.* New York: Macmillan, 1951.

Susan Estabrook Kennedy. *The Banking Crisis of 1933.* Lexington: University of Kentucky, 1973.

Robert F. Lanzillotti. *Banking Structure in Michigan, 1945-1963.* MSU Business Studies, 1966. East Lansing: Michigan State University Bureau of Business and Economic Research, 1966.

James Stuart Olson. *Herbert Hoover and the Reconstruction Finance Corporation.* Ames: Iowa State University, 1977.

Robert G. Rodkey. *State Bank Failures in Michigan.* Michigan Business Studies, Vol. 7, No. 2. Ann Arbor: University of Michigan Bureau of Business Research, 1935.

A helpful overview of Stoddard banking policies and innovations is provided by Lyle W. Miller, "Howard J. Stoddard and the Beginning of Michigan National Bank," an unpublished seminar paper written at Central Michigan University, December 1970, 24 pp.

The relevant judicial decisions in the anti-branch banking lobbying case of the 1940s are 318 Michigan 645, 320 Michigan 477, 163 Fed (2d) 288, 332 US 801 and 323 Michigan 490. The 1960 Saginaw Peoples Savings Bank decision is 359 Michigan 297.

Howard Stoddard received considerable press coverage, not all of it laudatory. The Lansing *State Journal* was a Michigan National Bank booster, and the local papers in the other M.N.B. towns were generally neutral or friendly after the initial adjustment to the bank's arrival. The business editors of the Detroit *Free Press* and the Detroit *Times* probably did more than any other commentators to publicize the "maverick" image; their interviews and in-depth stories were sometimes hostile in the 1940s and usually friendly by the 1960s. Another business publication, *Michigan Manufacturer and Financial Record*, of Detroit, devoted the cover and three pages of its October 1964 issue to the most readable and informative overview of the Stoddard career to appear in the Michigan press. Its title reflects its favorable tone: "Stoddard's Billion-Dollar Banking Empire Built In Less Than 25 Years."

# Index